Eternally Inspiring Recollections of our Divine Mother

Sahaja Yogis' stories of Her Holiness Shri Mataji Nirmala Devi

Volume 4: 1987 - 1989

Other books by the author:

Published by Blossomtime Publishing:

Eternally Inspiring Recollections of our Divine Mother,
Volume 1: Early Days to 1980

Eternally Inspiring Recollections of our Divine Mother,
Volume 1: Early Days to 1980
Black and White Edition

Eternally Inspiring Recollections of our Divine Mother,
Volume 2: 1981 – 1983

Eternally Inspiring Recollections of our Divine Mother,
Volume 2: 1981 – 1983
Black and White Edition

Eternally Inspiring Recollections of our Divine Mother,
Volume 3: 1984 – 1986

Published by Checkpoint Press:

The Awakening of Navi Septa, Book One: The Keys of Wisdom
The Awakening of Navi Septa, Book Two: The Mountain Mouse
The Awakening of Navi Septa, Book Three: The Swarm of Bees

Eternally Inspiring Recollections of our Divine Mother

Sahaja Yogis' stories of
Her Holiness Shri Mataji Nirmala Devi

Volume 4: 1987 – 1989

Linda J. Williams

Blossomtime Publishing

This edition is published 2013

by Blossomtime Publishing

Copyright © 2013 by Linda J. Williams

Cover design & Layout © by Sylvia Udar

Eternally Inspiring Recollections of our Divine Mother
Volume 4: 1987 – 1989

ISBN-13: 978-0-9573769-7-7

Blossomtime Publishing
69 North End Road, London, NW11 7RL, UK
blossomtime.books@gmail.com

This book is humbly dedicated to our Divine Mother,
Her Holiness Shri Mataji Nirmala Devi

That Your name may be ever more glorified, praised and
worshipped...

Thank You, Shri Mataji, for the warmth and simplicity and all the many ways in which You showered Your love upon us. And thank You for the great play of Shri Mahamaya that helped seekers to love and trust You, often without yet understanding the truth that You were and are.

The heart of this book is to remind us of the magic of Sahaja Yoga. The spirit of this book is to help our brothers and sisters all over the world, and also in the future, to know a small part of the beauty and glory of You, Shri Mataji, as a loving, caring Mother whose wonderful power of divine love dispelled and continues to dispel all our uncertainties.

Sift now through the words that we found when we tried to remember. What follows is our collective memory, our story together. We ask Your forgiveness if our memories are less than perfect, but our desire is to share with others the love that You gave us, as best we can.

Contents

Acknowledgements

The editor would like to humbly thank all the people who have made this book possible. First and foremost we bow to Her Holiness Shri Mataji, who is the source and fulfilment of all, and who graciously encouraged the collection of these stories.

Chapter 1

1987: January to March India

Shri Mataji at Mr Dhumal's farm

India Tour 1986/87 – Mr Dhumal´s Farm

We were on the Maharashtra tour going east to Rahuri, and Mr Dhumal invited all the yogis to stay the night at his farm. We arrived quite late, tired and hot as usual from the long journey.

I had a desire to take a photo of our Mother and saw an appropriate opportunity, as Mother was approaching us towards the house, I quickly went ahead of Her and crouching on the ground in the garden I took this photo.

All the yogis gathered in a big makeshift tent with a podium set up for the music programme. At first we were all expecting to have dinner, at least our stomachs were telling us logically that we were hungry. Instead the concert started with Indian classical music. After several performances, we were offered green sprigs of channas or chickpeas. Eating them was like manna from heaven, we truly enjoyed the offering, with the hope that dinner will be served soon. The music just continued and went on for hours as our attention sometimes got lost in the thought of the dinner. Meanwhile the vibrations was working and balancing us, we started enjoying the music and completely forgot about time and our hunger.

Our Mother accompanied us in the concert and was aware of everything and nothing escaped Her attention. After several hours the music stopped.

'You have enjoyed the beautiful music, at first your attention was on the dinner, but the vibrations took your attention away from the food – now the dinner is waiting for you,' Shri Mataji said. We all had a gratifying smile on our faces.

Joaquin Orús

Around the villages

We were in a village in Maharashtra on one of the India tours in the mid 1980's and the electricity broke down when Shri Mataji was about to give an introductory talk. She had some of the Sahaja Yogis sing Adi Ma and Jogawa, and then just asked the people to put their hands out and feel the cool breeze, which they did. Also, at that village where there was a procession with Shri Mataji on a bullock cart, and She later told us what the driver had said to Her. He spoke so eloquently about Her; it was like the devotional poetry of Kabir, even though he was a simple countryman. She also said he had been a great king in a past lifetime.

About Paithan – a village which was originally called Pratishthan and had been the capital of the Shalivahanas' kingdom – or Satavahanas as they were sometimes called - Shri Mataji's ancestors. We went there once on the tour in 1987, and there were a lot of ruins and it was a very poor village now. Shri Mataji gave a talk, a public programme to the villagers. They did not even have electricity and someone fanned Her with a folded up newspaper, and after the programme we went and had tea in the headman's house.

Mother told us this instructive story about the sort of misunderstandings created by Westerners. There was a missionary who went to an Indian village. He told the villagers they were sinful and guilty, but they would be saved if they confessed their sins. When the missionary came to leave, the village headman said: 'Thank you, sir, for telling us something we did not know. You have told us that we are guilty. We did not know that before.'

Linda Williams

Pasta for everyone

In January 1987 Shri Mataji invited 300 Western yogis from the India Tour to stay at Pratishthan. She graciously enquired what they would like for lunch. The Italians, who were rather homesick, promptly responded, 'Pasta!' There were only ten packets of pasta in the kitchen and each packet should serve about six people. Shri Mataji started cooking. Everyone had the pasta, and the Italians ate several helpings, yet there was enough left for another meal.

Yogi Mahajan

It was done by silence

My husband and I went to India to look at textiles in Gujarat, not for Sahaja Yoga. When we got back to Delhi we found there was going to be Shivaratri Puja. Shri Mataji asked to see my husband and I went along with him, thinking I would sit outside and wait for him. However we both went in and sat with Mother and somebody had brought the kind of fabrics that we had been looking at in Gujarat. Mother described much more to us and taught us about the symbolism of the designs that these simple fabrics had. I found that relaxed me a lot, looking at something that I had already seen. It was amazing the way Mother worked on me because I was much too shy to say anything. She took Her shawl off and it was very, very soft. She said it was so soft that it would pass through my wedding ring and yet it was as warm as a blanket.

'Feel it,' She said. My husband and I held it.

Then Shri Mataji held it and it was as if the silence was complete. I just felt as if Shri Mataji was saying, 'I've got you.' I remember this complete feeling of peace and thinking, 'I wish everybody could feel this idea that we really are just held by Mother.'

She didn't say anything to me. It was just done by silence and holding Her shawl.

Rosemary Maitland Hume

So tuned in

In 1987, when we were staying with Shri Mataji at a Sahaja Yogi's house on Prabhat Rd, Pune, a lady called Mrs Bhikule was there and she was so tuned in to Shri Mataji that she would suddenly wake up in the night.

'Ji, Shri Mataji,' she would say, and would go to Shri Mataji's room.

'I was just about to call you,' Shri Mataji would smile and say.

Deepa Mahajan

A cautionary tale

In the eighties, Shri Mataji came to live in Pune.

'Shri Mataji now that You have come to live here all will be well with Pune,' I said to Her.

'No, it does not happen like that. In My presence all the bhuts come out,' She replied.

'Shri Mataji, You must come to my house and have food,' a Sahaja Yogi from Delhi would ask Shri Mataji daily. She would avoid by making some excuse or the other. One day he insisted.

'Shri Mataji my house will be blessed by Your coming,' he said.

'No son, it is not like that. Sometimes skeletons in the cupboard come tumbling out. You must be careful never to insist on My coming. If I want to I will come,' She told him.

This fact was confirmed when Shri Mataji came to Pune before Pratishthan was built and stayed at the house of a Sahaja Yogi. She could not sleep and was very uncomfortable for two days. On the third day She told us there was something there that was disturbing Her. She told us to look around. Then She pointed to a picture of Her on the wall and said that something was not right with it. One Sahaja Yogi took it off the wall and behind it was a photo of a major false guru, a rakshasa from Bangalore.

'See, all these bhuts come tumbling out before Me,' She said, then left the place immediately.

Deepa Mahajan

He insisted on thanking Shri Mataji personally

It was in 1987 and Shri Mataji invited some of us from Dehra Dun to meet Her in Pune. She was staying in a flat there and overseeing the building of Pratishthan. When we reached Mumbai, one of the Sahaja Yogis from Dehra Dun, Ashwini Koorich, arranged for the five or six of us from Dehra Dun to stay with his Mumbai brother-in-law, an industrialist with a large clothing factory. During the night Ashwini gave realisation to his brother-in-law and gave him vibrations. By the morning a serious spinal defect which he had had from childhood had disappeared and he insisted on driving us up to Pune to thank Shri Mataji.

When we reached Pune we went to the flat where Shri Mataji was staying, and I was a bit nervous, because we had arranged for the Sahaja Yogis from Dehra Dun, but not the Mumbai gentleman, to come and see Shri Mataji. She asked to talk to me in private first, and I explained that our host had insisted on bringing us up, a five hour drive on a working day, and that he had had a miracle and absolutely insisted on coming and thanking Shri Mataji personally. She was very touched, and said it was quite in order, and that She wished other people would do the same.

Linda Williams

This is the atma tattwa

I came to Sahaja Yoga in 1986, but in a way was not a Sahaja Yogi, even though indirectly I did a lot of Sahaja Yoga work. I heard Shri Mataji's tape on the guru tattwa and all the Adi Guru incarnations, and realised what Sahaja Yoga really was. I had read a lot but not experienced before.

One day in 1987 I had the chance to present some of my poetry to Shri Mataji at Pratishthan. About twenty people were sitting there. I started reading it and when I finished I looked at Shri Mataji and She was weeping - the tears were there. Then She opened Her eyes, looked at me, then looked at the ground and I saw that all of us had tears on our cheeks.

'This is the soul, this is the atma tattwa which is one. This is the experience,' She said. I was shocked! Then I realised it is not my poetry but it came from somewhere else.

Although Urdu is not my first language I wrote in Urdu and presented the poems to Shri Mataji. She was very pleased, and liked them very much. She asked other people, including Baba Mama, to talk with me about this. She started explaining what poetry is. She gave me such a nice example.

'How do you feel when the moonlight comes through your window? How do you feel when you see a flower in blossom. How do you feel when the bird is flying down? These feelings have to come in your poetry,' She said, and explained to me the importance of the Swadishthan. Art comes from the Left Swadishthan.

In the Mahabharata there is a character called Eklavya. He wanted to be a student of Drona, the great archer. But he was not allowed to be Drona's pupil because of his low caste, even though his dedication was true. Shri Mataji explained to me that if your guru is not there physically but your surrender and dedication is true and thorough you can become your own guru. For this your Swadishthan works a lot. The Swadishthan gives you creativity, and the creativity comes through the guru. In this way you can be your own guru. This is what happened with Eklavya, and he became his own guru and he learnt so well, that he was even better than Arjuna, who had Drona present. Eklavya's dedication was greater, but he lacked humility.

Shri Mataji then said there will be a day when She will not be there and even Her photograph will not be there, but Sahaja Yoga will be there. These were Her words - that Sahaja Yoga cannot be destroyed because it is a living thing. It is an energy.

I wrote a book called The Two Goblets and it was on the news, and Shri Mataji saw the news and the next day called me and gave me a lot of blessings. She often asked me to sing and recite poetry in Urdu in front of Sir CP because he had his education in Urdu

Most of my poetry is about Sahaja Yoga, for example after reading Shri Mataji's lecture on Krishna Puja, or Fatima Puja, or Hanuman Puja, but one time it was the other way round. One of the leaders took a poem of mine to Shri Mataji and She explained the poem in the puja talk - it was Shri Buddha Puja.

Prakash Khote

Just do it!

In 1987 I was at Pratishthan with my father-in-law, who was an architect. Shri Mataji was building it and at that time it was basically a construction site. Shri Mataji used to sit in the centre of the main hall, which was open at the sides. She would sit on a chair, which was on a large blue carpet. Around Her were hundreds of doors from Taiwan, bathroom fittings, construction workers, and all sorts of things. The front of the house, from a Rajasthani palace, had just arrived and was going to be installed.

At some stage Shri Mataji called me over and said She had a job for me. She presented me with a long rectangular piece of sandstone which was in pieces. It was like a big window, hand carved, with daisy like flowers in a lattice shape, in three pieces and all broken. She wanted me to glue it together with Araldite glue.

The first mistake I made was to think that it was impossible to glue something together so heavy with Araldite. The second mistake was to listen to the suggestions of all sorts of people over the next few days, who would say, 'Why don't you do it this way?' and so on. Then some of us were sitting around with hacksaw blades trying to cut up the sandstone, which was hundreds of years old.

After three days, there was a small and spontaneous Diwali Puja. Shri Mataji called me over to Her.

'Just do it!' She said firmly.

Within half an hour, this thing, which had been in many pieces all over the floor, was glued together with Araldite and a little cement, and the next day it was put up on the wall of Pratishthan, where it still is. What I learnt from this is that Shri Mataji wanted me to see this job through to the end, and make sure it got done as She wanted it, and if we do this all the negativity will just disappear.

On the day of the puja, when I was working on the sandstone, I looked around, and all the Pune Sahaja Yogis had arrived. It was the Shri Lakshmi day of Diwali. They had bought a lot of food and drink and wanted to give this to Shri Mataji because She had never had anything in the house up to then. So we offered Mother a small puja – coconuts and rice, then they offered Mother a cup of tea and something to eat. They also asked Heir for the blessing of rain, because there had been a drought for three years. We all watched through the window, towards the mountains which Shri Mataji said are the Sahasrara of Maharashtra, and watched the rain come over those mountains, and it poured down in Pune for three days and broke the drought.

It was the most beautiful time to be in Pratishthan because Shri Mataji was building it, and you could see She was working it out. You would go there one day and there was a staircase being built, and the next time you went it had completely come down. She was working on so many things. It was like She was working on the universe, and it was being made and rebuilt and destroyed and rebuilt, and there were so many yogis from all over the world and also from India, working on different aspects of Pratishthan. Shri Mataji was so gracious.

Another time we were sitting in Her room and She was talking, and I was there with my young son. Shri Mataji had a bowl of roasted channa (chick peas) next to Her, as She often did in those days. All of a sudden my son got up and walked up to Her, and picked up the channa and started to hand it out to everybody as prasad. I was trying to tell him to come back and sit down. Then Shri Mataji raised Her hand.

'It's all right,' She said, and he walked around giving out channa to everybody. Then he put the bowl back on the table and sat down.

Gillian Patankar

Divine singing lessons

I heard Shri Mataji singing many times in Pune when She was teaching the Sahaja Yogis the song 'Ma Teri Jai Ho' and 'Bhaya Kaya Taya', and She taught us others too.

Deepa Mahajan

Shri Mataji gave vibrations for a few minutes

In 1987 we were celebrating Shri Mataji's birthday at Mumbai and Debu Chaudery was invited. But when he came, his hand was fractured and he told Shri Mataji he could not play. So She asked to see his hand, and gave vibrations for a few minutes. Then he was able to play the sitar for over an hour.

Videh Saundankar

Chapter 2

1987: March and April England and Italy

Where have you been?

The first clear vivid memory I have of Shri Mataji is when I was introduced to Her at the airport in London, in March 1987. David Prole introduced me, and Mother took my hand and said something very nice to me.

'Where have you been? Lost!' She said then and at that moment my life flashed through my mind and I thought, 'Where on earth have I been all these years?' When I got my realisation that feeling of coming home was so completely natural and I felt, 'Why did it take so long to get here?' When Shri Mataji said that to me I felt my Sahasrara blow open – whoosh! All this bliss, I couldn't sleep for some days.

Steve Jones

One of the moments I think about

A few days after meeting Shri Mataji at the airport, in 1987, She had a programme just for the Sahaja Yogis in Friends Meeting House, Covent Garden.

We were all lining up to give a flower to Mother. She had a big beaming smile on Her face and again She said something really nice to me. I bowed down in front of Her and when I got up She said my left side needed working on. She invited me to sit next to Her and took my left hand, then She looked straight ahead with a Shri Mahakali pose and gave a bandhan. I felt all these vibrations pouring through my left side. I was blissed out, like a little child looking up at its mother, and completely enchanted by Shri Mataji and looking into Her eyes. I could have stayed there forever. I was in heaven.

Mother has said that whenever we feel down or lose that connection just think about Her for a moment that we've been with Her, and that is one of the moments I think about a lot.

Steve Jones

A lovely cozy ashram

There was a time in the mid-eighties when Shudy Camps, near Cambridge in England, had just been purchased and was in the initial stages of renovation. Rumours abounded that Shudy Camps was the New Jerusalem and Mother wanted Hounslow sold as soon as possible. This was upsetting for those of us who lived there and loved the place. Shri Mataji had stayed there, and many foreign brothers and sisters too, as it was conveniently near Heathrow Airport.

One early evening, I heard someone entering the ashram and when I went to greet them in the hallway, I was amazed to find Shri Mataji Herself walking towards me. She refused Her special chair and sat on a very ordinary stool in the dining room. She played with the four children we had there, who offered Her everything they could find, including their toys. Yogis were returning from work and found themselves suddenly at the Feet of Shri Mataji. We had a number of Her belongings stored upstairs and She described a jacket of Sir CP's which She wanted, so yogis went up to find it. Meanwhile, She spoke with everyone, giving little bits of personal advice.

'What a lovely cozy ashram this is! Such loving vibrations, such a nice hospitable, family feel and now they want to sell it. I don't know why,' She said very clearly. Sir CP's suit jacket was duly found.

'Yes, that's the one,' Shri Mataji said, and then asked for it to be put back again where it had been found. She spoke personally to some more of the yogis and then left.

Marilyn Leate

Shri Mataji knew exactly what was there

The first time I really spoke to Shri Mataji was in 1987. That was when She came and visited Shudy Camps, when we were all working there on this beautiful house. In 1986 Mother had given everyone presents. They all got watches. I was quite sad because I had been there for six or seven months, and I did not get a present that time. In 1987 Shri Mataji came again, and She gave me a watch, the same watch that everyone else had got the year before. I can't remember Her exact words, except that She said She was happy that I was there. I felt completely at home, and it was wonderful.

Shri Mataji told everybody in detail what to do – such as removing internal walls and so on. Mother only inspected the house once, and She would explain exactly what to do in a part where She had never actually been. She would tell them to look for areas which had been hidden, such as false ceilings. The rooms were all so small, one could hardly use some of them, but Mother knew exactly what was there. It was quite amazing. The whole situation was as if Mother had designed the house long in the past and knew where every nook and cranny was.

'Where did that space come from?' we would say, when we were asked to do something which didn't seem possible.

Hardev Bhamra

A school in India

The first time I saw Shri Mataji was when She arrived at Rome Ashram, at Easter in April 1987, She sat in the central room and all the children gathered around Her, one sitting on Her knee. She told them that She was going to make a school for them in India where they could have lots of fun and climb the trees.

'Would you enjoy that? Would you like to climb the trees?' She said.

Lyn Osterholzer

Shri Mataji and the architect

The photos on the next page are of Shri Mataji at the Campagnano land, near Rome, in the spring of 1987. She was explaining to Hermann Haage, the architect, how to make the changes to the existing projects.

Alessandra Pallini

The drawings on page 21, done by Shri Mataji, were for us in the ashram at Guidonia, where She explained how to do the roof, the arches, the style of the house, what kind of plants to put in the garden and so on.

Alessandra Pallini

Shri Mataji visiting Campagnano, 1987

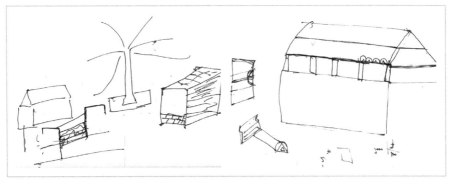

Shri Mataji's drawings for an ashram near Rome (not constructed)

Shri Mataji on the Via il Prato, Florence, 16th April 1987

Easter in Rome, April 1987 (email report)

Shri Mataji spent Easter weekend in Rome, and Sahaja Yogis came from all over Europe to sit at Her Lotus Feet there. It was originally intended to be more or less a private visit with Mr Srivastava, to celebrate their fortieth wedding anniversary, which occurred a few days previously. When it was known there would be a puja, people were invited from all over Europe.

Shri Mataji arrived from London on Friday morning in Rome airport, to be greeted by the Sahaja Yogis who had already arrived, not least the small children of the ashram, about twenty-five of them, who ran up to Shri Mataji with flowers and then ran back to the adults for more flowers which they then ran to present to Shri Mataji again. The sky was an impeccable blue, as it remained all weekend, except for some fine clouds like silk threads of vibrations which appeared after the puja, and this seemed to match Shri Mataji's sunny mood; Mother seemed very relaxed and happy the whole time. Shortly afterwards Shri Mataji departed with Her husband for a private visit to Florence.

Meanwhile hosts of Sahaja Yogis were arriving from all corners of the continent. Puja day was Sunday, and Shri Mataji arrived at the ashram from Her flat in Rome about midday. A platform had been built the previous day for the puja to one side of the house, so that Shri Mataji would be in the shade and we would all be sitting in the garden facing Her. She spoke about materialism and how people became dead with their attention going on dead material objects, and She told us how Lord Jesus had countered this tendency, He being pure Spirit.

The puja continued with bhajans and with small children washing Shri Mother's Feet and with the married ladies decorating Her. She was radiant the whole time. At the end She said how pleased She was with the show of unity between all the European nations which She had witnessed that weekend; it was really a very collective happening. The Europeans will all meet in ten days' time for the Sahasrara Day Puja in Alpe Motta. Shri Mataji had found the most beautiful and best place She had ever been to for puja.

Another relaxed afternoon followed, and in the evening after dinner Shri Mataji was so kind as to come again to the ashram, accompanied this time by Mr Srivastava, for an evening of bhajans. All the children of the ashram, aged between three and four years, gathered around the Lotus Feet of our Divine Mother to sing the Indian song 'Queen of the Universe' and to see some of the girls from the ashram perform an Indian-style dance. We finished off with a few more bhajans including Jogawa. The mood of the evening was relaxed and happy, like the whole weekend.

On the following day, in the afternoon a message came that Shri Mataji would like to see the national groups before She left for India. First were the Swiss. Most of us had already left by bus the previous night, but about ten of us were left, and we drove to Shri Mataji's flat where She received us in Her sitting room. She spoke to us for about fifty minutes about Switzerland and the evilness of its institutions, mainly the banks, and how we should now be quite uninhibited and fearless in proclaiming Sahaja Yoga. She also kindly advised us on how to handle the media in Switzerland. A Sahaja Yogini's article had recently come out; when I was in London last week I was able to present a copy, with translation, to Shri Mataji. Also, two Swiss Sahaja Yogis appeared recently on a radio show to talk about Sahaja Yoga. When I told Shri Mataji about it in London She said it was miraculous. She indicated that things might move much faster this year in Switzerland, and when we told Her that we hoped soon to start the new ashram in Givrins and to move in October, She seemed very happy indeed.

Phil Ward

Everything just works out in Shri Mataji's presence

The first time I saw Shri Mataji was Easter 1987, in Rome about six months after I got my realisation. We Austrians all went in a bus from Vienna. We stayed in a school, all the girls and ladies squeezed into a room, sleeping on the floor. We arrived in the dark and I remember hearing the birds singing in the middle of the night, as if nature herself was jubilant in anticipation of the arrival of Shri Mataji, just as much as we were.

We went to the airport to receive Shri Mataji and there was a big crowd of yogis, and I was in the back and could not see properly. I got a small glimpse of a top of a head and black hair, and I knew it must be Her. She was not tall, which surprised me.

The puja was held in the ashram in Rome, and I was amazed at how humble everything was. I had expected gold and marble, and there was this ordinary, if nice Italian house, and the makeshift stage was small, in the garden at the back of the house, and the decoration was made of a few cotton saris. We sat on the ground and had the Easter Puja. Shri Mataji was presented with a live lamb.

Later, there was a musical evening, and we sat in the hall. I was in pain and very uncomfortable, as my back was hurting badly, and thought I might get ill from the cold, but after a few minutes of sitting there, all the pain vanished, being sucked into the stone floor. That was one of my first strong experiences of Shri Mataji in person; to see how everything just works out and negative thoughts or feelings just vanish in Her presence.

Sigrid Jones

Chapter 3

1987: May - Australia

The streets were littered with diamonds

At Brisbane Airport, in 1987, I was standing near the entrance, with a book in which were photographs and written information regarding Sierra Leone.

'What have you got there?' Shri Mataji asked me as She came past, so I walked with Her into the lounge area and we discussed the information and viewed photographs. She said it was my destiny to go to Sierra Leone. I asked if Patrick Sheriff, who lived in Sierra Leone, and received Realisation in October 1985 could come to India.

'No!' Shri Mataji said. 'He can come to Shudy Camps and the English must pay.' This did take place at the subsequent Guru Puja in the UK.

Shri Mataji then told me that five English scholars wrote that if a person was black skinned then he or she was primitive, this circulated from England and apartheid took hold. Shri Saraswati who resides in Africa, is the sister of Shri Shiva, so if the English help Africa then He will be pleased. She went on to say that I should arrange a flight and passport for Patrick and have the cost carried by England

The day that Patrick flew out of Freetown, Sierra Leone, West Africa, it rained very heavily that night. It was even reported in the Brisbane Courier Mail that on the following morning the population all over Sierra Leone found the streets littered with diamonds due to torrential rain, the road surfaces were washed away and apparently 14,000 mining licences were issued during the next few days.

Peter Corden

Shri Ganesha is walking ahead of us

In May 1987, in Brisbane, my blessing was to escort Shri Mataji from the car to the stage of the Ithica Auditorium at the Brisbane Town Hall. As we stepped into the foyer I noticed the floor pattern contained multiple swastikas.

'Shri Ganesha is here!' I said to Shri Mataji.

'Shri Ganesha is walking ahead of us!' She replied.

Peter Corden

The vibrations have got better

The first time Shri Mataji came to Canberra in 1987, when She got off the plane She could barely walk because the pain in Her Swadishthan was so bad. We were having Sahasrara Puja up in the mountains at Thredbo and She had to come through Canberra to get there. It was autumn time and we had arranged to drive Her through the trees to show them to Her

'What's wrong with these trees, why are they all dying?' Shri Mataji said. When we got back to the ashram She asked me what I thought of Canberra, and whether I was happy in Canberra. I said I was.

'How can you bear it here?' She said.

The last time Shri Mataji came to Canberra we went on a picnic, and She spoke about Mother Nature and the beauty of the place. She came three or four times and the last time She praised the place, because the vibrations got better every time She came. She spoke a lot about Berny Griffin, who designed Canberra, and said it was similar to Delhi. He designed some places in Delhi as well.

Sarah Frankcombe

Look how far you have come

We were from Sydney, and received a phone call that Shri Mataji was speaking to the yogis in the Canberra ashram and to come quickly. We got lost in Canberra's traffic circles and I felt, as we finally crossed the lawn into the ashram that if I was more surrendered, we would not have been late. We duly sat down.

'If you have trouble surrendering, just look back, look how far you have come since you got your realisation, and you will have no trouble surrendering,' Shri Mataji said at that moment.

Heather Jeffrey

We're going to have a miracle!

In May 1987 Shri Mataji visited Australia. For the Sahaja Yogis, the height of Her visit was a weekend programme in the Snowy Mountains, in the town of Thredbo. Everyone had gone to a great deal of trouble to have a flower to give to Shri Mataji when She arrived on Saturday night. This was not easily done, as florists are few and far between in the Snowy Mountains, but we'd all managed somehow. We all had our flowers ready, but Mother made Her way straight to Her room without taking them. When Shri Mataji came from Her room, She went directly to the meeting hall and spoke to us for quite some time, after which we had a musical programme. Then Mother spoke to us again. By this time, most of us had been holding our flowers for three or four hours and were giving up hope.

'I see that you have some flowers for Me,' Shri Mataji sweetly said, just before leaving. 'Would you like to give them to Me now?' So, torn between the horror of offering these dead flowers and the longing to give something to Mother, no matter what, we gratefully and humbly gave the dead blooms to Shri Mataji. They were hanging down and completely finished. They were completely dead: not just slightly dead, but utterly dead. Shri Mataji went back to Her room. After a little while, She asked for the box of flowers to be brought in.

'Bring them into the bathroom,' She said. 'We're going to have a miracle. You'll see, it will be a miracle. Fill the bath with very warm water. Fill it just as if I were going to have a bath.' As the water was running, Mother was putting Her hand into the bath, vibrating the whole thing.

'Now put all the flowers into the bath,' She said. 'Make sure all the stems are down in the water.' When all the flowers were in the bath, Mother said: 'See, they're already looking better.' And they were. 'You wait,' She continued, 'and see in the morning. We'll use these flowers for the puja.' Next morning all the flowers were fresh and blooming.

After Shri Mataji has stayed in a place, the auspicious thing is to leave Her room exactly as it is for nine days after Her departure. This was done after Mother's departure from Australia in 1987. Every day, the ladies would just go in and check the room and each day there would be an indentation of the quilt on the same side of the bed as Mother had slept in. Each day they would shake the quilt and smooth it out, and each day the indentation would be there again, as though She were still sleeping there throughout those nine days.

Matthew Fogarty

Sahasrara Puja, Thredbo, 1987 with the revived flowers

A beautiful double rainbow

In 1987 Shri Mataji and all the Sahaja Yogis were at Thredbo in the Snowy Mountains, Australia, for Sahasrara Puja. A newish Sahaja Yogi was going through some personal difficulties, and prayed to Shri Mataji for a sign as he stood outside the hotel gazing at the mountains.

The next moment a beautiful double rainbow appeared, arching from Her room at the hotel, across to a nearby mountain. It stayed there for a long time, finally disappeared, and then came back again.

Judy Dobbie

You'd better hurry

We were meeting Shri Mataji at the airport, which was something Australians weren't used to doing. I had been given the honour of presenting Shri Mataji with a beautiful garland. It was a very long garland, as high as Shri Mataji. I was holding this garland and it was so heavy and all of a sudden the string broke. It fell on the ground and I was horrified. I picked it up and put it together as best I could, but I was thinking, 'How can I offer this to the Goddess, because it has been on the ground?'

Eventually Shri Mataji arrived and I was still wondering what to do, when Mother turned round.

'Well, if you want to give it to Me, you'd better hurry,' She said.

Barbara Napper

The order of the names of the deities

On one occasion when Shri Mataji came to Australia in the late 1980's, I found there were discrepancies in the order in which we said the names of the mantras. One of the common ones was that people would always say Shri Mary-Jesus. The answer came this way.

'I'll tell you about it,' Shri Mataji said. 'When it comes to Shri Shiva-Parvati, there is no one else but Shri Shiva, so Shri Shiva always comes first. However when we go onto the Vishnu line, Shri Vishnu incarnated in different forms as time goes by. When we look at Shri Lakshmi-Vishnu, it goes with Shri Lakshmi first because they were a married couple. Likewise when it comes to Shri Sita-Rama, Shri Sita comes first because they were a married couple. When it comes to Shri Radha-Krishna, again they were a married couple so Shri Radha comes first. When we come up to Shri Jesus and Shri Mary this was not a marriage so He goes first.'

When we go to Shri Brahma, to the other line, it is Shri Brahmadeva-Saraswati, so Shri Mother clarified which comes first. Shri Brahmadeva comes first. On the Vishnu line it varies according to whether they are married or not.

Peter Corden

Editor's note: on other occasions Shri Mataji asked people to say the mantras in a different order. It seems nothing is fixed.

They have noise laws here

After the public programme in Brisbane, we went back to our house, where Shri Mataji was staying. She was seated near the doorway into the hall. The lounge-dining room was quite large and was filled to capacity with yogis, visitors and musical instruments and we were to have an evening of entertainment and bhajans. I was slightly behind and to one side of Shri Mataji.

The music started quite reverently, however as the evening progressed, it became louder and louder. I put a bandhan around the noise factor because some noise pollution laws had recently been passed, and the cut off point for noise was ten o'clock, and in a quiet suburb on a week day night, with the loud bhajans, I was definitely a contender for complaints from the neighbours. I was becoming quietly concerned that this might be an all-night do, and that the neighbours and even the police might come round, as the enthusiasm and momentum of the bhajans showed no sign of abating.

'We will finish up now, because they have noise laws here,' Shri Mataji said, at precisely ten o'clock.

Albert Lewis

It's part of My plan

After Shri Mataji's first visit in 1985, we decided to find a sensible restaurant to take Her to after the public programme, the next time She came, in 1986. We found an up-market place by the river, and they had a good singer – a young lady with a beautiful voice who would sing modern devotional songs.

Shri Mataji arrived for Her next visit on a Monday, and the next day She went shopping in the Brisbane arcade, and bought a suit for Sir CP and

Shri Mataji being welcomed into Norman Park House, Brisbane in 1987

Shri Mataji receiving and giving gifts at Norman Park House

clothing for various members of Her family. In the evening the programme was at the Brisbane Town Hall and after that we all went to the previously vetted restaurant. We made sure Shri Mataji had the best seat, and all the attending yogis settled around the table.

When the meal arrived, Shri Mataji did not start eating, and we were all waiting for Her to begin, because it is inauspicious to start before the Goddess. I was becoming a little anxious, as two of us had to leave, because on the evening Shri Mataji came we were to do a live radio broadcast on the 4EB station. (Shri Mataji was apparently delighted with this new way of spreading vibrations)

Two Indian Sahaja Yogis with us explained that Shri Mataji has no desires and therefore we had to invite Her to eat. We did this, She began to eat, and we all tucked in to the delicious food. The dessert was served and the singer began singing, all was flowing as arranged, and the other Sahaja Yogi and I excused ourselves and left for the radio show.

We arrived at the radio station and began our presentation of 'Good Vibrations'. The vibrations were good, and the show went without a hitch. We felt a little pious that we were doing 'God's work', and drove home. As we entered the driveway a young Sahaja Yogi came out and told us Shri Mataji had been verbally attacked by the singer at the restaurant! Instant beads of sweat appeared on my brow, and in trepidation I went into the house where Shri Mataji was.

I quietly asked a Sahaja Yogi what had happened. He said that after the singer had finished Her songs She had been introduced to Shri Mataji, and had verbally attacked Her. I apologised to Shri Mataji for what had happened.

'It's alright; it's part of My plan. They'll expose themselves,' She explained. I felt a little better.

Albert Lewis

Anyone who asks for help in God's name will be answered

We were again in my old car. I was in the back with Shri Mataji and in the front were the driver and another Sahaja Yogi, who told us the following story about a priest who was caught in a flood and was sitting on the roof of his church praying to God to be rescued.

Along came a man in a rowing boat and offered to rescue him, but he refused, saying God would rescue him. The floodwaters kept rising, and the priest kept praying. Along came a helicopter and offered to rescue him, but again he refused, saying God would come and rescue him. The floodwaters kept rising and eventually the roof of the church was covered and the priest drowned. The priest found himself at the pearly gates of heaven, and he asked the gatekeeper why God didn't rescue him.

'Well, we sent you a boat and a helicopter, but you refused to go in them,' replied the gatekeeper.

At this point everyone in the car was laughing, and Shri Mataji was chuckling to Herself.

'Anyone who asks for help in God's name will be answered,' Shri Mataji said, almost under Her breath.

On one occasion Shri Mataji came late for a puja, and then apologised to the assembled yogis. She explained that She had had Her attention on people who were not yet Sahaja Yogis, because anyone who asks for help in God's name will be answered.

Albert Lewis

Shri Mataji's second precious visit

Shri Mataji's second precious visit to New Zealand was in May 1987. This followed the Sahasrara Puja in Australia. Shri Mataji stayed at the new ashram in Valley Road, Mount Eden, very close to the mountain itself. The first public programme was held at the Pioneer Women's Hall in the centre of Auckland. It was full, a beautiful event. Near the end a young Maori girl stood up and sang a Maori song.

Shri Mataji came to our country with Her elder brother Bala Sahib, who was such a humble, gracious man. He was a High Court Judge, so wise, very appreciative and down to earth.

There was a morning interview with Leonie Breznehan on Radio New Zealand. The interviewer was very polite and humble towards Shri Mataji, and so it also was an auspicious event and an excellent interview.

After Shri Mataji came back, She sat down in Her puja chair, about 10 am. She was so composed whilst we prepared the puja around Her. This was appropriately to Shri Ganesha, and was New Zealand's first puja. That evening the weather turned bitterly cold and squally.

David and Trisha Sharp

Shri Mataji's brother saw the Kundalinis rise

Shri Mataji's brother Bala Sahib accompanied Her to New Zealand on Her second visit. He hadn't previously taken to Sahaja Yoga but he participated in the puja we performed at the ashram, sitting in a chair at the back. After the puja had finished he announced that during the puja when everyone had bowed down to do namaskar he had been able to see the Kundalini in everyone's back rising.

Maybe, Mother had said, later, that he had gained his realisation during the puja.

Bryce Clendon

Shri Mataji and Her brother Bala Sahib

There should be another island

During Mother's second visit a visiting yogi asked Her a question about New Zealand. She replied that New Zealand is Shri Ganesha's trunk when it goes to the left, which represents auspiciousness, and also that there should be another island somewhere.

Bryce Clendon

The thali at the Shri Ganesha Puja

New Zealand in the thali

The second time Shri Mataji came to New Zealand, we were privileged to host a Shri Ganesha Puja, and for most of us it was the first time we had ever attended a puja with Shri Mataji. We were all busy getting ready and the announcement was made that Shri Mataji was already sitting there ready waiting for us. There was a great flurry and we all immediately headed to the front room of the ashram. A beautiful talk followed.

'Look! There is New Zealand in the thali,' Shri Mataji commented, when the amrut was poured over Her hands, 'and very clearly you can see the shape of the North Island and tip of the South Island.' The thali is the dish in which the liquid falls during the puja. Shri Mataji also had us photograph the soles of Her Feet, and She commented on how white they were.

Janie Frith

During the puja when the ghee or honey was poured into the thali over the previous elements, Shri Mataji pointed out that the puddle had formed the shape of New Zealand's North Island and the tip of the South Island. Photos were taken to record this before the puja continued.

Bryce Clendon

We have to keep up with the rocket

After a puja, during an early visit to New Zealand, Shri Mataji likened evolution in Sahaja Yoga to a missile, a rocket. One booster pushes us so far, then drops off, the next booster takes over and the rocket goes faster. This happens again and again, and in the process, the rocket gains height, overcoming gravity. We are at the stage where another boost is due, Shri Mataji said, but if we keep hanging on to the used booster then we will be discarded with it. We have to keep up with the rocket.

Brian Bell

He was ready for his transformation

During an early visit to New Zealand, Shri Mataji was interviewed live by a well-known radio personality who had a reputation for cynicism and aggression. The exchange began with some hard-hitting questions about religion, the world situation and other contentious subjects. Shri Mataji answered with Her usual relaxed aplomb.

Health became the topic and the interviewer admitted that he was diabetic. Shri Mataji talked about the causes of diabetes and the way in which it can be overcome through self realisation, which She explained. As the interview progressed, the interviewer became more sympathetic and positive.

'Are you a Messiah? A prophet?' he eventually asked. Shri Mataji didn't reply and suddenly the interviewer started saying, 'I can feel this coolness on my hands! When I bring them together it feels as if I'm holding a ball of cool wind!' He explained how, at the beginning of the interview he was very sceptical, 'but now I can feel it.'

The workers at the radio station couldn't believe what they were hearing. What the interviewer was saying was so out of character. They crowded around the studio window to watch and listen.

Later the interviewer said he could feel the coolness in his head.

'What about everybody else?' he asked.

'They can get it too,' said Shri Mataji. 'Just tell them to put their hands out to the radio and they will get it.'

That evening She told us that although the interviewer had a bad reputation, underneath he was quite humble, and so was ready for his transformation.

'That is why he felt it so strongly,' She said.

The radio programme prompted a number of newspaper articles, all very respectful of Shri Mataji and very positive about Sahaja Yoga. Shri Mataji has told this story many times around the world.

Brian Bell

Shri Mataji at the havan in Auckland 1987

The shawl was a gift from the New Zealand Sahaja Yogis. After the havan Shri Mataji gave presents to all the ladies.

A havan in the garden

On Her second visit a havan was performed, at Shri Mataji's request, in the back garden of the ashram. Later in the afternoon, She came and sat on a chair on the lawn near where we had had the havan.

I don't remember if everyone went before Shri Mataji, but I finally had the opportunity to present Her with a small ceramic bowl I had bought a long time before. I used to keep it in a drawer, wrapped in tissue-paper, and would occasionally take it out and admire it. It was quite simple, but had pretty blue hydrangea flowers painted on it and some piercing near the border. The last time I had taken it out to look at it I was amazed at the blast of vibrations that came off it. When I had shown it to our leader, Brian, to ask if I could offer it to Her his immediate remark was, 'Wow, this has accumulated some vibrations!'

Shri Mataji didn't pass comment on the bowl but accepted it graciously.

Bryce Clendon

The cactus flower

While living at the second ashram in Auckland I had a small cactus in a pot on the front veranda. I had had it for a long time yet it never seemed to look any different. Three days after Shri Mataji left I noticed it had a yellow flower fully opened right on the top like a Sahasrara.

Bryce Clendon

The Ganesha-like lawyer

This is the story of a case filed against the order of the Pune Collector on 28th May 1987 for demolishing Pratishthan, as the authorities assumed it was a temple, and if so could not be constructed in an agricultural zone. Shri Mataji's plea was that it was Her personal farm house and not a temple. (Shri Mataji grew both rice and sunflowers on the land, both agricultural crops).

When the matter came up for hearing in the High Court, Her lawyer was not in the court. From nowhere a young boy, dressed as a lawyer, appeared before the judge and requested him to dismiss the case, but also to postpone the hearing by an hour. The Ganesha-like lawyer somehow managed to trace Shri Mataji's lawyer, who was arguing a case in another court, and brought him to the High Court. After the case was decided in Shri Mataji's favour, the Ganesha-like lawyer disappeared. No one knew who he was and no one had seen him before.

Yogi Mahajan

Chapter 4

1987: June to August England and America

A visit to Hounslow ashram

We were in London in 1987, and had been trying without success to get an appointment with Shri Mataji. She had asked us to see Her and report on our visit to Sierra Leone. However, the circumstances relayed back to us indicated that Shri Mataji had so many people on Her list to see that it would probably not happen. While living in Hounslow ashram, around 10.30 in the morning I answered the phone.

'Shri Mataji here,' Wow! Kristie was stunned into speechlessness, but managed to reply something coherent.

'I am coming around to Hounslow to look in the attic at some saris I have stored there, and I will be there for lunch,' She said.

Panic! What to give Shri Mataji to eat? Coming from Australia this was a big deal for me, however, Marylin Leate came to the rescue. The English were used to Shri Mataji's menu, so off we went to the shops to buy lamb cutlets. Marylin said Mother liked them in mint and vinegar. So yes, we prepared a feast for the people living in the ashram, and then word got out and other yogis started to arrive. Shri Mother enjoyed Her lunch.

'What's wrong with South Africa?' She then asked us.

'I don't know what's wrong with South Africa Mother, but West Africa is very good,' Peter replied.

With that Peter produced photographs of the West African yogis and their children. Shri Mataji was keen to learn the story of the yogis there, and the land that we had purchased to build an ashram on.

'How much did all this cost you?' She asked.

'$1000, USA,' we replied.

'Go and get the money,' Mother said to a leader who was with Her.

'No Mother,' we said.

'You Australians!' She replied.

Kristie then asked if could Patrick Sherrif, one of the Sahaja Yogis from Sierra Leone, come to England for a puja.

'Yes,' She nodded and said.

How wonderful this play was that was being worked out, and Shri Mataji never got to look in the attic for the saris. The lunch went until late afternoon.

Kristie Corden

A bliss casualty

In 1987, the year I received the gift of self realisation from Shri Mataji, something slipped in my lower back, trapping a nerve and causing me to walk around with a bit of a limp. After the Thursday night programme in Hampstead we received a message that Shri Mataji was arriving at Hounslow Ashram and we were allowed to receive Her.

I'm not sure exactly how, but suddenly I found myself in front of Shri Mataji discussing my back issue. She asked me to sit down with my back towards Her and placed Her Foot on my right Swadishthan area for some time while She worked on other issues. This was an extraordinary experience for me as I felt the millions of molecules that constituted my physical body were dancing with joy at the streams of divine nectar that pulsed from Shri Mataji's Foot into my being. After She had finished working on me I got up.

'Look at his face, he is a bliss casualty!' Mother joked. I can assure you, I definitely was!

Steve Jones

Now your love has taken form

Practically everyone had arrived by the Friday evening for the Guru Puja weekend, 16th July 1987, and the main item on everyone's agenda was preparing the house of Shudy Camps for Shri Mataji's arrival, and preparing the stage for puja. During the week there were at least fifty people working on the house, and this swelled to 700 by Friday, and work continued right until the last minute. At the same time, a number of large marquees were being erected in the garden. The men slept in one and the ladies and babies in another. The stage was beautifully decorated, overhung by a cloth in white and green colours as backdrop, with a gold-embossed disk at the centre. The backdrop was a splendid painting of the parting of the waters in the Red Sea.

On Saturday the main concern was the preparation of the house. People had been working night and day for several days previously, and it seemed as though the work would never end. Marble arrived from Italy for the main staircase on Thursday evening, and had been set by the time Shri Mataji arrived. As the sun was setting on Saturday evening, all the Sahaja Yogis made their way to the front of the house to await the arrival of our Divine Mother. We could still see the people working away inside the house to make the final preparations and arrange Shri Mataji's bedroom. A group of younger Sahaja Yogis made their way to the end of the driveway to lead Her car to the front door by dancing in procession, as in India. The rest of us waited, some holding flags of the countries represented.

Suddenly the setting sun broke out from behind a bank of cloud to cast a brilliant ruddy light on the façade of the house, and Shri Mataji was there. After leaving Her car and waving to the assembled Sahaja Yogis, She went into the house and made Her way upstairs to Her bedroom, where we could see the workers doing namaste to Her. Then Shri Mataji came to the window, and for a long, silent minute or two stood there, Her hands joined in namaste, Her head bowed, and Her eyes closed, towards us. Then She opened Her eyes, leaned on the windowsill, and slowly looked at all of us, smiling, Her glance moving throughout the assembly. It was a wonderful moment. Later She commented on the pink colour of the sky at that moment, saying that it was Shri Mahalakshmi's colour; Shri Mahalakshmi was showing Her contentment. We all moved to the back of the house, where after a few minutes Shri Mataji appeared again.

'Now your love has taken form,' I heard Her say.

The next day, Sunday, was puja day. During the puja Shri Mataji talked about the older forms of yoga, in which either one renounced all things to go and sit at the feet of the guru, or one lived a normal life at the end of which one renounced one's property - Sankhya Yoga. During the puja itself, Shri Mataji was presented with a trident and a wooden shepherd's crook. At the end of the puja the vibrations were very strong, and Shri Mataji told us as She was leaving that we should all remain sitting there in meditation to absorb the vibrations.

Phil Ward

The best gift of all

A man called Patrick Sheriff from Sierra Leone was sponsored by the English to come to Guru Puja in 1987, and he was looked after by the English for six weeks in the UK. He brought with him pictures of a mud brick ashram that was being built in Sierra Leone. When he went to Mother after the puja, She was so delighted to see these photographs, and made the comment that we can bring Her all the riches, gold, silver but to see the photos of an ashram going up in a farfetched place like Sierra Leone was the best gift of all.

Following my time in Sierra Leone I went to Austria and Shri Mataji spoke to me. She asked me to tell Her a couple of stories about Sierra Leone. One was when Patrick had got his realisation in 1985

'My fingers are talking,' he had said. I told Shri Mataji about the following day, when I took a photo of Her to him and asked Patrick who the lady in the photo was.

'It is very simple, God is our Father, Jesus Christ is the Son of God, and this lady is the wife of God,' he said. So Mother was very pleased.

'Feel the vibrations,' She said.

'What is Sierra Leone?' I asked Shri Mataji. She said that it is a ductless gland and a remote control. So obviously Sierra Leone had to be treated for some other parts of the Virata to work out.

At Shudy Camps, Shri Mataji explained that in the past five English scholars had justified the slavery of the people of Africa and also apartheid, citing very racist reasons. Shri Mataji said apartheid came because of these five scholars. When scholars from the UK write it circulates because it is the heart pumping through the system and Shri Mataji pointed out that

Shri Saraswati is the sister of Shri Shiva, and the situation was very offensive, that the country that is the home of his sister was put into slavery.

At one time Shri Mataji said She could not save the world while apartheid stood. A year or two after that it came tumbling down thanks to Mandela. Shri Mataji said that Shri Saraswati resides in Africa and She is the sister of Lord Shiva. Due to the fact that the British had done this work and put Africa into strife, Shri Saraswati would then be quite distressed with them. So the responsibility falls on England to redeem the situation by helping Africa. Shri Mother advised that if we organised that the English do some work in Africa, Shri Shiva will be pleased and the heart will be warmer, and the UK will get warmer. And the whole world will benefit.

Peter Corden

Shri Mataji talked about music

In the evening there was a sitar concert by Debu Choudhuri, who had come all the way from Delhi for the occasion. He played two ragas, and finished with a third, Rag Swanandeshwari, which he had composed some years before at Shri Mataji's request. Afterwards Shri Mataji talked to us about music, how in Western music certain developments such as in the field of harmony had been made, 'which was a good thing', but that modern music was completely degenerate, even much Indian music. The old ragas had been directly inspired by the unconscious. She described the difference between the Karnatic music from South India, which uses microtones (shrutis), and the Hindustani from Northern India, and talked about how many great Indian musicians had played before Her and had such respect for Her.

After the musical recital came the dramatic performance, prepared by the English. This presented the different incarnations of the Shri Adi Guru, with music from a sort of rock group, and a son-et-lumière. Shri Mataji much enjoyed the production, and at the end, when some of the girls finished with a graceful dance, She showed the girls how to dance together the opening of the Sahasrara, holding their saris high above their heads to produce the effect of petals.

Phil Ward

My heart just ripped open

The first time I came to Shudy Camps was for Guru Puja 1987. A group of Austrians came by plane, and we were picked up from the airport by coach, and travelled through the night to Shudy Camps. We arrived there tired, but when we got there the atmosphere was absolutely electrifying. There was this mansion, in the middle of the night, in the quiet country-side, and absolutely every window was lit, and people were working on the house. It was magical; even though there was all this activity, there was this wonderful glow of sweet calm and serenity. My heart just ripped open, and I completely fell in love with it all.

Everybody worked to finish the renovation work on the house until the very last minute. Shri Mataji arrived at the front of the house in the car, and the sky just burst with this most amazing sunset, everything lit with a soft glow. Mother got out of the car and looked around and said that this must be the New Jerusalem.

She slowly proceeded towards the house and Her rooms, talking to people, and accepting flowers, and while She was taking Her time, upstairs the work was still going on. Shri Mataji was at the bottom of the landing, and they were still laying the carpet at the top of the stairs! Of course Shri Mataji's timing was perfect as always, and when She reached Her rooms everything was ready.

Sigrid Jones

A custody issue

At Shudy Camps, in 1987, a Sahaja Yogi asked Shri Mataji whether She could help him with his personal situation. He was contemplating suing his ex-wife for custody of their son. Shri Mataji said She would help.

Before the details of the case were related to Shri Mataji, She explained to him that in English law the custody of a young child is usually decided in favour of the mother, unless there are exceptional circumstances. Shri Mataji then enquired whether the mother was unfit or addicted to drugs or mentally unwell. The Sahaja Yogi said that she was not, but that she had always had custody of the child, and now it should be his turn to have custody.

'When was the last time you sent money for the child?' Shri Mataji asked. The Sahaja Yogi could not remember. Then She asked, 'When was the last time you visited the child?' Again the Sahaja Yogi could not remember. Then Shri Mataji said, 'Do you think the child would rather live with you than with his mother?' The Sahaja Yogi said he had no idea.

Now Shri Mataji was ready to give advice.

'I think I can help you,' She said. 'Give up completely the idea of suing your ex-wife for custody of the child. You will save yourself a lot of grief, and a lot of time and money.'

The Sahaja Yogi felt very despondent that Shri Mataji had not given him the answer he wanted to hear, and sat in a corner of the room.

'Are you still sulking?' Shri Mataji told him, 'Can't you see that it is not fair to remove a small child from the mother?' But still he was not uplifted, so She tried another angle. 'If you lose the case, your reputation as a good father and a caring person will be destroyed, even your reputation as a good Sahaja Yogi would be affected because it is clear that you neglected your child, isn't it? Do you feel comfortable dragging down the name of Sahaja Yoga to the courts?'

At last this Sahaja Yogi realised that Shri Mataji had the welfare of all concerned in mind and he too was being helped, and a big smile appeared on his face.

Luis Garrido

Shri Mataji at the Shri Vishnumaya Puja

It is very important to wear an undershirt

It was August 1987, Shri Vishnumaya Puja in New York. We were meditating on the grass outside the house where Shri Mataji was staying. She asked us to come inside and we were all in a small room with Shri Mataji. She asked my father to massage Her Feet. She didn't say anything to me until we were about to leave.

'Beta (son), why are you not wearing an undershirt? It is very important to wear an undershirt.' I had just taken off my undershirt before I went in, because I was perspiring! She said it is very important for your centre heart.

Mohan Gulati

Shri Mataji was very concerned

In America, at the New Rochelle ashram, New York, I used to have to go down when Shri Mataji came, and baby sit for the children of the people living there, or make the tea or something. One time I was asked to put a hot water bottle into Shri Mataji's bed. She was sitting alone in Her room and She had just come back from a public programme. She asked me what I thought about it.

'I thought it was wonderful,' I said, or something like that.

'This city (or maybe country) was completely abandoned,' She replied. She was obviously very concerned that it would work out.

Another time, at the Shri Vishnumaya Puja in Connecticut, I was looking after the Kalbermatten children, and everyone was busy getting everything ready. We were walking along to the road and a car drew up with Shri Mataji in it. She corrected all the yogis, because our attention was not on Her, and we were not there to receive Her. We were all into planning, in our ego and into getting the puja hall ready.

Pamela Mathews

She was literally caring for my health

I was having a period of illness and fatigue and generally low energy. I had tried a lot of different things, but was still having trouble and getting sick a lot. At one point, Shri Mataji was visiting, and She opened Her own medicine kit and took out some medicines and prescribed for me on the spot what I needed for this sort of lethargy. She took the medicine from Her own kit and gave it to me to use and it was great.

She was literally caring for my health with Her own medicine.

Phil Trumbo

Sahaja culture and personal details

When I was still new to Sahaja Yoga, Shri Mataji always had a way of verifying for me that She was with me all the time. When I would be in Her presence, She would sometimes comment about something that She only could have known if She were inside me. I had been in Sahaja Yoga about a year and a half and one day at my work place, which was Chemical Bank in those days, I got a telephone call from Shri Mataji Herself. It was really a shock when you get a phone call from the Adi Shakti!

'Why not try to get your relationship back together again with your husband? He has the vibrations of a seeker, and if he got into Sahaja Yoga your children would get into Sahaja Yoga, and what more could a mother want?' She said. How did Shri Mataji know I was divorced and in great agony about this? I had never discussed it with Her out loud. I was utterly flabbergasted and yet overwhelmingly happy to have the opportunity to try and redeem myself. She gave me some strategies for how to communicate with my ex-husband. I went to live in Washington for about six months, but my husband didn't want anything to do with it. Nevertheless it transformed all of us. After about six months Shri Mataji said that I had given my ex a chance, my children had forgiven me, and I needed to come back to New York.

That telephone conversation came when Shri Mataji came on a surprise visit with Sir CP, who came to attend a fortieth birthday celebrations of the United Nations. Shri Mataji decided to join him at the last moment, and we didn't get the call that She was coming until She reached there. They were booked into an international hotel near the UN. We had a tiny ashram out in New Jersey, at Bergenfield.

All the yogis came, from Boston, Maine and Ohio, and Shri Mataji would come out of the ashram and sit in the one comfortable chair we had. She must have spoken to us for ten hours on Sahaja Yoga culture almost in a chat form. The house was filled with yogis sitting at Her Lotus Feet with such awe. She spoke about Sahaja Yoga culture and we had a little puja in the basement and She talked about personal details with us: career suggestions, ashram suggestions, and we would get involved, marriages and so on. Shri Mataji looked over all the marriage applications, and when She came to mine She looked at me.

'Carolyn Vance, I would like to marry you Myself!' She said. I was in my forties and everyone else was much younger so I hadn't taken this marriage business too seriously. She was just trying to say something nice!

Carolyn Vance

The kindest of the kind

Another time, I was still a new yogi and was beginning to realise more fully the horror of the problems in America. Shri Mataji had come to New York and as we were so few I had gotten the chance to ride with Her in the back seat of Her car.

'Don't feel so responsible for America,' She said to me after a long silence. 'You weren't here for all your lives, you know.'

I immediately relaxed and felt the joy. Shri Mataji knows exactly what our worries or obstacles are and She removes them instantly. She is the kindest of the kindest. Her grace is the most gracious. Her love and compassion make it impossible for anyone to feel anything but joy when one is in Her physical presence.

Carolyn Vance

Shri Mataji's divine attention

Shri Mataji gave us a great deal of support and advice about establishing ashrams. She was accustomed to changing Her place of residence about once a year – usually in order to better accommodate Sir CP's diplomatic needs. She said the good part about moving often is that it stops our habits from getting too entrenched.

Nearly every year, Shri Mataji would help us reorganize our ashram situation in New York. In Her talks to all of us, She would try to raise our awareness of the important role the ashram played for new people — how they would be learning about the culture of Sahaja Yoga from us and how important ashrams were for our own individual ascent, as we dealt with our own ego reactions and could learn to transcend the material, and know the importance of love.

At one point, She said there are a certain minimum number of yogis needed in the ashram to be able to solve the problems easily. At that time, the number was eight. The highest joy of all the experiences of ashram living was the fact that the divine attention was on us all the time.

Carolyn Vance

The divine diplomat

Shri Mataji especially liked to shop in New York City. We set out from the ashram and it was quite a long drive into town, so first we went to a Chinese restaurant and had lunch and had a huge table.

Most of Shri Mataji's shopping had so much purpose – a training for us, and it was also for the resources of the world and the shopkeepers. Once She found a particular shop She liked in Chinatown. It was so small that the whole group of yogis accompanying Her couldn't fit inside. We took turns watching Her selections and hearing Her comments about the art and craftsmanship of the items – small to massive cloisonné urns, ceramic horses and other figurines, jade flowers, horses, rings, etc. She would look at them, and after about ten of these, the shop keepers closed the shop to other customers. They got Shri Mataji a chair, brought Her some tea and got us some Coca Colas.

The husband and wife, the Chinese shop owners, were delighted to have such a generous patron and felt they indeed had an honoured guest. She would have them explain how the items were made, what part of China they came from. They were deeply knowledgeable and involved in the fine art, culture and literature of China and were proud to tell us about the craftsmanship that went into these items. They also had a bookstore that imported Chinese literature. So now we could see how the divine diplomat was working to improve our relations with China.

The same process kept happening with each group of items until the entire lot was removed. Finally, the shopkeepers ran out of items and had to bring in more from the small storage space in the back and She bought those too. With each group of selections, I was more and more awestruck at Her generosity. These were gifts Shri Mataji was selecting for Her family and the yogis.

The vibrations inside the tiny shop became stronger and stronger until it felt like a puja. In this magical environment, the bargaining began. The shopkeepers were extraordinarily respectful and also very generous so Shri Mataji received an excellent discount. She would not bargain, but the shopkeepers loved Her so much that the discounts were amazing. We also made some really good friends, and every shopping trip I went on with Shri Mataji was like a training ground on the Laxshmi tattwa. She would be lecturing a little and pointing things out and hoping we would get the point of what She was saying. After the purchase was made and the prices all agreed on - by the time they got to that stage they all loved Shri Mataji so much that bargaining wasn't even necessary.

Before we could leave the shop, some logistic issues had to be worked out. Being still a new yogi, I thought it would be impossible to get this huge inventory to India without the normal gross amount of red tape. How to get these very large and plentiful items overseas to India? All the yogis began looking at one another with furrowed brows, but Shri Mahalakshmi smoothly took over and organized everything in such a simple way that She removed our headaches before we even got them.

Any time She was shopping, She was constantly teaching us – about generosity, about appreciation for handcrafted items, about another country's culture, about how shopping for things that we can give others shows our love, how it helps to change the economy, about discretion, about handling money.

Carolyn Vance

Art history lessons from Shri Saraswati

In the course of living in New York City, and Shri Mataji visiting there a number of times, we would go out with Her on various shopping experiences. To call it shopping was like calling the ocean a big body of water – it doesn't quite describe it. In many cases, Shri Mataji was buying gifts for people in other countries, and She would pick out gifts for hundreds of people. They were all appropriate, and very aesthetic. But the main thing about these excursions with Her was aesthetics.

I had a background in Fine Art, and Shri Mataji would take us to shops that had a gallery quality, such as carpet shops, sculptures and glassware. She would examine them critically, vibrationally and from the point of view of aesthetics. We were with Shri Saraswati, getting art history lessons – telling us about the origin of silk, carpets, bronze sculptures, carvings of wood and stone, and what part of the world they came from. Shri Mataji had a great deal of knowledge about the people involved in this. When She looked at an object and felt the vibrations She was able to see a direct line to the creative spirit of the individual who had made it, to that creativity, and all this in some shop in a busy corner of New York City. It was a transformative experience.

Shri Mataji uses art and beauty to transform things through vibrations. It is not just that things are superficially beautiful, but the way She arranges Her homes - the way She arranges the aesthetics, the way She directs the visual, the textural, the colour and even the materials that Her homes are built with. They are all built with a sense of harmony and the correct materials. Sometimes She would use styles that you wouldn't think would work together; wooden screens from Rajasthan with stone work from another area. They would work together marvellously well. She would take classical European Italian Baroque decorative images and patterns and use them together with those of the east. There was always an amazing balance, such as one sees in the Sistine Chapel.

Part of Her role on this earth is to bring back the Shri Saraswati principle, a sense of aesthetics, of taste. She does it in art, music, dress, and architecture. Meanwhile She raises the Kundalini of the whole world, a pretty amazing undertaking!

Phil Trumbo

Showing us how to spot beauty

Another amazing incident was when Shri Mataji paid a surprise visit to New York. She was staying in a hotel with Sir CP in Manhattan. My job was there, so at lunchtime I came down from my office and got ready to go to Shri Mataji's hotel. I thought I'd wait outside Her window to get some vibrations. I headed for the revolving door of my building, but who should come through it but Shri Mataji.

'I came to get you,' She said, and took me by the arm.

She said we should go and find another Sahaja Yogini who was working a few blocks away. There were two or three men with us, so we all went over to the other lady's building. We went up in the elevator to her office and she was also overcome with shock, surprise and joy.

Then we walked up and down Fifth Avenue looking at things in the stores, handmade things, embroidery on a towel, a piece of artwork. It was Shri Laxshmi training – showing us how to be able to spot beauty. Shri Mataji wanted to rid us of right-sidedness, especially when we were conducting programmes for Her.

Carolyn Vance

Shri Mataji knew exactly what to do and when to do it

Shri Mataji had one of the Sahaja Yogis clean up Her rings, and She was leaving for California.

'What is this community we are coming to?' She asked we got on the road. I explained that this was a Hasidim Jewish community and they generally deal in diamonds and/or electronics. As I finished saying the word 'diamonds,' Shri Mataji turned to my wife.

'Where are My rings?' She asked, and we had to go back and pick up Her rings in the flat.

It so happened that Shri Mataji explained to us later that the way we were going, we would have got to the airport sooner than the yogis but with this little delay, by the time we had got back and picked up the rings the traffic had built up. So when we got to the airport, all the yogis had time to get there to greet Her.

She knew exactly what to do and when to do it, so sweetly.

Michael Petrunia

The baby at Shri Mataji's holy Feet

Where there's a will, there's a way

After a puja in California in 1987, a group of yogis were sitting in a living room in Los Angeles, and Shri Mataji was talking and laughing with us. I was holding my daughter Adya, who was under one year old, and had recently been gifted with her new name from Shri Mataji. Adya seemed very restless and wouldn't sit still, having just learned how to crawl. I let her go for a moment, only to look up and see her make a beeline for Shri Mataji. Once she arrived at Mother's Feet, she sat down, and then proceeded to behave so sweetly and quietly, as long as she could sit at Mother's lotus Feet. However often I got up and brought her back, the first opportunity she had, she quietly got up and went back to Shri Mataji's Feet again.

Mother thought this was very sweet, and leant down and stroked her hair, and was very happy to let her sit there. I went into the kitchen to get Mother something to eat, and when I came back I noticed that She was wearing a shawl exactly like mine. I was so pleased and thought, 'Oh I have a shawl exactly like that one.'

The next thing I knew was my sister came up to me and whispered in my ear. 'Shri Mataji was getting cold, and She asked for a shawl, and I saw yours nicely folded on your luggage, so that is the one I gave to Her.' I was amazed, because there was my daughter sitting at Her Feet, and Shri Adi Shakti wearing my shawl – and drinking Diet Coke. It was such a nice gift.

Mona Dale

Look at my watch

One time in Los Angeles, a large group of people assembled to see Shri Mataji off as She departed the city. We were waiting near the departure gate. The person next to me pointed to her watch.

'Oh look, it's five minutes until the flight and Shri Mataji's not here,' She said.

'That's interesting. The flight is expected to leave on time,' I added.

Within a minute or so, we saw Shri Mataji coming. She was walking down the hallway, greeting the crowd of yogis, which had grown. As Shri Mataji walked, She stopped and spoke to individuals, one at a time and spoke for some time to each person, never rushed. I didn't count the people, but it had to be at least thirty. She also accepted the flowers from many people, graciously and slowly. Then She got on the flight and it took off. The person who showed me the time before Shri Mataji arrived pulled me to the side.

'Heidi, come here. Look at my watch,' she said. It was five minutes later.

'Oh my!' we said together. We smiled, because there was no way all that could happen in five minutes.

Heidi Zogorski

Meeting my guru

A couple of months after receiving my self realisation, in the summer of 1987, I met Shri Mataji for the first time at the Lakewood house/ashram in San Diego. The leader at the time introduced me to Her.

'I know who he is,' She interrupted him, waving Her hand while She did so.

During our brief conversation She commented that I looked like an Indian.

Stephen Day

Chapter 5

1987: August England and France

Tell her that I love her very much

As a melodramatic youngster, there was a short time in the summer of 1987 when I banished myself into the wilderness for not going through with something I thought Shri Mataji wanted me to do, until She called me back in Her own unique way, with Her own light and loving touch. How limited my understanding of Her unconditional love - just as an ant can never understand a human being, how could I understand God's love? That was when I first learnt I could be near Her when not physically in Her presence.

During this time I did some voluntary work in Scotland. One day I took a lunchtime stroll on my own in the nearby fields. I looked up at the clouds, imagining I could see all sorts of shapes - an elephant, 'Shri Ganesha', I said aloud. Then I saw Her holy face smiling down on me and heard Her voice speaking from within my heart.

'You are alright,' She said with great kindness, 'you mustn't worry - do what you want to do - I love you!' The vibrations were gushing up from my feet to my head and tears of joy were rolling down my cheeks.

Before the age of mobile phones, I had to wait till evening to call my mum from one of those charming red phone boxes in the village. As soon as she answered she was bursting to tell me her own news. She had woken that morning with a strong desire to see Shri Mataji and was lucky that this desire coincided with Her midday arrival at Heathrow. At the same time as my magical stroll, my mum was standing at the back of the crowds with her bunch of flowers. Mum also mentioned feeling shy because she too had decided to be quietly away from the Sahaja Yogis for a while. Of course, anyone who stood at the back was much more visible to our compassionate Mother (the shepherd more attentive to those lambs out in the cold) who made straight for my mum, greeting her joyfully, asking how she was. Then Mother asked about me, my mum informed Her I was working in Scotland.

'Very good! Scotland has very good vibrations!' She said, and taking my mum's hand held it for a moment and simply said: 'Please, just tell Danya one thing, that I love her very much.'

When I finally managed to find my voice, the phone box misting up considerably, I was only able to say: 'I know!'

Danya Martoglio

Mother is calling you

It was a programme with Shri Mataji at St Martin's Lane, London, soon after I had been away from the collective in Scotland for some time. I was still a bit shy to come forward into the crowds so arrived late and stayed at the back with the mums and babies, in the doorway.

'Please let me have just one glimpse of You, Mother,' I said in my heart.

Shri Mataji had reached the point in Her discourse when She would offer the yogis a chance to ask questions and very subtly, sweetly and gently She wove my name into the names of the yogis to see if they had any. I bowed in answer.

'Danya, you never had any ...' She then said.

The next experience was at the Diwali Puja, I was at the back of the hall with my head down into my bhajan book - where there was a beautiful printed photo of Her Lotus Feet that I was focusing on as I sang Ai Giri Nandini, as I couldn't really see Mother on the stage. I said to myself – 'Maybe if I clear myself for a year, I will again have that golden opportunity of decorating Her Feet.' Then someone tapped me on the shoulder. I was so busy looking at Her photo and singing my heart out, I hadn't realised that She was calling me! 'I need you to show them what to do,' She said when I went up on the stage.

I am sure I was trembling - with emotion, gratitude and due to the fountains of vibrations flowing from those dear and tender Holy Lotus Feet.

Danya Martoglio

A crown above the bed

In 1987 Shri Mataji was coming to Paris and we were looking for a hotel to receive Her, as the puja was too far from the ashram. We had a specific idea about how to decorate Her bed. We wanted to put a crown and a white veil above the head of the bed, but as it was a hotel we thought that it wouldn't be possible, because we couldn't make holes in the walls. So we surrendered and forgot about it.

One week before Shri Mataji came we found a beautiful hotel which had just opened a month before. This was already a miracle because it had the same style as Shri Mataji's house of Shudy Camps, and the cook was on holiday for the week when Shri Mataji came so we were allowed to cook for Shri Mataji. They also had two huge bedrooms. One was more for a lady and the other more for a man, and as Sir CP was also coming, this was perfect. But the best was that when we first entered the room for Shri Mataji, to see if it was acceptable, there was a crown above the bed with a white veil, exactly as we wanted. When Shri Mataji arrived, we told Her about our desire, and how the crown and veil were there automatically and how the kitchen was free.

'Yes, the Goddess is always preparing Her own place when She is coming,' She answered.

Trupta de Graaf

Shopping with Shri Mataji

Nearly every time Shri Mataji came to Paris, in 1985, '86 and '87, She asked us to take Her to Marche St Pierre, an area with lots of material shops, and especially one called Marche Saint-Pierre, which has four or five floors of different materials. Shri Mataji would look at everything and touch nearly every single roll of material. One time She bought a lot of synthetic material to offer to some Indian Sahaja Yoginis. She said they like synthetic because it is practical. For us it was strange, because at that time we were quite fanatic and only liked natural fibres like silk and cotton.

It was wonderful to be there with Shri Mataji and to order all these metres and metres of material, to witness Her generosity and to see Her vibrating everything. Also this area is very busy and there are people from all nationalities. These were the best shopping days of my life.

Trupta de Graaf

Shri Mataji vibrating the clothes and materials

I was too full of vibrations

One day after a public programme which Shri Mataji gave in Paris in 1987, we came back to the ashram and after dinner, and talking with some yogis Shri Mataji asked me to stay with Her in Her room. She lay down on the bed on Her side and asked me to sit beside Her and put my right hand on Her leg above the knee. She had Her back towards me, so I sat and as soon as I put my hand on Her, She put Her left hand on my hand very softly and stayed like that. It seemed She was sleeping, although we can't really know what Shri Mataji is doing.

I thought I had better not move at all, otherwise Shri Mataji would take away Her hand. I was not really sitting comfortably but wanted to stay like that for ever. As there was a little light in the room I could look at Her hand and see a difference of skin colour. Shri Mataji's hand was darker than mine, but with a tint of dark blue*. I was in complete bliss and although I only had the chance to stay alone with Shri Mataji a few times, this was one of the most special moments, as I felt that I could really absorb Her vibrations. I wished all my sisters in the world could be there. I don't know how long I stayed like this, but it was at least two hours, and went to bed around three o'clock.

In the morning, I got up for Shri Mataji's breakfast and was sitting in Her room with another yogi, while She was having tea. I could not think and was a bit dreamy. Shri Mataji looked at me and said I better go to bed, because I was too full of vibrations from the previous night and could not absorb any more. I indeed was feeling full of vibrations.

Trupta de Graaf

Editor's note: Traditionally, Shri Krishna's skin had a bluish tinge, and this blue has been seen in many miracle photos of Shri Mataji, and briefly experienced by many Sahaja Yogis when looking at Shri Mataji.

Shri Mataji at Chartres cathedral

During the Shri Krishna Puja seminar of 1987 in France, Shri Mataji sent a message encouraging the Sahaja Yogis to visit Chartres cathedral. She and Sir CP also paid it a visit. Whilst inside the cathedral She was asked whether the fabled veil of the Virgin which is kept there is genuine. Shri Mataji took a little time.

'Yes it was Mine, I can remember it now,' She said.

Having spent a long time inside the cathedral Shri Mataji exited and was greeted by a crowd of Sahaja Yogis who had just arrived on several buses.

'This is a very beautiful place, have a nice time,' She said to them.

She then added some words, the gist of which was to remember that all this beauty in the church was created spontaneously over many years, and

Shri Mataji at Chartres Cathedral

was not the result of following a rigid plan, and the artisans were allowed to express their devotion and the exuberance of their art. A Sahaja Yogi asked Her permission for a photo shooting event. Shri Mataji posed for a photograph surrounded by all the children outside the cathedral.

Luis Garrido

A very strong rose perfume

For several years following my divorce in the 1980's, I had fallen into a state of total exhaustion and acute mental and physical anguish, but one morning I woke with a strange premonition that something good would happen. I had an immense desire to go to Chartres cathedral to see the Virgin Mary there.

In the cathedral I prayed before the statue of the Virgin. Immediately I smelled a very strong rose perfume, so intense that I turned to see where it was coming from. I walked around the cathedral and the scent followed me round the whole building. As I left the cathedral and stood in the open air in the square by the entrance, the scent was still there. A few yards away from where I was standing I could see an Indian lady wearing a white sari getting out of a car. She looked at me and smiled, and I felt attracted to Her. Suddenly my head emptied of all thought and I could only see this lady, as though nothing else was there. She was still smiling at me. I approached and asked one of the people with Her who She was.

'You don't know Her? Why are you standing here?' one person said.

'Because there is such a beautiful scent,' I replied. 'Roses, can't you smell them?'

'It's Shri Mataji, don't you know Her?' said the man.

'No,' I said.

'Well, She is here for truth and She can protect thousands of people, like Christ did.'

I felt an explosion of joy within myself, since I already knew somehow this lady was very great, and this was what I had been waiting for. I could not move away now.

'Why don't you join us?' my neighbour suggested.

I followed the little party into the cathedral. As we walked, I felt a pleasant tingling sensation rising from my feet, through my legs and throughout my body. I had a feeling in my heart which I can only describe as expansion or fulfilment. The rest of that day was spent in joy and bliss and from then on, my sickness and depression disappeared.

Paulette Oddo

Editor's note: The beautiful cathedral at Chartres, like so many in that area, is dedicated to Notre Dame – Our Lady, Mother Mary.

It was an important moment

Just after Shri Krishna Puja in 1987, in France, we had a meeting at the ashram at Le Raincy, and Shri Mataji was there with a number of Sahaja Yogis. She was commenting on the puja and at some point a young girl asked for an Indian name.

'Yes, why not?' Shri Mataji said, and found a name for her. Then She said, 'Who else would like a name?' and we were sixty-three people in the big room at the ashram. Very patiently Shri Mataji gave a name to almost every person. It took a long time because She explained the meaning of every name, as She really wanted to find the right match for every yogi there.

I was a member of this big team of yogis and Shri Mataji gave me the name of Siddheshvara. She explained that it was a name of Shri Kalki, and the main significance of it was that I had the power to give realisation. Some of those yogis are, even today, known only by these names that we were given by Shri Mataji on that day, so it was an important moment.

Shri Mataji at the Shri Krishna Puja 1987

Siddheshvara Barbier

We saw Her Feet on the suitcase

In Paris, in 1987, we were in a hotel with Shri Mataji. I was with Rosie from Australia and Shri Mataji was going to leave, so She asked us to pack Her suitcase. She was sitting in Her chair quite far from us, about four metres, and was telling us where to put what and how to pack a suitcase. We took about half an hour to get it balanced on both sides – the case had space on both sides, then finally we wanted to close it but it was quite full, so it was very difficult. We were pushing on all sides together, very hard, for some time, and all our attention was on the case.

'Push!' Shri Mataji was saying. We were a bit gentle because it was Shri Mataji's suitcase and we didn't want to break it. Suddenly we saw Her Feet on the suitcase, close to our hands, and in one go She closed it with Her Feet. We did not hear Her coming over to us and were completely surprised. We looked up and Shri Mataji was standing smiling.

Trupta de Graaf

It is good you sold the houses

About 1987, in Paris, I was with Shri Mataji in Her room, and suddenly She said it was good I sold my houses. I couldn't remember mentioning to Shri Mataji about the houses I had inherited from my family. She just knew, without my telling Her. My brother and I had inherited a house in Paris, a farm in the South of France, and houses from my grandparents, all of which we sold. I was quite relieved when Shri Mataji said that because sometimes I wondered if my brother and I had been a bit fanatic in selling everything, but She confirmed that it had been a good choice. We wanted to get rid of our past, which was hanging on in these houses.

With the money we got, we went to pujas, sent the children to the Rome and India schools and never regretted it. So with this one little sentence, 'It is good you sold the houses,' Shri Mataji helped me to clear more of this heavy past.

Trupta de Graaf

Sound business advice

Shri Mataji asked me about a Sahaja Yogi's work and I told Her that he had started a company but it didn't work very well. She said that when you start a company you must start very small and grow slowly.

Trupta de Graaf

After the programmes

In Paris in 1987, Shri Mataji went to the Ladies Room on Her way out and I accompanied Her. There were a number of ladies there and one was a young Sahaja Yogini from Paris who was normally quite shy, and Shri Mataji asked her how she was. This girl, probably from nervousness, started to laugh and could not stop laughing. Shri Mataji also started to laugh, and then we were four or five ladies all laughing in the Ladies Room.

After another programme, Shri Mataji was going out of the hall, I was walking beside Her, and at the exit door a man came to talk to Her. He was obviously a drunkard, the way he was talking, with a very red face and old clothes. He started to tell a long story to Shri Mataji, something like his wife had died and she was still hanging around him as a ghost and he could not get rid of her and missed her. Shri Mataji listened patiently and said it was time to get his realisation and ask his wife to leave him, and reincarnate and get her realisation. Shri Mataji was very kind and gave him a lot of Her time. It was a very good lesson of patience and compassion, to see with how much love She gave to this man even though he was in a really bad state.

Trupta de Graaf

Like a big tree

I was in Shri Mataji's room in the Paris ashram in the 1980's and there were a few yogis. Shri Mataji was talking with us very kindly and answering our questions.

'You see,' She told us at some point, 'even when I am always surrounded by so many of you yogis, actually I am all alone, because I am like a big tree and you are little flowers at the foot of the tree. Even if the big tree is surrounded by these little flowers, the big tree is alone.'

This is the meaning of one of Shri Mataji's names, the word Ekakini – meaning alone.

Ruth Eleanore

Protocol

This was in Paris in Le Raincy ashram. Shri Mataji called me to massage Her Feet when She was going to sleep, maybe after a public programme or something. I massaged them for a little while but felt very tired. I decided that Shri Mataji seemed to be sleeping, so I tiptoed out of the room and also went to sleep. For a long time I reproached myself that I should have stayed until She sent me away, because so many yogis stayed and massaged Her until She sent them away. So I do not know what is less or more protocol.

Ruth Eleanore

Our attention should be like Arjuna's

In about 1986/87 Shri Mataji was going to visit us in the ashram of Le Raincy, Paris, and we were preparing for Her arrival. At that time we didn't have a special service for Shri Mataji, cups, plates and so on, so we went to buy one in the Rue de Paradis near the Gare de L'Est. We found a shop where they sold imitations of expensive services and we bought a nice red one with some gold on it.

When Shri Mataji came She really liked it and asked to go to the shop where we bought it because She wanted to buy some more, as the price was really good compared to the quality. So we went and while the shopkeeper was busy finding things for us Shri Mataji sat on a chair and started to talk about the sari She was wearing, as we had made a remark that it was very beautiful. It had some archers on the border and also on the sari itself.

As Shri Mataji was talking we sat at Her Feet in the middle of this nice shop in Paris, and She told us the story that was on Her sari. It was about Arjuna. His guru, Drona, asked the five Pandava brothers to have a shooting competition. They had to look at a tree and tell what they saw. The other brothers saw different things: one saw a tree, another said that in the tree were some branches, then some leaves and on a branch a bird, and on the bird an eye. Only Arjuna answered that what he saw was the eye of the bird. He shot directly at the eye of the bird, while the others missed it. Shri Mataji explained that this story meant that our attention should be the same as Arjuna's. It should be on the Spirit, in the same way as Arjuna's, as he only saw the eye of the bird and not everything around.

It was a very special moment, just the three of us sitting at the Feet of Shri Mataji, and like in the story, we were only listening to Her and were not aware of what was going on around us.

In the end Shri Mataji bought two services, one for Sir CP and one for Her family.

Trupta de Graaf

Chapter 6

1987: September to November - India, England and Europe

They are Your children

It happened that in Kolkata we met Shri Mataji again, in September 1987. At that period She had a puja almost every year there. At the airport we used to go and say goodbye, because often She would be going on to Australia or somewhere like that. We were there at the airport, and Shri Mataji was talking to us all one after the other. She spoke to my mother.

'Your children are very sweet, very nice,' She said.

'They are Your children,' my mother said.

'No, they are your children,' Shri Mataji said.

Another year, again in Kolkata, I used to write songs and poems for Shri Mataji and whenever there was an occasion I would perform them. One time I was performing in Kolkata, and after the performance She asked me to stay back, near Her, while another Sahaja Yogini, a violin player, came up to perform. Shri Mataji was listening to this beautiful music.

'What raga is this?' She asked me, and I didn't know what to say, because I didn't know about all that, I had never learnt classical music.

'I don't know,' I replied.

'Ask her,' Shri Mataji said so I did. The lady was Bengali and had a Bengali accent, and she was playing 'hamsa dhoni' so she said, in Bengali, 'homsha duni' so I turned to Shri Mataji and said what I heard.

'It is hamsa dhoni,' Shri Mataji said.

Then later I asked whether I should go on studying – whether to do arts or sciences, and then She said I should take up a career in journalism, because we need a lot of journalists in Sahaja Yoga. So far, I have not done that, because I got married after my bachelor's degree.

Shoma Arcilio

Some rose-oil perfume

On the 13th of October 1987, Shri Mataji blessed the Gumpi ashram in Vienna with Her visit. She kindly allowed the ladies of the ashram to wash Her Lotus Feet, after which we offered Her some rose-oil perfume, bought in India, to put on Her Feet. Shri Mataji put some on the back of Her hand and told us all to smell the backs of our own hands. Everybody could clearly smell there the scent of the perfume.

'Now you have to believe that you are all in My body,' Shri Mataji said to us.

We were all amazed and delighted.

Brigitte Saugstad

I got completely lost in the vibrations

This happened in Vienna, at a public programme, and I was asked to do the introduction. Because of this I was very close to the stage when Shri Mataji came. She came to the stage, sat down and started to speak. I was sitting close to the stairs of the podium, and there I got completely lost in the vibrations. I felt attached to a huge, thick, solid column of light. There was nothing between me and this light and it kept me completely thoughtless.

Gunter Thurner

Shri Rama Puja, 15th October 1987 (email report)

By the Grace of our Divine Mother, the Shri Rama Puja was celebrated on Sunday at the Centre International des Avants, an old hotel on the hillside above Montreux, overlooking Lake Geneva. Shri Mataji arrived on Saturday morning from Bombay, to be met by two leaders at Zürich Airport. They flew on with Shri Mataji to Geneva Airport, where Shri Mataji was met by hundreds of Sahaja Yogis, all crowded into the small arrivals hall and holding flowers. Smiling, Shri Mataji walked through the mass of yogis, accepting flowers from each person present. She was so fresh and radiating joy that you would not have believed that She had just had a fifteen hour journey from Bombay, including two late planes and a missed connection in Zürich. As Shri Mataji moved about the terminal building She was followed by yogis singing Kundalini, Kundalini. Everything was remarkably peaceful; the terminal staff and the policemen appeared to enjoy the whole thing, or at least not to be bothered. Shri Mataji then left for Les Avants, with a fleet of cars following.

An hour and a half later, we all arrived, to find that our Divine Mother was not yet there. She had stopped on the way at a motorway service station overlooking Lausanne, for some refreshments, and someone in the car with Her later told us how in the car they had been playing a cassette of songs, with Shri Mataji translating all the words for the people accompanying Her in the car. Shri Mataji finally arrived about an hour later, to the strains of Swagata Agata Swagatam and more offerings of flowers, and went up to Her room to rest.

In the evening it was suddenly announced that Shri Mataji was coming down to the dining room to have dinner with us. Since the dinner was in two shifts of which we were on the second, we were a bit disappointed that we would not immediately be seeing Her, until someone suggested that Shri Mataji should be entertained by music during Her meal. So in we trooped, clutching harmoniums and various others holding tablas, tambourines and bells, and sat down on the parquet floor in front of the table at which our Beloved Mother was sitting taking Her meal in the centre of the large, bright and airy semicircular room, surrounded by tables which seemed to radiate away from Her at which Sahaja Yogis were dining. She smiled at us, and we started to sing and play the old favourites. From time to time Shri Mataji would comment on how a song should be played, how for instance just after climaxes in a bhajan there should be a moment of silence before the music takes off again. When the shift came to an end Shri Mataji told us that we should now take our food, and we were replaced by other groups of musicians who came together informally from a number of different countries - France, Spain, Austria and Germany. The music went on for the whole of the second serving of the dinner.

Next morning the Sahaja Yogis assembled in the puja hall, a long, narrow hall, but from which everyone could see clearly our divine Mother on the stage. A beautiful set had been constructed on the stage. Shri Mataji was to be seated on a golden throne about six feet with red silk cushions, whose legs were supported on carved kneeling lions. Behind Shri Mataji's head was a large silver disc again inlaid with beads and brilliant as it reflected the video lights. Over the throne was hung a beautiful golden canopy, with a silk cloth draped over the back of the throne. Shri Mataji later commented how comfortable the throne was. To either side of the throne were marble pillars, actually made of covered wood, but very realistic; Shri Mataji said, smiling, that She was surprised that there was so much marble here! Behind the throne was a cotton screen behind which would be seen a 'forest' of bamboo shoots, back-lit, to symbolize the forest from which our Divine Mother was emerging after the fourteen years exile.

Shri Mataji entered the puja hall majestically, to music from the film Chariots of Fire. She spoke before the puja about the qualities of Shri Rama: 'sankoch' or the formality of the heart, being extremely diplomatic. He was born of the Solar dynasty and is on the right-hand side of our subtle being, and so was extremely mild to counteract its excesses. He controls the inner workings of a number of organs in the head such as the eyes and the lungs and the certain aspects of the throat. Shri Mataji talked for nearly an hour, and then the puja got under way. At the climax of the puja, a golden crown was presented to Shri Mataji. Visually the puja was extremely dramatic and magnificent. For aarti we sang Raghupati Raghava instead of the more usual Sabko Dua Dena. In the evening Shri Mataji was so kind as to join us again for a session of music and poetry. Arneau had written a number of beautiful poems and we combined these poems with live music and a slide show. Shri Mataji enjoyed it very much, particularly the poems.

Next morning Shri Mataji left for Geneva about lunchtime. A few of us were on hand to say goodbye to Her, standing in waiting holding the bamboo shoots which the previous day had been on the stage, to make an arcade through which our Beloved Mother passed on Her way to the car. That evening was the first programme in Geneva.

Phil Ward

A narrow escape

Mother's Divine love was protecting me even before I knew of Her existence. In the early 1980's a friend asked me to write the script for a documentary on religions in Kashmir and Ladakh. As part of my research, I made an appointment to interview a well-known Tibetan false guru but it fell through at the last minute. A few months later, I was acting in a play in The Hague. As I arrived at the venue I saw posters announcing that this false guru was giving a public programme in the hall next to the theatre and would receive any members of the public, but it was exactly the time I would be on stage.

I only realised what a narrow escape I had had and how lovingly Mother had guided me away from all the pitfalls I had been heading for when I got realisation later that year and met Her face to face for the first time. I went up onto the stage with other seekers after a public programme in Geneva.

'This is a new yogini, Mother,' a yogi said, and She looked at me and smiled.

'I know,' She said.

She took my hands in Hers and I melted. My heart was filled to overflowing. Oh Mother, how can I thank You enough for all Your loving care and attention over the years! May I always feel You in my heart and mind and may others see You in me. May I be a worthy instrument for You to work through. May Your will be done, Mother, on earth as it is in heaven.

Elizabeth Matera Matthews

You couldn't have carried it all anyway

A small miracle happened when Shri Mataji was travelling from Geneva to Brussels in October 1987 as part of Her European tour. Her baggage was loaded onto the plane and our Divine Mother left with two Sahaja Yogis, carrying copious hand luggage.

When they arrived in Brussels, there was no sign of Shri Mataji's beauty case at the baggage claim and Johan went back to the aircraft to search the cabin, without success. Shri Mataji by this time had already been welcomed by the assembled Belgian yogis and was asking very concerned questions about the whereabouts of the beauty case. No one had taken it as hand luggage and in Geneva we could clearly remember that it had not been checked in with Shri Mataji's suitcase. All of a sudden, an Indian gentleman appeared out of the crowd, carrying Her beauty case and gave it one of the Sahaja Yogis who had accompanied Her.

'I think this is yours,' he said. He disappeared back into the crowd. Shri Mataji later said that this was Shri Hanuman.

'Well, you couldn't have carried it all anyway,' Shri Mataji said to Bill.

Bill Hansel

The majority felt the vibrations

After the programmes in Antwerp and Brussels, in 1987, the next evening, a Friday, was Amsterdam. We were warned of the dreadful vibrations of Amsterdam, and were very surprised to see four or five hundred people come to the programme, which took place in one of Amsterdam's most splendid hotels. We were also impressed with the quality of the people attending, who nearly all seemed to be very intelligent and humble, ready to listen to the advice Shri Mataji and the Sahaja Yogis had to give them. There were one or two conspicuous exceptions, one of whom Shri Mataji asked to leave the hall, which he did. A large proportion had been to false gurus or taken drugs or both, and there were some quite heavy vibrations at first, but at the end of the programme, when Shri Mataji told all the new people to come and sit at the front, on the floor, to receive vibrations, the majority of those present had felt them.

Phil Ward

Brussels and Antwerp (email report)

I had the privilege of attending public programmes in Antwerp, Brussels, and Amsterdam, in 1987. The programme in Brussels took place in a town hall on the outskirts of the city; about four hundred people came, and Shri Mataji stayed until midnight, talking to new people and giving them vibrations.

Next evening in Antwerp, in the huge auditorium of the General Motors factory on the outskirts of the city, about two to three hundred people came. At the end all the new people who wished came to the front of the hall and sat on the floor in rows, while the Sahaja Yogis gave them vibrations and Shri Mataji gave them attention individually from Her place on the stage.

Phil Ward

Let's go to McDonalds

It was Shri Mahakali Puja in Munich, 1987. I was supposed to cook for Shri Mataji after the puja, but I don't know what had happened to me. I had no ideas as to what to cook and started to panic a bit. Then after the puja, I was with Shri Mataji in the car to go back to the ashram. In my mind, I was going through what we had bought to cook for Her.

'Who will cook for Me now?' asked Shri Mataji.

'Me, Shri Mataji,' I said and thought, 'This is it.'

'After a puja one should not stay in the kitchen and cook. Let's go out and have something to eat in the restaurant,' She said and smiled at me.

My heart was overflowing with love and relief, but all the restaurants were closed because it was early afternoon. The driver of the car mentioned that only McDonalds would be open and this would not be appropriate.

'Why not?' Shri Mataji said. 'Let's go to McDonalds. The chicken is good there.'

So we went there and it was brought out to Shri Mataji, who stayed in the car, chips and Chicken McNuggets and Coke. We ate with Her and laughed like children and could hardly believe it. It was so incredible, joyful. Even the blue October sky seemed to feel the same and expressed it in little puffy white clouds.

'Look up in the sky and see the clouds,' She said, noticing it. 'Even the sky seems to be bubbling with joy.'

Afterwards, Shri Mataji went directly for shopping to town, without going back to the ashram and having a rest. The swastika was still on Her Feet and we were all in our saris.

Annegret Kaluzny

The 108 holy names of Shrī Mahākāli

Aum twameva sākshāt Shrī Mahākāli sākshāt
Shrī Ādi Shakti Mātājī Shrī Nirmalā Devyai namo namah
O Divine Mother, You are verily Shri Mahakali. Salutations to You!

Mahākāli...................................... *You are... The dark goddess, the immaculate desire of God Almighty*
Kāmadhenu............................. *The divine wish-fulfilling cow*
Kāma–swarūpā........................ *Love itself*
Varadā.................................... *The bestower of boons*
Jagad'ānanda kārinī................. *The cause of the total bliss of the universe* 5
Jagat–jīva mayī .... *The life-energy of the whole universe*
Vajra–kankālī........................... *Terrifying to behold with your thunderbolt and skeletal form*
Shāntā.................................... *Peace*
Sudhā–sindhu nivāsinī............. *The one who dwells in the cosmic ocean of nectar*
Nidrā...................................... *Sleep* 10
Tāmasī .... *The one who presides over the Tamo guna (pure desire)*
Nandinī................................... *The pleasing daughter of Kamadhenu*
Sarv'ānanda swarūpinī .... *The embodiment of universal joy*
Param'ānanda rūpā .... *The highest form of supreme, divine bliss*
Stutyā..................................... *The most praiseworthy* 15
Padm'ālayā .... *The one who resides in the purest lotus*
Sadā–pūjyā.............................. *Always worshipped*
Sarva–priyan–karī.................... *The one who showers love and kindness on all*
Sarva–mangalā......................... *The auspiciousness of all things*
Pūrnā...................................... *Perfect and complete* 20
Vilāsinī .... *The supreme enjoyer, charming and playful*
Amoghā .... *Infallible*
Bhogawatī .... *The one who enjoys the universe*
Sukhadā .... *The one who bestows perfect happiness*
Nishkāmā .... *Desireless* 25
*Madhu-kaitabha hantrī........... *The killer of Madhu and Kaitabha*
*Mahish'āsura ghātinī............... *The slayer of Mahishasura*
*Raktabīja vināshinī .... *The destroyer of Raktabija*
*Narak'āntakā .... *The destroyer of Narakasura*

Ugra-chand'eshwarī .... *The terrifying goddess of wrath and fury*

Krodhinī .... *Cosmic wrath*

Ugra-prabhā .... *Radiant with fury*

Chāmundā.............................. *The killer of Chanda and Munda*

Khadga-pālinī .... *The one who rules by the sword*

Bhāswar'āsurī .... *The goddess whose fierce radiance destroys the demonic forces*

*Shatru-mardinī....................... *The one who destroys all enemies*

Rana-panditā .... *The master of the art of war*

Rakta-dantikā .... *The one whose teeth are red (with the blood of demons)*

Rakta-priyā .... *Fond of the blood of demons*

Kapālinī .... *The one who holds a skull in her hand*

*Kuru-kula-virodhinī .... *The one who confronts all the evil of the world (such as the dynasty of Kauravas in 'The Mahabharata')*

Krishna-dehā .... *Dark-coloured*

Nara-mundalī......................... *The one who wears a garland of human skulls*

Galat-rudhira-bhūshanā .... *Adorned with the dripping blood of demons*

Preta-nrutya-parāyanā .... *The one who dances upon the dead bodies of the fallen and during the cosmic dissolution*

Lolā-jihvā .... *The one whose tongue hangs out with an insatiable thirst for the blood of demons*

Kundalinī .... *The coiled energy (the residual energy of the Holy Spirit in the sacrum bone)*

Nāga-kanyā .... *The virgin serpent (kundalini)*

Pati-vratā .... *The faithful and devoted wife*

Shiva-sanginī .... *The eternal companion of Shri Shiva*

Visangī .... *Unaccompanied*

Bhūta-pati priyā..................... *Loved by the lord of the living (Shri Shiva)*

Preta-bhūmi krutālayā .... *The one who dwells in the land of ghosts and ghosts (where Shri Shiva rules)*

*Daityendra mardinī................. *The slayer of the chief demon*

Chandra-swarūpinī .... *The cooling radiance of the moon (Ida nadi)*

Prasanna-padma-vadanā........ *The one with an auspicious lotus like face*

Smera-waktrā .... *The one with a smiling countenance*

Sulochanā.............................. *The one with beautiful eyes*

Sudantī .... *The one with perfect teeth*

The place of Maria

This story is from 1987, when Shri Mataji was in Munich, at the ashram there. I opened the door to a man who had been knocking. He was a journalist, and wanted to interview Shri Mataji. Mother was in Her room sleeping at that time. I asked the man how he had arranged the interview because we didn't know about it. He told me that he had been in the Marienplatz, in the centre of Munich, that morning.

'The Marienplatz is the place of Maria,' he said to me. He said he had heard about Shri Mataji a long time before. He always wanted to interview Her, but had never managed it.

When he had been in the Marienplatz, although the day was very hot - because it was the middle of August - he suddenly felt very cool. He turned round and there was Shri Mataji in front of him, and he immediately recognized Her. There were a few other people with Her because She had been out shopping. He was so surprised and went up to Her and asked if he could interview Her.

'Of course,' Shri Mataji had said, and gave him the address to come to. He was writing a book about Mary at that time and seemed to recognize Mary in Shri Mataji.

At the ashram, She came downstairs and was happy to see him. The interview was beautiful and was for the magazine he was working for, New Age 2000 or something like that. The man had a problem on his leg and all the time he was interviewing Shri Mataji, about two hours, She worked on his left knee.

Mara-Madhuri Corazzari

Shri Mataji at Graz, Austria, in 1987

These pictures are from Shri Mataji's visit and programme to Graz, Austria on October 14, 1987 and from the subsequent Shri Mahakali Puja at Schloss Blutenburg (castle of blood), Munich, Germany on October 16th, 1987.

Shri Mataji took a very small plane from Graz to Munich, a short but spectacular flight across the Alpine mountains in Austria.

Shri Mahakali Puja 1987

Shri Mataji at Graz Airport, 1987

Shri Mataji at Graz 1987

How alone She must be

On the way to Graz Shri Mataji rested in a yogi family house in Gleissenfeld, in the countryside. Near the farmhouse was a mountain, with some rocky cliffs almost looming over the premises. Then the yogi told Shri Mataji that the rock was named Tuerkensturz, because apparently a Turkish man had fallen to his death from those cliffs. Shri Mataji looked at the mountain, and gave it another name, changing the atmosphere of the mountain from a gloomy to a benevolent presence.

She took a rest and I was passing the corridor outside Her room when She came out and asked for some water. I brought the water to Her room where She was sitting on the bed, and was overcome by an overwhelming awe. How alone She must be, Who created everything and us, and how small and insignificant are we, trying to impress and please Her.

Sigrid Jones

Seven red bangles and a pair of silver anklets

In 1987 I was living in England and was very sorry that I missed Shri Mataji's programmes in Austria. In October some Austrian yogis came to visit us in England and told us how beautiful it was with Mother in Vienna. Suddenly I had a big, big desire to see Her before She left the UK for another country. I decided to pack my year old daughter Sita into the bus and go to the airport to see Shri Mataji off. The desire grew and grew over the next few days until one morning the phone rang.

'Mother would like you to come tonight to Her house to translate something,' the leader said.

Oh, my God, I had to write it down on a piece of paper to convince myself it was not a dream! I baked an apple cake, made a nice posy of flowers and off we went to London. Shri Mataji came to the door to greet us, we were asked to enter the living room and I found myself sitting next to God on the big settee. Sita looked at Mother.

'Ah, she doesn't recognise Me because I don't have a bindi today,' Shri Mataji explained.

My husband ended up talking to Sir CP about stereos. I had nothing much to do except worry about Sita toddling all over the apartment with chocolates in her hand.

'You see how difficult it is to be a mother..... and I have so many children!' Mother said, or something like that.

Before we left we were presented with chocolates and Mother gave me seven big red bangles and a pair of silver anklets - exactly those (with little hearts) which She wore at a puja on the photo which I always carried in my handbag. We stood there, receiving these presents, I looked at Mother's Holy Feet and saw the whole universe - unforgettable, most precious memories.

Waltraud West

One of the Chinese lions

The Chinese guardian lions

Shri Mataji and Sir CP went to China during the cold war; they had received an official diplomatic invitation which made it possible. Whenever time permitted, Shri Mataji would buy ceramics and other works of art and crafts from the countries She visited. This way Shri Mataji assembled an impressive collection of ceramics that represented all the places She went to and the many people She met. Her memory was incredible and if we asked Her about any object She knew exactly what it was and what it meant, the history and the cultural tradition behind it. We were all very impressed with Shri Mataji's knowledge and understanding of different countries and traditions and the extent of Her interest in their history, art, culture, current aspirations and even the current political affairs, and everyone She had met in all those years of travelling.

She never had a house big enough to display this collection of ceramics and other works of art, and the bulk of it was kept in storage. She told us She was extremely busy as a diplomat's wife and also with Her mission of spreading Sahaja Yoga, and had not seen some of these objects for twenty years. The plan was to display the whole collection on a permanent basis in India so people who didn't get a chance to travel abroad could see and enjoy them.

In 1987 Shri Mataji was planning to move back to India from the UK and the whole collection had to be packed for shipping, at Shudy Camps.

This also required preparing a detailed inventory for customs' purposes. Being a large collection and Shri Mataji's time being limited we all tried to be very efficient and organised. She asked for every object to be shown to Her prior to being packed, took great pleasure in seeing them because they brought Her back special memories and She told us about every piece. Meanwhile time was passing and not much packing was being done.

Once the objects had been shown to Shri Mataji they were taken to the next room for packing. There, the person in charge started telling us off for taking so much of erHer time and asking Her so many questions about every object, so we did our best to accelerate matters. At one time I brought, from the attic, a pair of Chinese guardian lions to show Her. I was stopped by the Sahaja Yogi in charge of packing.

'What is the need to show this monstrous ceramic piece to Shri Mataji, let's just pack it, and not waste Her time. This is so ugly, surely not a piece of art.' He held onto one of the lions for packing and I escaped with the other to show to Her.

'Ah, what a beautiful piece of art! This is from China - I haven't seen it for a long time, where is the other one that goes with it?' She exclaimed.

Nowadays these two lions can be seen at Pratishthan, guarding a set of doors.

Luis Garrido

The divine marriage counsellor

In 1987 at Shudy Camps there was a couple whose marriage was about to break down. The wife, who was not a Sahaja Yogini, felt that if her husband had not joined Sahaja Yoga her marriage might have been more successful. Shri Mataji advised the Sahaja Yogi to give up Sahaja Yoga completely for a time, and to do his utmost to save the marriage. She also explained to the lady that all marriages are sacred.

At Shudy Camps I asked Shri Mataji Her opinion about divorce.

'Divorce is very inauspicious and only to be contemplated as a last resort, when all efforts towards reconciliation have failed or when people are fighting badly all the time, then it needs to be allowed,' She told me.

A Sahaja Yogini was upset that her husband always refused to accompany her when she attended a Sahaja Yoga function, and she felt like divorcing him.

'Instead of wanting to punish your husband, why not forgive him instead of divorcing him? You must feel sorry for this poor man and he has done nothing wrong,' Shri Mataji told her. Later the husband became ill and this Sahaja Yogini felt very privileged to stand by his side, nursing him as a devoted wife.

Another Sahaja Yogi complained that his wife refused to practice Sahaja Yoga and how upset he was with her.

'I remember you introducing your wife to Me,' Shri Mataji told him, 'she is a very nice, good person and you are lucky to have her. Never pressure her into joining Sahaja Yoga and enjoy your marriage.'

Luis Garrido

Fragrant moments

Speaking of fragrant memories, those familiar scents like Diorissimo and Rose can evoke the Divine; yet it was Her own special fragrance that came from the very essence of Mother Earth – that is the one we all cherish; the one no perfume house could ever match! Sahaja Yoginis who had the blessed opportunity of caring for Shri Mataji's vibration-drenched saris will verify that the longer She wore a garment, the more fragrant it became.

I am remembering when Shri Mataji allowed me to prepare the white, satin silk saris She needed to take for Her long realisation tours abroad. Sometimes Her request to wash and iron up to a dozen saris came at very short notice - especially when trips had been spontaneously decided. Then the whole family would eagerly await Antonio, Shri Mataji's trusted gana, to drop off the familiar burgundy Samsonite suitcase.

On arrival, we would then place it on the sofa beside the altar and tentatively open the treasure chest ... as soon as it sprung open, there it was; Mother's sacred fragrance! A fragrance that immediately infused us with Her grace and brought tears of gratitude to the eyes. We would leave the job till the last possible moment simply so we could keep the fragrance flowing and permeating the house. Also, I am not sure if it was coincidence, but often the request came at a time when I was feeling a bit unsure of myself.

I recall sitting anxiously outside Mother's bedroom at Shudy Camps once, expecting to be told off for some foolishness, my head sheepishly low when suddenly the door opened and there She was - 'Ah good, there you are! I've got some white saris I need you to wash ...' Phew, no telling off. Spending many hours through the night, washing the holy garments, becoming more cleansed from within as I worked the soap into each tiny kumkum mark ... the symbolism was not lost on me!

Danya Martoglio

An old film

In late 1987 Shri Mataji asked my wife Ruth to come up to Her house in Rosary Gardens in London to help make some curtains. One day while she was staying there, Shri Mataji, Ruth, and another yogini had lunch together. Then Mother switched on the TV. Just at that moment, the titles of a film were coming up. It was Gaslight, a 1940 production.

'This is good, let's watch it,' said Mother, and they watched the film.

The plot of Gaslight revolves around a man's attempt to drive his wife insane in order to have her committed to an asylum, at which point he will be able to claim some jewellery that is hers by right. Shri Mataji remarked on the clarity with which the actors and actresses spoke in these old films, and also commented on how sweet the heroine was and how dignified she looked in the clothes of that period, particularly in the sweeping, off-the shoulder ball gown which she wore in one scene. The husband almost succeeds in his plan, but at the last moment the young wife is rescued. Then it is her turn to stand up to her husband and tell him what she thinks of him.

'Yes, yes, that's right, go on, tell him!' said Mother.

The whole incident was intimate and delightful: the ordinary raised to a higher power.

Chris Greaves

The people looked radiant and transformed (email report)

It was Diwali, at the end of October 1987, about a hundred Sahaja Yogis mainly from Italy, Austria, and Switzerland went to Linate Airport, Milan, to welcome our Divine Mother to Italy and to enjoy Her darshan. As usual, Shri Mataji kindly accepted flowers from all those present and was then driven to the flat in Milan where She would stay. We went to the cinema where the evening programme was to be held, and started to rehearse, and had an awful rehearsal. The cinema stage was black, the seats were black, the walls and floors were black and the vibrations weren't terribly good. Meanwhile the local Sahaja Yogis were busy transforming the cinema; three bandhans of flowers around the chair of Shri Mataji, baskets of flowers along the front of the stage, and we felt a little better.

By half past six, when the programme was scheduled to begin, we found ourselves becoming as if by magic more relaxed and joyful, and not too worried. As Shri Mataji entered the hall, we sang Namostute followed by Swagata Agata, Shri Mataji taking Her seat on the last line of Namostute. Then Shri Mataji, smiling, asked us to sing an Italian song. It had never occurred to us to do so, so the performance of Churi Churi was completely spontaneous and enjoyed by everyone. The hall, full of about five hundred people, looked radiant and transformed. We had the privilege of staying on stage with Shri Mataji during Her discourse, leaving it only when She gave realisation, and returning afterwards to sing Namostute again and Adi Ma. Shri Mataji said afterwards how pleased She had been with the singing and that it had opened the hearts of the audience.

Phil Ward

Only a Mother could do the job (email report)

The Friday of the Diwali weekend in 1987, a programme took place in Piacenza, south-east of Milan. This was organized by the local Rotary Club and was by more or less by invitation, so mainly local aristocratic and business families came. It took place in a local palazzo, a large, old, and splendid town house hung with Persian and Indian carpets and other decorations and full of beautiful sculpture and paintings.

Here again a vibrational transformation took place; the video crew, the first to arrive, said the place caught at first from head to foot, but by the time we arrived the vibrations had settled down. Shri Mataji was visiting the rest of the house and had not yet come into where the programme was to be held, a dark and lofty room with some tables and benches laid out amongst statues and rolled-up carpets, and with frescoes of angels on the ceiling, which gave very cool vibrations, as later we all held our hands high and asked, 'Are these the vibrations of the Holy Spirit?'.

As we sang songs Shri Mataji was in the next room, putting Her divine attention upon those present and working on a number of people. At one point a lady came in and declared that she had been completely cured of lumbar problems she had had since her childhood, with tears streaming from her eyes and to the cheers and applause of all present.

One really impressive thing about this programme was the quality of the new people. There were maybe eighty to a hundred people present, including twenty or thirty Sahaja Yogis. Some of the new people were aristocrats, but many came spontaneously to sit on the floor before our Divine Mother to receive realisation from Her. Very humble and dignified people; Shri Mataji commented that other countries, the English, Germans, and 'the Swi-iss', She said, smiling at us, had much to learn from the Italians. Incredible questions were posed to Shri Mataji, who talked about Her Divine Nature as I have rarely heard Her talk before in a public programme.

It was asked, is it not dangerous for a female incarnation to come on the earth at this time? What was the need of a Mother? Shri Mataji replied that with modern, complicated, and impure people, Lord Krishna would just have killed them with His Sudarshan chakra, and even Lord Jesus, although the essence of forgiveness and love of humanity, would have lost patience and used His destroying powers, of which He had eleven and just one was enough to destroy the whole creation. So only a Mother, with Her love and compassion and patience could do the job.

After Shri Mataji's talk, which took the form of answers to questions posed to Her by the lady chairman of the meeting, a televised interview took place with a journalist who had come and got her realisation, and many people came forward to shake Mother's hand and express their gratitude. It was very intimate and with the backdrop of the carpets and the high, ancient walls it could have come from some Rembrandt painting of the Divine Mother surrounded by Her listeners.

Earlier in the day Shri Mataji had held a press conference which had been attended by eight journalists, who insisted on having their realisation first and then asking questions. There weren't many questions, but those that came were good ones.

Phil Ward

Diwali Puja 1987 (email report)

On Saturday we all made our way to the place of the puja, a hill resort in spectacular scenery (jagged rocks and sheer cliffs like a Chinese painting) north of Lecco, about half an hour's drive. Four hundred Sahaja Yogis from all over Europe met in the puja hall to wait for Shri Mataji, who arrived from Milan about 11pm and kindly came to join us.

Mahabhajans it turned out to be, with each national group singing at least one song, with an Indian bhajan between national groups. The French song was particularly beautiful. Before the singing started Shri Mataji talked to us for a while, and gave presents of ties to all the leaders present. The bhajans went on until 4 am., without anyone feeling tired.

Shri Mataji told us a funny story about Rustom Burjorgee. He had once suggested to another yogi that he should ask Shri Mataji to become nirakara, formless, to hasten his spiritual growth. This yogi did so, but She told him that this was not proper. Shri Mataji was at that moment travelling by plane to Calcutta with some leaders. When they got there the people who had assembled to greet Mother could not see Her, or any of those travelling with Her. They had indeed become nirakara, and so completely invisible. Shri Mataji gave a bandhan to the driver of the car so that at least he should see them.

The puja was announced as starting at midday, but shortly after midday we received instructions from Shri Mataji to go for our lunch, and return at 3 o'clock. Our Divine Mother finally came for the puja towards the end of the afternoon; after all, Diwali is a puja to be celebrated at night.

During Her discourse She spoke first about innocence, how after realisation we now have both innocence and knowledge, which is divine knowledge, not worldly knowledge by which we know how to manipulate, dominate, and oppress. Then She spoke of the dangers we face and the wrath of God. During the puja Shri Mataji spoke about the aspects of Shri Lakshmi, as we said their mantras to Her. Then there was more music, particularly Tere Hi Guna Gate Hai, and at the end of the puja, Shri Mataji expressed Her wish that all the musicians should come to India; one or two who would not be able to go otherwise would not have to pay the tour fees; after all, as Shri Mataji said, the musicians are working for the rest of the folk on the tour. The puja ended with the aarti being sung.

'See you in India!' Shri Mataji said as She bid us farewell.

Phil Ward

Like when Christ or Socrates spoke

As an infant in the 1970's I lived tantalisingly close to Shri Mataji's house in Surrey, but it was not until a few days before my twentieth birthday that I finally encountered Shri Mataji Nirmala Devi and Sahaja Yoga.

Shri Mataji had just arrived back in London from the Shri Rama Puja in Switzerland and a few days later, on the 16th November 1987 She gave a public programme at Porchester Hall. It was one of the rare occasions when She stood to address the audience. I remember thinking that it must have been like that when Christ or Socrates had spoken and I was enraptured by Her talk about the Spirit. After giving self realisation Shri Mataji invited the new people to come onto the stage, so I went to meet Her.

Shri Mataji was in a very joyous mood. She greeted me and talked very much like a mother or a friend. This surprised me as I was very much in awe of Her and could feel that She was an enormously powerful personality. She was all the time gentle and very loving and asked me whether I had felt it. I had, but so far my experience had not been as strong as before, when I first received my self realisation, and I didn't know why. Shri Mataji then took my right hand in Hers, stroking my palm as She talked and drew the sign of the cross with Her finger on my palm several times.

'You have to forgive,' She said to me, very simply.

'Yes, yes, Shri Mataji,' I immediately replied, because this seemed to me to be so obviously the right solution.

'That's it,' She looked at me and said, and before I knew it, I was sitting on the floor at Her Feet being worked on by another yogi, with vibrations absolutely blasting through my Sahasrara and in as deep a state of meditation as I have ever been!

Tim Bruce

As you are, so the world will be

It was in London - at Porchester Hall in the mid 1980's. It was close to the end of a meeting, our Mother had given Her talk and I was standing near the stage.

'As you are, so the world will be,' She said, referring to the yogis as a whole.

Chris Greaves

The origin of the affirmations

The affirmations started with Shri Mataji giving realisation with affirmations at Porchester Hall in London, in the mid 1980's. After that they were developed by yogis and were based on Mother's words that She had spoken on different occasions about different chakras.

Grazyna Anslow

Someone who tells the truth

On November 16th 1987 I headed for Porchester Hall in London. I was not quite sure what to expect - someone had given me a poster the day before. I walked into a grand hall full of people and immediately felt at home. There were all types of people, all ages and races, children running, lots of joy and chattering. I sat down, waited for something to happen and enjoy. After a while someone told us we will all get our realisation later. This worried me a little bit, as I had read that one could never get one's realisation in this lifetime. Suddenly everyone got up and a lady wearing a cardigan and a headscarf came in and She reminded me of my grandmother. This lady, who was Shri Mataji, started talking and made so much sense to me that after five minutes I thought, 'Here is someone who is telling the truth.' I knew She was the teacher I had been seeking. We did get our realisation.

'You have to be honest and if you feel something, admit that you have felt something,' Shri Mataji said.

I did feel the cool breeze and I somehow knew that it was something very important. We were invited to go to the stage to meet Shri Mataji. As I got closer to Her, I became very nervous and everything seemed to be in slow motion, I realised much later that it was the strong vibrations. Shri Mataji said a few words to me, did some bandhans on my hand, then burst out laughing and told me to bring sugar the following evening.

I spent the rest of the evening sitting in the front row watching Shri Mataji. I kept wondering, 'Who is this beautiful lady? She is so genuine, greets everyone with such grace and smile, I have never seen such a smile!'

After the programme I walked home, overwhelmed by all that happened. Next morning, I spontaneously never smoked again, and I had been trying to stop for years.

Annie Calvas

Shri Mataji worked on the left Vishuddhi

At one of Shri Mataji's programmes at Porchester Hall, I arrived burdened with an unduly large left Vishuddhi catch. In those days Shri Mataji would attend to all the new people individually and then receive flowers from the regulars. The Vishuddhi catch was so bad that even after the talk and realisation session I felt in no condition to get too close to Mother.

After a time of sitting there quietly I saw someone at the end of the queue who I needed to speak to, so got up and went and had a word with this person. By the end of the conversation the queue had moved on and was now close of Shri Mataji. I now felt better, and that giving Her a flower was not such a bad idea. Soon the queue got to the person just in front of me and Shri Mataji asked him how he was. He replied, mumbling that he had a catch on his left Vishuddhi.

'I beg your pardon?' Shri Mataji replied. Again he mumbled something about a bad left Vishuddhi.

'What is he saying?' She turned to me and asked.

'He says he is catching on left Vishuddhi Mother,' I replied, loud and clear.

After that Mother worked on the person's Vishuddhi, and got up and left without attending to me directly.

Bernard Rackham

I had entered a new dimension and 'come home' at last

In 1987 I was forty-two years old and spiritually on my knees, having tried and abandoned drugs and some other seeking paths. One day at a Narcotics Anonymous meeting somebody heard me say, 'Like a lotus grows clean and pure out of the mud,' and he homed in on me. I was struck by his happiness - he was always happy. One day he mentioned, 'I meditate,' and then he put a leaflet into my hand which said, 'Shri Mataji in person at Porchester Hall'.

Shri Mataji arrived dressed in white, Her long black hair flowing down over Her shoulders, and walked down the centre aisle of the audience. It was as if everything stopped, or faded away and I just saw Her. The hairs on my arms and at the back of my neck stood on end and I could feel my heart beating. I thought, 'What's going on here, who is this?'

She spoke, – such sense – almost voicing my own thoughts and feelings that I had never been able to articulate. Then I discovered She was going to give the experience of self realisation. We all went through the exercise of putting our right hand on different chakras, and She asked us to say different things within ourselves. Then She blew over the microphone.

'How many people felt the cool breeze coming from the top of their heads?' She asked.

I looked around the hall, and everyone raised their hand. I was sitting near the front. Had I been singled out not to ever see or glimpse God? I felt my bottom lip tremble as my despair and disappointment began to well up. Then Shri Mataji's eyes met mine.

'Don't worry, it's alright, if you didn't feel it come up here to Me,' She said. I knew She was speaking to everyone, but She was looking at me and somehow had felt my desperation and to me that was a rope to a drowning soul. I went up to Her.

'I'm so tired of searching,' I whispered. She asked me what I'd been doing, where I'd been seeking and I mentioned a couple of things. She tutted and shook Her head. She held my hand and stroked it for ages and put Her hand on my stomach, all the time looking right into me. Suddenly I felt my forehead open up like the opening of a cage, there seemed no top to my head

'Oh my God, it's true!' I thought. It was wonderful beyond words.

'Ah, she's got it,' Shri Mataji said to some people standing around Her. She said a few other things that I will keep in my heart, but what She said proved that She knew me, that I had entered a new dimension and 'come home' at last.

Jenny Brown

I am eager to be with My children

Travelling from Barcelona to Madrid with Shri Mataji in 1987, we were about nine Sahaja Yogis, and Mother's bags were checked in together with the bags of the Sahaja Yogis travelling with Her.

Arriving in Madrid, the signs said that the bags were to be collected on belt number 1, where the Sahaja Yogis went. I was standing alone with Mother in proximity to belt number 10.

'Javier, please collect My bags that are going around here on belt 10,' Mother said. I told Her that our bags were going to be collected by the yogis at belt number 1. A little disappointed Mother said, 'Please pick up

My bags because I am eager to be with My children who are waiting for Me outside.'

To my surprise Shri Mataji's two bags were indeed the only ones turning on belt number 10. Mother went outside and collected all the flowers offered by Her Madrid children, who were waiting for Her, and only when Mother sat inside the car were the rest of the bags delivered. My daughter Anita told me the same thing happened on a trip with Mother in South America.

Javier Valderamma

A chance to be close

When I was a very new Sahaja Yogi I travelled to Spain in November 1987 to see Shri Mataji at the puja. In my heart I really longed to be close to Shri Mataji because I had heard of all the beautiful moments people had spent with Her. I told the other yogi who was with me, 'All those Sahaja Yogis are very lucky, I wish one day that I might have a chance to be close to Shri Mataji.'

We came to the ashram where Shri Mataji was residing. The sweet thing was that this puja was on my birthday. I saw the Sahaja Yogis waiting outside the house for Her to come out and when She did She smiled at both of us.

'The Swiss are there already,' She said. But there were only us two. Then Shri Mataji went into the car to leave and we all namaskared, and suddenly the car stopped. One of the drivers was waving his hand and calling one of the Spanish Sahaja Yogis. He ran over, wondering what was happening. Shri Mataji wanted the Swiss to come shopping with Her. I couldn't believe it. It was what I had wanted in my heart, and what I had told my Sahaja brother only two hours before.

So there we were in the car with Shri Mataji, spending the whole day with Her. She took us to a restaurant, it was amazing. Eight or ten Sahaja Yogis and Shri Mataji ordered the food for us; we were like little children loving our mother, and She treated us like little kids. Most of us were around twenty years old.

'We have too many choices and we shouldn't spend so much time ordering the food,' She said. 'Everybody, hamburger with french-fries.' I was told we were not supposed to eat beef in Sahaja Yoga, so I was surprised to hear Mother order it for Herself, but with no egg. She said it was not good to mix egg and beef as it was too much protein or calories for Her.

It was an incredibly relaxed atmosphere and. I couldn't believe that I was sitting there with Shri Mataji.

While we were eating our hamburgers, french-fries, Coke She started to tell how in 1970 She opened the Sahasrara, and explained how the Kundalini shot up and how She could feel it like a volcano and all the colours. While Mother was describing this we sat there with knives and forks in our hands and our Sahasraras completely opened. It was the most amazing thing; there was this mix of complete divinity of Shri Mataji and Her total motherly love.

'Now you all have to have some sweet things,' She said. I felt like I was five years old. 'All of you, chocolate ice-cream,' and we all had chocolate ice-cream. So we had had hamburger, beef, egg, french-fries, Coke and chocolate ice-cream. Normally my liver would have exploded! But when I had the chocolate ice-cream I felt my Nabhi become so cold, because the whole food was vibrated. It was if Mother was filling us with food and vibrations at the same time making the Nabhi and Swadishthan become cool. So that was my first experience of Shri Mataji as the all-pervading power. She knows everything that is in all of our hearts and is ready to answer all our wishes if we have the desire within us

Pascal Shrestaputra

Coca-Cola

When Shri Mataji came to Madrid in 1987, She stayed at my house. It was a small and humble house because there was no better possibility. We had prepared everything with much detail and we really did our best, and had bought everything we thought Shri Mataji might need.

We were in a car on the way to my there, I was on the back seat with Shri Mataji and there was another person in between us. I felt very nervous to think that She was coming to my house and didn't know what to do. I started to say mantras inside. After a while Shri Mataji leaned towards me, behind the person between us.

'Very good,' She said.

When She arrived we duly performed all the welcoming protocol. We wanted to offer Her something to drink and She asked for water. Oh no! We had no mineral water for Mother! Luckily there was a shop nearby and we quickly went out to buy some.

'Oh, it doesn't matter, I'll have Coca-Cola. I just asked for water because I knew that it was missing,' She said, when the person was explaining all this to Her.

Spanish Sahaja Yogi

Cristian's healing

Our son Cristian was seven years old. From his birth he had had problems with his throat and his ear, which caused general suffering. The doctor wanted to operate and take out his tonsils.

'Wait a little, as our spiritual master is about to come and we have a great faith in Her,' we told the doctor, who went silent and a little sceptical.

Shri Mataji came to Madrid in the autumn of 1987, and blessed us with a Shri Ganesha Puja. It was celebrated in a cottage in the suburb of Soto de Viñuelas. This puja was more international and there were more people than the preceding ones. We, Cristian's parents, left the problem to Mother's attention. In our heart, we hoped that Mother would heal our boy. While the puja was being celebrated, Cristian went to give Mother a flower garland, and, at that moment, our request came up spontaneously, 'Mother, please, heal our child.'

During the puja, Cristian's mother offered Mother a 'jota', the traditional song from Zaragoza and surroundings. We then asked Mother for a spiritual name for Christian's little brother.

'Ganesha,' Mother raised Her head and said, after some seconds.

Some months later, Cristian was feeling perfect the doctor told us he was cured from his serous otitis. We felt comforted and grateful to our Mother.

Joaquín Orús

Why did the plane not take off?

Once, we were returning to India from Milan, via Rome in the late eighties. Sir CP was also with us. The flight got late and we missed the connection at Rome. So the airport authorities made us stay in their hotel near the airport. From the hotel Shri Mataji went shopping and told another Sahaja Yogi and me to wait for Her at the hotel.

The flight departure was at 7.20 pm. We waited for Shri Mataji up to 7.00 o'clock, then went to the airport thinking that now She would directly come to the airport. When we reached airport, there were many Sahaja Yogis waiting for Shri Mataji and the baggage was already loaded by a Sahaja Yogi who was working there. On the public announcement system they were repeatedly announcing our names telling that the flight was being delayed on account of us. The aircraft could not take off because our baggage was in it. Just then Shri Mataji arrived at the airport.

'When I told you to wait for us at the hotel, why did you leave without us?' She asked.

We explained our reason, and then She spoke to every one of the Sahaja Yogis who had come to see Her off and received flowers from them. We boarded the aircraft at about 8.00 pm. As we entered the aircraft, all other passengers and air hostesses booed us. Shri Mataji did not say anything. She just sat down in Her seat. We also sat down.

To our surprise, the plane could not move for two hours after that, due to a technical snag. Shri Mataji told us to go and ask these ladies who were shouting at us, why the aircraft did not take off.

Suresh Nigam

Chapter 7

1987: December India

The Queen of Sahasrara

I attended my first India tour in December 1987 after a year in a half in Sahaj. After landing in Mumbai, a shock for most of the Westerners, driving past kilometres of slums, we were taken to an enchanting fishing village called Alibagh, a few hours away. It was unlike anything I had known before and felt we had been transported back hundreds of years.

We slept in a coconut plantation near the pristine sea with kilometres of unspoiled beaches. The villagers' lifestyle was in harmony with nature in a way long forgotten in the West that made a deep impression on me. Men would go fishing in their small boats while women in colourful saris would catch fish using nets and wading into the sea.

The whole village was practicing Sahaja Yoga and in the evening they organised a procession to welcome Shri Mataji, with music so joyful one could not resist dancing. While waiting to see Her, the vibrations became stronger and stronger and I felt very moved by the music. Then loud 'Jai Shri Mataji's' were heard and we knew Mother had arrived. The crowd parted to let Her pass and She came walking slowly, so graciously She was almost gliding. When Shri Mataji was in front of me, I bowed to Her in a low and deep namaskar. When my head was bent down with my Sahasrara directed towards Her, I felt a rush of cool breeze through the top of my head as if it was completely opened. The vibrations were so cool and intense that it felt like a stream of water was pouring out.

This was an obvious manifestation of Shri Mataji being in total control of the Sahasrara chakra: because at that moment I had completely accepted and welcomed Her, She had fully opened my last chakra and blessed me with this incredible sensation of lightness and bliss. There was only joy within me and all the yogis around also seemed to be bathing in it.

Mother went into the bungalow that was to be Her residence and after a few minutes came out onto the balcony. The music started again and such a torrent of joy was felt that Shri Mataji started to dance a few steps. After that, a Sahaja Yogi, Mr Koli, came onto the balcony too and showed a unique painting of all the gods dancing in front of the Adi Shakti. Shri Mataji was very pleased with it and compared the yogis dancing in front of Her to it, and said that every yogi should have a copy. Since then a reproduction has been used in some mantra books, and poster copies were given out at some later pujas.

I will never forget that evening where, for the first time, I truly started to realise who Shri Mataji was.

Pascal Sreshtaputra

A great honour

I was on the India tour, 1987, when it was mainly around Maharashtra, and we were at a small village called Rahuri. I was coordinating the video team that was documenting Shri Mataji's tour. It was mainly getting a group of people into a bus, getting there on time, making sure the equipment ran, making sure the local electricity wasn't out at the moment and trying not to be intrusive on the experience. It was fun but quite a gruelling adventure.

We were at an event where some musicians were playing qawwali, and part of it was going up and making an offering of rupees to the performers. After doing that, Shri Mataji suggested that people go up and make a symbolic offering of a few rupees to the people who were operating the video and audio equipment for the work that they had done. At the time, I was sitting a bit back and wasn't actually operating the equipment, and wasn't on stage or anything. People were given this honorary donation at Shri Mataji's request. It was quite sweet, a symbolic gesture. I didn't receive anything because I was out of sight.

After the programme I was at a low point, tired and feeling a bit left out. Even though it was a small symbolic gesture of no economic value, I was feeling bad emotionally because somehow I hadn't rated the acknowledgement of this reward from my Mother. Finally something clicked in my head and a voice seemed to say to me, 'Your Mother would never do anything to make you feel bad, would never do anything to displease you and make you feel bad about yourself. So know that if you are having this feeling, it is not coming from Shri Mataji.' I just cried tears of joy, knowing this, believing it and feeling I would always have this trust from Her, even though I hadn't gotten the outward sign of this approval.

The next day it was time for the Sahaja Yogis to leave and we were having a going away ceremony. Shri Mataji was giving advice to the newly-married people in very humble surroundings at a little farm at Rahuri. She gestured towards me and there was a garland to be offered to Her as She left. I came to the stage and the organizer, Mr. Dhumal gave me the garland and I was able to garland Shri Mataji and She smiled quietly as I did. No one had spoken to Her about my disappointment or the fact that I hadn't been rewarded for my efforts or hadn't been recognized. It was this subtle knowledge on Her part that I had been on the video crew and I was rewarded in a way that I never imagined.

It was a great honour to be able to put flowers around the neck of your creator.

Phil Trumbo

She was Shri Mahamaya

On the India tour in 1987 we visited Aurangabad. Shri Mataji's older brother was living there and he invited all the three hundred or so Sahaja Yogis on the tour to his house. He gave all of us a cup of tea and a piece of cake, and also gave all the ladies a rose. He had a picture of Shri Mataji on the wall.

In the evening there was a music programme at a school hall and we were all sitting and waiting for Shri Mataji and Her brother to arrive. I had to go out for a short time, and when I came back there were Shri Mataji's brother and a lady sitting on the sofa on the stage. It looked like Mother in physical appearance, but somehow She looked like an Indian lady, the sister with her older brother. She was Shri Mahamaya, because somehow She was being a sister.

Maggie Burns

The integration of all incarnations

There was an Indian boy from Aurangabad who asked a very good question in a public programme. After answering him, Shri Mataji wrote about it in Her diary.

I was with Shri Mataji, and the diary was a little away from Her on the table. I wanted to get up and get the diary for Her, but She told me not to. She Herself bent to the left side and pulled it towards Her. I wanted to write down what Shri Mataji would say, but Mother said just to listen.

'One boy asked Me a very good question in the Aurangabad public programme,' She told me, 'and that I wrote in My diary and I will tell you. The question was, "This Paramchaitanya is beyond feeling. How can we feel it nowadays?"'

'From time to time,' Mother said to him, 'one by one, incarnations came on this earth and gave Their divine messages. But this incarnation, which is Shri Mataji,' at this point, Shri Mataji held Her right Vishuddhi finger towards Herself, was in an off-white sari with a red border and I could see Her as the Virata, 'is the integration of all incarnations, has taken incarnation and is doing the divine work. That is why we feel vibrations, even if they are beyond the feeling of human beings.'

Shakuntala Tandale

This humble 'celebrity'

The first time I ever saw Shri Mataji was at Ganapatipule in December 1987. Before arriving at Ganapatipule, I had already heard a lot about Her and how one could feel amazing vibrations and that one felt amazing when one saw Her.

At Ganapatipule we were waiting for Her arrival at the music programme. When Shri Mataji came onto the stage I was thinking that She just like my Nani (maternal grandmother).She was very motherly, relaxed, loving and simple, just like a grandmother. And of course I did not feel any vibrations. Actually at this stage I did not know what vibrations were and how they feel, but Her simplicity and detached humble personality were obvious.

After that, there were many hours of Indian classical music, much to my dislike because I was a typical westernized teenager, although I was Indian. When Shri Mataji was leaving people were bowing to Her, but She had Her hands folded in namaste longer than anyone else. I was amazed at this humble 'celebrity' (I was quite young and was into celebrities/Bollywood style, at that stage).

When She had left the stage, and I looked at the empty chair, I felt I was seeing an amazing sight. The stage glowed in a golden light. I looked again and again, rubbed my eyes and looked again. It was glowing. I am unable to express it in words. It was nothing supernatural but it felt like I was looking at the seat of God as it would be in heaven. And no one had told me that She was divine!

Mahima Saxena

Editor's note: if we see lights like this it means we are a bit off centre.

What name do You suggest?

The first darshan I had of Shri Mataji, and the first time I spoke to Her, was at Ganapatipule in 1987. The marriage ceremony was over. Mother had blessed the couples one by one, the last couple was about to leave and She was in a joyous mood. I took the opportunity to speak to Her.

'Shri Mataji, our daughter is born. She is one month old. What name do You suggest?'

'Purnima,' She replied. This means bright full moon in Sanskrit. I put my head on Her Lotus Feet, and was conscious of a sweet smell.

Now started a mental upheaval. My ego reacted, because Purnima is a traditional name with an ethnic tinge and not much used in modern society. After a month I had a dream, and saw the face of Mother in the form of a very big full moon, bright and glowing and smiling at me.

'You do not like the name,' She said in the dream.

'Mother,' I replied, also in the dream, with folded hands, 'You have sent a great yogi to us.'

Virendra Verma

Editor's note: Mr. Verma and his wife had been married for many years, but it was only after they both became Sahaja Yogis that they were blessed with a child, a beautiful daughter.

Chapter 8

1988: January to March India

1987 - 88 India Tour

Ah! The white tents on the beach at Ganapatipule, camping under the palm trees.

'Let's go early and help with puja preparation,' my friend said, on the day of the puja.

We set off and ended up making modakas with the Indian ladies in front of a little grass hut. Then as we headed into the pendal to help arrange flowers on the path Shri Mataji would walk, we realised we did not have our puja saris. Somehow we were able to borrow saris and get ready. During the puja, when fourteen married ladies were called up, no one moved. They asked again. Still no one moved.

'Well, goodness, I'd like to go and do puja!' I thought.

So I calmly stood up and walked to the front. Somehow by the time I got there, another girl and I were numbers fourteen and fifteen, the last two to arrive. We looked at one another, then looked up at the pujari, then again looked at one another. The pujari waved us both on stage. It was so amazing to do puja to Shri Mataji in Ganapatipule. Not only were we blessed with that experience, but we were also blessed as Shri Mataji gave each one of us a 'peasant-style' mangal sutra of silver.

Pramod Shete

It was like moonlight

My desire was to awaken the Kundalini. I tried following steps of Patanjali on my own, but gave it up and then in November 1987 I came to know about Sahaja Yoga. Somebody told me it was the spontaneous awakening of Kundalini. It seemed impossible.

'No, try,' they said, so I went to the Safdarjung temple in Delhi and, just by looking at the photo of Shri Mataji, I got my realisation.

On the 1st January 1988, I saw Shri Mataji for the first time in Maharashtra. They announced that She was not coming that day, but would come the next day. I was disappointed because New Year's Day was special, but then they announced that Shri Mataji was coming and then She came and I saw Her for the first time. At that time, the Ganapatipule programme was in in the village of Malgond, and I saw Her coming out of the car and then on the stage. It was like moonlight, watching Her.

Nirmal Gupta

This photograph knows everything

Saint Namdeva wrote many songs and my father sang one of Namdeva's songs to Shri Mataji. The song is about a saint who meets another saint and Namdeva explains the beauty of the meeting. Shri Mataji really liked this song and explained about his poetry and said he was a great saint. He went to Punjab and his poetry is in the book of the Sikh community, the Guru Granth Sahib. Shri Mataji said She wanted a book of Namdeva's bhajans and my father happened to find one, and bought it the very next morning, and presented it to Shri Mataji that very day. She was surprised that he had managed to find one so quickly. She was very pleased and often asked him to sing that song again.

At Ganapatipule in 1988 my father was accompanying a great singer from Aurangabad. The performance went very well and they went to bow to Shri Mataji afterwards and She hugged this lady and gave her Her own necklace, and Her photograph.

'Keep this photograph with you, because this photograph knows everything,' She said. 'Whatever you want to tell Me, tell it before this photograph, and I will come to know.'

Ravindranath Saundankar

A husband from anywhere

The first time I met Shri Mataji was at Ganapatipule in 1988. I had filled in the form for marriage, but it had got lost. My mother was with me and she was worried because I was twenty-four and wanted to get married.

We gave a lot of bandhans and on the last day she spoke with one of the leaders of Pune and he talked with Shri Mataji. In the evening Shri Mataji called my sister and me because she also wanted to get married. There was a music programme going on and we were on the stage at Shri Mataji's Feet. She asked us many things and I remember She asked us about our studies and where we would like a husband from, and we said anywhere.

Nanda Tagliabue

Shri Mataji very patiently showed me how to do it

I am a musician, a conductor, and some people call me a maestro. On one of the earlier India tours, about 1988, Shri Mataji gave all the yogis who were there little cymbals; the ladies had smaller ones and the men bigger ones. Almost by chance I was sitting opposite Her when we were singing bhajans and on the stage. I was playing these cymbals and was not playing them the right way.

She looked at me, and with Her hands made a gesture for me to give Her the cymbals, and She showed me how to play them. So here was I, who am supposed to be an accomplished classical musician, and Shri Mataji very patiently showing me how to do it. When I finally got it right, She nodded at me very strongly with Her head, to make me understand that it was the correct way.

Very recently I was organising a concert with choirs, and the children had to sing a traditional song from Japan, and one little girl had to play cymbals. I was able to give her some Indian type cymbals and taught her how to play. If anyone had asked me who taught me this, I was ready to admit that it was God Herself.

Siddheshvara Barbier

She was so comforting and so normal

It must have been 1988, when we went back from Ganapatipule on the boat with Mother from Jaigad to Mumbai. Jaigad was a little place near Ganapatipule, with a tiny quay and one little building on it, and there were only about twenty of us. We were with the Dehra Dun people and a few Sahaja Yogis from England, not many at all and there were loads of tiny jellyfish clustered round the quay. Mother was sitting there drinking Limcas, waiting for the boat to come and we were all sitting round Her and I think the harbour master got his realisation. I remember the feeling of utter peace of being there with Mother at that little port, a fishing village and all those little wooden buildings.

Later that night, we were up on the deck singing bhajans to Mother and it was a really beautiful calm night. All the Sahaja Yogis were on the deck around Mother. I don't know what had happened to all the other passengers, the hippies from Goa and so on, but it was a Shipping Corporation of India boat, so Mother got star treatment, even if they did not know She was the Goddess. The greatest memory of those times was that you knew She was the Goddess, but She was so comforting and so normal.

Auriol Purdie

It was just magical

We were at Ganapatipule and a few of us travelled via boat from a port near Ganapatipule to Mumbai with Shri Mataji. We got to a quay and were waiting for the boat so were able to have tea with Mother. The boat arrived around midnight. We followed Mother out onto the dock as the boat was there, and there were about twenty or thirty yogis. We were walking together, with Mother at the front wearing a white sari. As we went onto the boat, there was a plank you went over. Mother stopped so majestically as we went from the dock to the boat and I was just two feet away.

'See this. This is hell,' She said strongly to me and told me to keep away from the people on the boat, because one of them had tried to talk to me. She pointed, and didn't have to say anything. We just looked around in the dim light at the lower parts of the boat. There were people drinking alcohol and so on and it was just yucky, squalid. She led us up to the top deck, which was where they had First Class cabins. We were there with Her and our brothers and sisters were so sweet. They knew Shri Mataji had spoken strongly to me, so they let me come close to the front and I held the prasad for Mother to eat. It was just magical. The moon was full on the calm Arabian Sea as the boat was going up the coast.

Dattatreya Haynes

My best birthday

I can't remember if it was my twelfth, thirteenth or fourteenth birthday, but it was my best ever. My parents and my younger brother were traveling on a ship and about to arrive in Mumbai and I had gone to the docks to greet them. By a stroke of good fortune, I saw Shri Mataji, who was on the same ship. I went forward and bowed to Her but She stopped me and gave me a very loving hug and wished me happy birthday!

My heart skipped a beat. I was surprised and my happiness knew no bounds. I thanked Her and She asked my father to bring me to Her house in the evening to celebrate. I was very excited but later, my father said that while it was very nice of Her, we really shouldn't bother Her as She is so busy. I quite understood and was still very happy because the Divine had wished me happy birthday, so went to bed with a blissful smile on my face.

Next morning, when I woke up, my room was full of presents. My father said he was sorry because he hadn't realised that Shri Mataji had gone to the trouble of making arrangements to celebrate my birthday and all the gifts were from Her. She invited me over later that day. I was so touched that I had tears of joy in my eyes, for even as a child, I recognised Shri Mataji was an ocean of love and only She knew how to pour so much love on to all of us. Thank You, Shri Mataji.

Shruti Jalan Gupta

Because I am with them

When I went to Ganapatipule in 1987, it was announced that the programme was over and now we were going to Mumbai and on the 10th January 1988 there would be the Sankranti Puja in Mumbai. I felt the programme was over so soon and I had the desire to go closer to Shri Mataji, but felt I could not.

I went to the puja in Mumbai and was sitting towards the back and in my heart thinking, 'I want to go to Shri Mataji.' In the beginning the desire was very strong. Shri Mataji gave Her lecture and afterwards they were going to start the puja and once they started the mantras Shri Mataji stopped them.

'People sitting here are thinking that they want to come to Me. Why are they thinking like this? Because I am with them,' She said.

I was indeed thinking like that. I was amazed and thought, 'She knows everything,' because I had been thinking, 'I want to go to Her,' and then She announced this. I pulled my ears and that was it.

Nirmal Gupta

This music will reach every corner of the world

The best compliment Shri Mataji ever paid to me was in 1988, when She named me Roshan – the enlightened one. She once told me that I had the complete knowledge of Sahaj Yoga and She was very happy that I would be able to now write, compose and sing Her message for the whole world. I am still trying to understand what She really meant by that, but if God is to be seen on Earth today, it is Param Pujyaniya, Her Holiness Shri Mataji Nirmala Devi.

The recording of the bhajan tape Roohani Roshani was important because Shri Mataji personally supervised its making – right from the compositions, poetry and the pre-recording puja advice. At the recording time, She put Her attention to it and when it was recorded She checked its quality and made me redo certain portions where She felt it needed correction. I still remember Her remarks after I phoned Her to check She had heard the whole album, before it was formally released.

'I want you to know that I am very pleased with this work of music,' She said. 'This music will reach every corner of the world. You will not believe it, but your music will become so popular and in demand worldwide that your name will be remembered even a hundred years after you are dead and gone. Probably you will return to listen to your own work.'

I was completely dazed with Her words, spoken so very softly over the telephone. At that time, I was staying at a yogi's home in Mumbai. After the phone conversation the yogi put flowers around his phone and did a small puja to it. He would not let anyone call from this phone, as it had just been vibrated with Mother's voice. It was such a thrilling moment for both of us.

Sanjay Talvar

Shri Mataji made Her recommendations

This photo was taken in Mumbai in 1988, after Shri Mataji had heard my first professional audio recording. We had gone through each song, and She had made Her recommendations to improve upon them. Later I

Shri Mataji in Mumbai 1988

went back to the studio to make the amendments. The cassette was called
Roohani Roshani, named by Shri Mataji.

Sanjay Talvar

The pencil and the piece of cloth

Shri Mataji was explaining something. I remember very vividly when She actually took a pencil and a piece of cloth, and She poked the cloth. The following explanation was given to me directly by Mother.

'Do you know that this pencil represents the Kundalini?' She said. 'The cloth represents your attention, and this attention is actually lying on the diaphragm on the seat of the Nabhi. It's always around the Nabhi, because we are worried about our existence, our sustenance and how are we going to survive and all that, so the attention is all the time there.'

So when the realisation happens it is an automatic process, the Kundalini like a pencil just draws that cloth of attention from the diaphragm and brings it to the level of the heart. At the heart it gets enlightened. Now at the heart when it gets enlightened there is a passage which connects the heart to the brain, and that passage goes through the left Vishuddhi. If there is no guilt, the Vishuddhi is clear; then this attention rises through, goes to the brain. And its light, its enlightenedness is now ready for projection. Then any yogi can project his attention through it anywhere, where it needs to work.

He can empower it with the desire, with the motive, with submission, and it can go there and can just disperse. It's like waves that reach the end of the sea and just disperse, they don't bring back any ripples, which means this attention can actually work, it can actually change things around. Whatever you have put it to use for, it affects. In a normal man who is not realised, his attention is on the Nabhi. When he tries to project it, it goes somewhere and it brings back a reaction like a projectile back to you. And then you go into a cycle of action and reaction. Whereas a realised person just disperses his attention, it is enlightened and it enlightens things wherever he goes.

Sanjay Talwar

How fortunate I was

I remember going to work at Pratishthan just after school, with my school uniform on. Sometimes I was very fortunate to get the holy darshan of Shri Mataji, who directed and taught the architects everything about divine architecture. She asked us yuvas to come and work there and I had just finished my tenth class exams and had studied hard.

'You have used your head a lot, now you should come to Pratishthan and work and learn to use your hands,' She told me, after one of the pujas.

'Yes, Mother,' I said, and bowed down.

Little did I know at that time how immensely fortunate I was to be directed by the Supreme One to work at Her house, for one of Her names erHis Kataaksha Kinkari Bhuta Kamala Koti Sevita, which means 'at a single glance of Hers, billions of Shri Lakshmis present themselves to be at Her service'.

Ajit Kulkarni

It is just heaven

When I was young I was at Pratishthan, playing with some other children. Shri Mataji was passing by and She called many of the kids and I just went close to Her. She put Her hand on my head and it was an experience of heaven. When She touched you or was close to you, you cannot describe it in words - it was just heaven.

Sahaj Singh

You are the only One who gives!

When I first went to Pratishthan to see Shri Mataji, She was very busy and we waited for some time for Her. When She came, Her first words were, 'Forgive Me that you had to wait for two hours.' I was very ashamed at hearing those words!

'Where do you come from?' She said and also asked what work I did, so I told Her. I explained I was new to Sahaja Yoga, and had come for Her blessings.

Shri Mataji asked me to put my hands under Her Lotus Feet, then She raised my Kundalini and gave me some tips. She asked some other Sahaja Yogis to feel which chakra was catching, and they said it was the Nabhi. Then She asked me get up, and I apologized and said I did not know anything about chakras. Shri Mataji explained it was something to do with my being a government servant, and told me to do ice treatment on the right side, on the liver.

When I visited again, Shri Mataji asked me if we ever had a problem of people behaving in a manner as if they had epilepsy, in our house. She told me that if this did happen, to burn ajwan in the house every evening. We did this for about two months and everything became all right. Then I again went to Pratishthan, and Shri Mataji asked me why I was afraid, and asked what I had in my hand. I told Her it was a ring with Her photo on it, and Shri Mataji said if ever I was afraid to show this photo.

On the way home, by mistake I got into the Ladies' Compartment on the train. I was caught by a Police Constable, and he tried to frighten me by saying he would take me to the lock-up. There were many other people who were also in trouble like me that he had also arrested at that time. On the way to the Police Station he asked me where I had been, and I said I had been to Shri Mataji's programme. I showed him Shri Mataji's ring and he asked me never to make this mistake again, and just let me go.

On another occasion, I was able to explain to Shri Mataji that although I had a good salary, somehow money never stayed with me. She asked me to build a house, but I did not know where I would get the money from. Anyway, I prayed to Her photo when I got home, and although I only had four thousand rupees to start it with, somehow people came and helped, and the materials were just there, and now it is finished and worth about 2,000,000 rupees.

We should pray at Shri Mataji's Lotus Feet that everyone should get a mother like that. You are the only One who gives!

Mr Raskar

Shri Mataji called me

When the construction of Pratishthan was going on Shri Mataji stayed in the front portion on the first floor. At this time the Pune Sahaja Yogis used to go there to help with the construction work. Once Shri Mataji was going out of Pune and the working yogis had assembled to meet Her. I was standing at the back of the gathering and She called me. On reaching Her with my son Sahaj, when I bowed at Her Feet, I felt Her body enlarging like Shri Virat, Shri Hanuman. I was like a tiny particle before Her. In my heart, I thanked Her for showing me Her Virat form.

Kamala Singh

A blessing in disguise

On 23rd January 1988 as per instructions from Mother, I went to Pratishthan with a Maths tutor for arranging tuition for Miss Aradhana, the grand-daughter of Shri Mataji. As Miss Aradhana had not come from college, we were sitting with Shri Mataji in the first floor room, near the entry staircase of the house.

This is the room where She used to stay when the construction of Pratishthan was going on. Shri Mataji was sitting on the bed with Her Feet on the ground and we were sitting on the ground. During the waiting period of about an hour, She was discussing all sorts of topics with us.

Suddenly I began to cough and fell at Her Feet, but soon recovered. We came back from Pratishthan without meeting Miss Aradhana, as she had not come. Later on I realised that from the moment of falling at Her Feet, my chronic chest problem had disappeared. I felt I had been called for this, on the pretext of arranging the tuition.

RR Singh

Her attention was on every stroke

In the late eighties, when Pratishthan was being built, as Yuva Shakti we used to go and do the work there whenever we could, at weekends, when there was no college. We were told people were required in a certain court-yard so we went there. We were handed little buckets of paint and small brushes. Shri Mataji had some cement plates cast which were adorning the beams and columns and She wanted to make them look like stone. We climbed up a ladder to do the painting and Mother took a seat behind us, even though we did not see Her.

'Jayant,' Shri Mataji called to me. I was surprised because I did not know She was there. 'Do it there,' I tried to do pranams but it was difficult, up there on the ladder. She pointed a finger to the left of where I had been painting. 'Do it there, but do it very lightly. I don't want the colours to be very dark.' Her attention was on every stroke. We were there with our hands, but Shri Mataji was looking at everything that was happening and was working through us.

Jayant Patankar

By Your Grace any raga can work for any chakra

I felt that in Sahaja Yoga music is essential and there is a relation between Kundalini shakti and music. I studied Indian classical music quite lot, and as I knew that Mooladhara is Shri Ganesha's chakra, and that is purity, so all pure notes come in Raag Bilawal. So I proposed this raga for Mooladhara. I wrote notes on the relations between Indian Classical Music, the subtle spiritual body and Kundalini shakti, and tried to relate the ragas with the chakras. In 1988 I met Shri Mataji at Pratishthan.

Shri Mataji watching the work

'Shri Mataji by Your grace any raga can work for any chakra - this is Your power, this is what I feel about the relation between the ragas and chakras,' I prayed. Then I read out what I had written and asked Shri Mataji to guide me, and She said it was ok, but for Nabhi I should use Gunakali

Shri Mataji demonstrating at Pratishthan

and for Vishuddhi Jai Jaivanti. I presented Her a book that I brought, which had some reference to the Indian classical music used in ancient prayers to God and She took it.

'I have no time to read,' She said, but She opened the book and pointed to one paragraph, 'see it is written here that in the ancient period, to please Shri Shiva, Bhairavi raga was used.'

Then later, in the year 2000 I presented another tape to Shri Mataji - Stotrangeli – at Pratishthan.

Videh Saundankar

She had never played like that before

It was in early 1988, and I went to a puja in Maharashtra. There were no other foreigners there and I did not understand much of what was said. There was a music programme and I sat upstairs in the front of the gallery, because I wanted to tape the music. I had a tape recorder which worked well. The lady who played for Mother was a Begum, a Moslem lady. The music was nice but nothing to write home about, but then suddenly, towards the

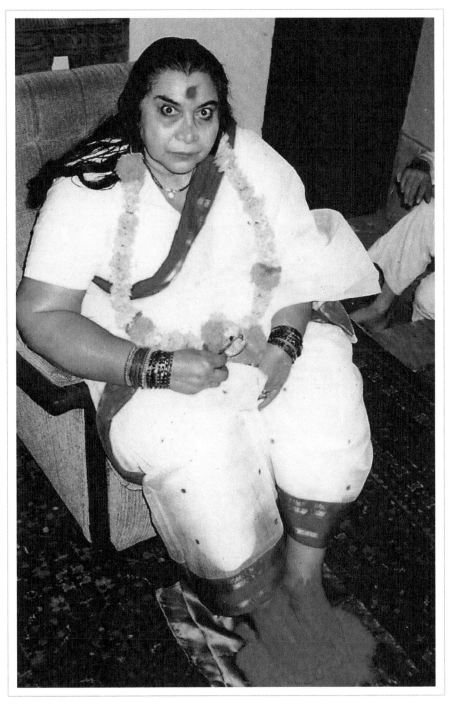

Holi, with the powder anointing Shri Mataji's Feet

end of the performance, I think when she was playing the Bhairavi which comes last, her playing seemed to take off and become a million times better.

After the performance I discovered that firstly I was not supposed to have taped the music, and secondly, nobody except me had in fact taped it, but both Mother and the lady wanted a copy of my tape. Mother explained that She had raised the lady's Kundalini at a certain point during the programme, and it was after that that her playing transformed. The lady said she didn't know what had happened to her - she had never played like that before. Of course I was honoured to give Mother the tape.

Linda Williams

Shri Mataji watching the workers and yogis playing Holi

Derek Ferguson diary entry Wednesday 1st March

Dr Rustom Burjorjee, the psychiatrist, arrived. He asked Shri Mataji lots of questions. She explained about dreams a bit, saying that they could be analysed and gave an example of how. Rustom had a patient who saw the Kundalini rising in a dream and also a serpent going round the Mooladhara. She explained that the patient's Mooladhara was damaged and that the dream he saw was trying to show him that, and he should take to Sahaja Yoga to get it cured. She told Rustom that he could explain that and could interpret other dreams also.

Shri Mataji spoke about a leader and said the reason he had gone down was because he had developed ego because of being a leader and also

Shri Mataji with the workers and yogis

because of complacency. Earlier he was very good and had a very powerful innocence. For example four men had tried to steal some sugar cane from his field, but they were caught and beaten by some big men whose faces were black and you could just see their eyes. The next day the thieves went back to the Sahaja Yogi and asked him what path he followed because they knew it was something divine. He asked them if they had been hurt and he told them he had not, and Shri Mataji said the big men were ganas.

She spoke about some angels helping Her. Shri Mataji went to a Mahakali temple to awaken the deity there and a tall fair faced man came and took Her in and around it then disappeared. She asked the people there who he was and they had never seen him and there was no one of that description there. She said it was an angel.

Another time Shri Mataji went to Jaganpuri temple and the Brahmins would not let Her in. Suddenly a little boy came and took Her inside past the crowds and then disappeared. Again She asked the people who he was and they said he had not been there before – he was another angel. She said angels come down like that to help with the Sahaja Yoga.

After this Shri Mataji started to work on one of the leaders and said his boss was like a rakshasa. Rustom said that most people have someone like that at work. Shri Mataji said we should rise above these things and not get affected by them. Rustom said the person had a bad Vishuddhi and Shri Mataji said Rustom also had a Vishuddhi problem, and that is why

She could not hear what he was saying properly, because She goes by the chakras and hears through the Vishuddhi and not the ears. She said that we should have a genuine dedication to Her from the heart to be able to rise.

Shri Mataji said the caste system is the curse of India and Shri Krishna tried to put things right but people have still not changed. No matter what caste you are, you can still commit the same sins. She also said that when the Hindu Indians change to Christianity they still have a caste system, so what is the use of changing? Even in Sahaja Yoga people from different castes try to club together. Only Sahaja Yoga can change that, because of the intermarriages. She said She could understand people clubbing together when they go abroad, because of language etc, and also in different states of India, but not in their own state.

Shri Mataji being shown a finished window made by hand, because there were no power tools at Pratishthan

A cure for a bad liver

During this time Shri Mataji went to England for Easter Puja. While She was away I became ill with jaundice. It took some time to completely get over the jaundice fully, but Shri Mataji really speeded the process up in a few sessions of putting Her Foot on my liver. At one time I was called to Her and as I sat before Her, there was a lot of activity in Marathi. Water was poured over Shri Mataji's Feet and that water was put into a bottle; ginger was vibrated and sugar and then all these things were given to me to treat my liver. I rounded up the other yogis, like Laurent Dumonet, and we sat in a circle and I shared out all of the vibrated things. We all drank it together and after drinking, we were all floating, just like we had drunk some kind of divine drink.

On another session Shri Mataji asked for a small bowl, called a katuri, of mustard oil. While She put Her hand in the oil, Shri Mataji told me to look into the mustard oil and nothing else. Shri Mataji took Her hand out of the oil and told me to keep looking. Now with the jaundice I had become completely yellow, like science fiction yellow. I remember getting such a shock when I saw myself in the mirror, but after looking into the oil 95% of the yellow went into the oil and I came out very much pinker than when I went in.

John Watkinson

Chapter 9

1988: April to June England and Europe

Easter Puja, Shudy Camps, April 1988

Shri Mataji's car entered the courtyard in the same cloudy English atmosphere that had prevailed all day long. When the car's door finally opened in the middle of the crowd who were waiting, the cloud cover opened and gently allowed a little space, right by the sun, to salute the meeting of the smiling Mother with Her devotees. It was the first time I saw Shri Mataji. As She slowly made Her way through the crowd, stopping at every step to receive flowers and give a little of Her attention to all, and laughing with the little ones, I could fill my eyes with the reality of Her incarnation. And then, too soon, She was in the house.

Staying behind the crowd of Sahaja Yogis that had accompanied Shri Mataji we now observed that, far from receding, the human flow kept crossing the threshold; people squeezed into the furthest corridors of the house. Shri Mataji had asked everyone to enter, as She wanted to welcome and address them. Hundreds of people! We couldn't help laughing at this incredible invitation. When would it stop? We went in, amazed to finally get a chance to stand not too far from the entrance door as more and more people squeezed inside. We discovered that Shri Mataji was not in a remote hall upstairs, but just seated there, and we were right in front of Her.

When it became clear that no more movement could take place, there were very few people left outside, and Shri Mataji was staring at us, at three metres maximum. I held a little girl in my arms, who couldn't otherwise have seen Shri Mataji, and Mother's eyes looked attentively at all the people. The next day Mother would mention in the puja talk that the Sahaja Yogis were getting younger and younger and She sometimes wondered, 'Who was the father and who was the son?'

The evening programme was in the presence of Shri Mataji. Zakir Hussein played Djugal bandhi with his brother, Asit Desai and his wife Hema and others were singing the Tulsidas bhajan Thirat kaha jana, and there was a wonderful santoor player too.

The next day, the sun had definitely taken over, and Shri Mataji had to interrupt Her talk as She felt too hot The previous week's weather had been extremely bad with gales and heavy rains, and it was supposed to get worse by the week-end. As usual the weather forecast had not considered the needs of the divine.

The puja talk, about Christ, was deep but also full of humour. Mother stayed a long time, receiving the gifts and giving Indian names to Westerners. While talking to every person one after the other, She would sometimes stop and stare in front of Her fixedly and you couldn't avoid feeling that this strong look was addressed to you and you only.

Devarshi Abalain

Shri Mataji moved the clouds

The Easter Puja at Shudy Camps took place on Easter Sunday, April 1988, in the back garden of our Divine Mother's house in the heart of New Jerusalem, under a marquee. Since Thursday Sahaja Yogis had been converging from all over Europe and beyond.

On Saturday morning Shri Mataji arrived in Her car around lunchtime, to be received by everyone standing outside the house in the spring sunlight. The weather, contrary to the expectations of the forecasters, was improving all the time. The following day Shri Mataji explained that She had been concerned that the weather should be good for the puja, since we were all staying in tents, and that She had arranged things in such a way that all the clouds which were supposed to be sitting over England were elsewhere. Later, we looked at satellite weather pictures in the newspapers, and there we could see the clouds, right over Newfoundland just as Shri Mataji had said. She was moved to make these remarks after feeling hot during Her talk, and remarking that the sun would annoy Her unless She talked about Him.

One of the miracle photos described in the story

Immediately after Her arrival, Shri Mataji went to sit down in the front reception room and asked everyone to come in. By some miracle we all managed to fit in, there were plenty of us and the room was quite small. Shri Mataji spoke for a little while about Her plans for future events in Europe: marriages in Milan at Shri Krishna Puja, pujas in Europe during the summer and a visit to North America. She also talked about Her house, how the transformations that had taken place were amazing and how the transformations that took place within the Sahaja Yogis were no less amazing. She said we must have confidence in ourselves. She mentioned some miracle photographs that had been taken in Ganapatipule and that She was having developed at the time to show us. In one all the deities could be seen sitting around Her, and in another a light could be seen emerging from the Sahasraras of the bridegrooms at the weddings, the filaments of which traced out our Divine Mother's name in Arabic script.

Phil Ward

A music programme

On Saturday evening we assembled in the marquee and Shri Mataji arrived for a music programme. Nothing but the best for our Mother! We were treated to bhajans from husband and wife Ajit and Hema Desai, who had a very simple and direct style - Shri Mataji afterwards praised the originality of their singing. They sang bhajans by Tulsidas and others, and at Shri Mataji's request, bhajans by Kabir. Kabir recognized that the ultimate transcended all religious identifications; the others had not managed this, for example Tulsidas only praised Shri Rama. Kabir could see the oneness of all of these incarnations.

Zakir Hussain and his brother Fazal Qureshi performed a tabla duet, which was fast and exciting, and the rapport between the musicians was beautiful. Shri Mataji was very pleased by their playing, and praised them very much after the concert. She said that She wondered if Zakir Hussain was not the reincarnation of the guru of his father, Ustad Alla Rakha, another very great tabla player.

'He is a Sikh, and a seeker,' Shri Mataji said; during his concert his Kundalini had risen, and She had felt the difference in his music from then on. He was extremely humble and respectful before Shri Mataji.

Phil Ward

May God bless them, they sang so well

The puja took place on Sunday morning, starting about midday, and Shri Mataji spoke to us for about forty minutes. After Her talk the Atharva Sheersha was read, and She was read the text of the Messiah, while Her Lotus Feet were being washed. Then the choir and orchestra assembled to sing the oratorio.

'May God bless them, they sang so well,' Shri Mataji said to those on stage near Her. Afterwards She suggested we should hire a hall and give a public performance.

The Viennese had prepared a choral version of some Johann Strauss waltzes, which Shri Mataji had very much enjoyed when She had visited Vienna, saying of Strauss's music that it was universal music that everyone could understand, bubbling with joy, but they did not get an opportunity to perform this weekend. In 1985 - the tercentenary of Bach and Händel's births – Shri Mataji had listened to some of their music at the Munich ashram, and had praised both composers very highly.

There were bhajans after the performance of the Messiah had finished, during which time Shri Mataji was receiving presents from the different nations and kindly giving names to a number of children and babies.

In the evening there was a 'play' by the little children of the Sahaja Yogis living at Shudy Camps, highly unrehearsed but very sweet, accompanied by an English Sahaja Yogi and your correspondent playing 'Old MacDonald had a Farm' and 'Humpty Dumpty' on synthesizers. Some sketches followed, with two professional actors portraying in comic fashion a yogi going to India, bestrewn with lemons and chillies, and the chaos of the marriage day but with everyone getting – in the end, after a great deal of mirth – lined up behind the veil opposite the right person. Shri Mataji appeared to enjoy it all very much, and at the end She spoke very beautifully and highly about the Sahaja Yogi children, how confident and innocent they were and how well they had done. By now it was about half past two, and time for dinner, so we took leave of our Divine Mother. The following morning Shri Mataji was seen off by all of us as She left Shudy Camps for Heathrow and India.

Phil Ward

Composed for some special occasion

We were at Shudy Camps for Easter Puja, 1988. The music for the puja was the Messiah by Handel. I am a musician and was in charge of conducting it. Every step of the puja – and at that time the pujas were pretty long – corresponded to a different piece of the Messiah, and when Shri Mataji was crowned, at exactly that moment, the choir happened to sing the Halleluiah Chorus, which is close to the end of the Messiah. The Halleluiah was composed for some special occasion, and this was it!

Siddeshwara Barbier

I had sung for God

In 1988, Sahaja Yogi musicians from all over the world prepared to perform Handel's Messiah, for Easter Puja. Singers and instrumentalists rehearsed in their home countries and finally put this wonderful puzzle together at the Lotus Feet of Our Mother. Being a professional singer, I not only conducted part of the choir rehearsals in Vienna but above all, prepared the soprano solo. During that time, the main question of my life was whether I should take to singing or acting.

We arrived at Shudy Camps, got everybody together and started rehearsals. Another Yogini had also prepared the soprano solo and she sang at a rehearsal, but was rather an amateur. I got very upset, inwardly – how could anyone offer such a poorly prepared performance for Shri Adi Shakti?

Suddenly, earlier than expected, it was announced that Shri Mataji was arriving. Completely caught up in my network of thoughts, grudges and despair, I nevertheless joined the others for the welcome in front of the entrance door.

Shri Mataji arrived, beaming as always, but I stood back, as I was so caught up that I did not feel anything. I was swept along with everybody else into the large tent where Shri Mataji took Her seat and started to talk. I cannot even remember what She said, and was unable to stop my thoughts and emotions. After a while Shri Mataji went up to Her room, and we all went out.

And there it happened, when I stepped over the threshold of the house: in a split second all my grudges, despair, and defiance disappeared, like a dark cloud that had been in front of the sun and was dispersed, leaving the sun in its full brightness. It had all been Maya. Detached, I could now approach the other musicians with a light heart and we continued rehearsing. The next day it was decided that I should sing all the soprano solo parts.

When I was a child I had always wanted to sing for God. I sang in church, but never knew if I was heard. Now I was very excited. Only once during the performance did I get tears in my eyes and my voice nearly failed, but was carried by this gentle wave, and could perform for the Goddess. From that day on, the question if I should become a singer or an actress was equally dissolved.

I had sung for God.

Andrea Wicke

Our small simple wish was realised

In May 1988, Shri Mataji came to France and we had a puja in Melun near Paris. At that time, my sister Sita and I were teenagers and were living in a town 400 kilometres from Paris. We came with some other Sahaja Yoginis by car. That was our second puja with Shri Mataji and it was fantastic. Shri Mataji asked for young girls to perform the puja and Sita and I could go on the stage to do the puja to the Devi. In France, we were very few teenagers at that time. Shri Mataji asked us to use our whole hand, not only one or two fingers, to paint Her Feet with kumkum, and then to apply this liquid kumkum on our palms. It was so light, we had no thoughts and only pure joy.

At the end of the puja, the ladies we came with left the tent where the puja was hosted, right after the aarti, and while Shri Mataji was still on the stage. They made gestures in our direction to ask us to collect our luggage and go with them. With a sad heart, pulling our ears, we obeyed them because we were young and if they wanted to leave, what would we do? When we were outside, we took our bags and waited on the side of the road leading to the tent, and the ladies who had called us disappeared somewhere.

We could hear the cheers, and the crowd shouting, 'Jai, jai, jai!' We were so disappointed because we were missing all this and we could not say goodbye to our Holy Mother. Then the most unexpected happened. A car came our way, and as it came nearer we realised it could be Shri Mataji's car. When the car reached us, yes, Shri Mataji was there in the car! She had a large smile and waved us good–bye through the window. I was so extremely happy that I jumped in the air and did a big wave back, while my sister bowed in namaskar. But the yogini who was standing with us, one of the people who had driven us and asked us to leave early, did not see Shri Mataji! Our small simple wish was realised and we felt so happy. It was for us really which filled our life for weeks together with light, happiness and vibrations.

Indumati Patil

Oh, Pranava!

The first time I ever met Shri Mataji was when She gave me my name. I was called Paul. Shri Mataji asked me to go on the stage. It was early May in 1988, in Italy. I sat down in front of Her and She asked what my name was and I told Her.

'Oh, Paul,' She said, and went into meditation. She closed Her eyes and stayed like that for a minute. For me it was eternity. It was difficult for me to keep my eyes open. Then suddenly She said, 'Oh, Pranava!' I didn't understand what this meant. 'You like it?'

'Oh, yes, yes, I didn't understand,' I said. I didn't realise this was my name and meant for me. She said it is like a mantra, both for me and for others when they say it because it means vibrations, chaitanya.

Pranava Fiorini

Peace for my country

On the first Friday of May 1988, yogis were preparing to go to Rome for Sahasrara Puja. Inside myself, I had put various desires to Shri Mother to be answered by Her. Then on the Saturday, Mother talked to the leader, who passed on to me that I had the answers to all my desires, by Shri Mataji.

The next day a beautiful Sahasrara Puja was enjoyed and then on the Monday afternoon a public programme was held with Mother in attendance. The hall was packed with yogis and new people, many of whom She gave self realisation to. At the programme's end, She asked those who desired to shake Her hand or speak with Her to come forward. A very long queue formed of new people. I had a strong desire to go forward and thank Her for whatever She had done for me, but stepped back to let the newest ones go forward. Before She began to meet anyone, She looked around and Her eyes lit on me.

'You, come here,' She said. I went to Her Feet and Shri Mataji hugged me warmly and held me. I felt it was the love of a real mother and incredible vibrations surrounded us. The leader was sitting beside Mother and translating. She then looked at me.

'It is your time to ask if you have any desire,' She said. It came to my mind that I wanted peace for my country, Iran, which had been involved with Iraq in a war that had been going on for ten years with great destruction to our people.

'I want peace for my country,' I answered.

'You can have peace.' This was a spontaneous request, not planned or even thought out beforehand from among the other desires I had previously put to Shri Mother, which were more personal. Following that, She began to receive new people and the yogis began to prepare to return to their cities after the wonderful weekend with their Mother.

Less than a month after this had happened, the news came out that the war had stopped between Iran and Iraq. So I had this desire fulfilled by Shri Mataji and the people who knew about what had happened in that public programme rang me in congratulations for Mother's work.

Reza Ghaffarian

A moment of ecstatic joy

The puja near Barcelona in May 1988 took place on top of a hill, with little more than one hundred Sahaja Yogis.

A miracle happened during the puja and was mentioned by Shri Mataji Herself. Balloons had been tied in rows above the Sahaja Yogis' heads. When Shri Mataji said it was our vibrations that made the balloons move, my sceptical mind started looking around to see where the wind was coming from. It was windy in this mountain landscape and if you looked at the far off slopes you could see the trees moving strongly, but I then looked at the little trees around the yard and nearby where the puja took place, and they were absolutely still. It would have been impossible for the balloons to move as they did without the little trees around the house moving too.

On Saturday evening, after Shri Mataji individually addressed several people, we listened to the Spanish yogis' bhajans and ended up dancing in front of Mother in this tiny chalet's hall. It was an exuberant moment of ecstatic joy that must be remembered to this day by everyone who was present then.

Devarshi Abalain

The all-knowing Mother

In June 1988 I returned to London from India after living there for six years. Before leaving I had made an arrangement with the Sahaja Housing Co–op that if I ever wanted a room at Chelsham Road, which was my house, I could have one. When I returned I discovered it was difficult to get anyone to live there, but one family had agreed to do so, with their five children and a nanny. However, that didn't leave any room for me and my children.

I was worried, because I had very little money, nowhere to live and needed to put the children in school. I decided to send a letter to Shri Mataji and managed to give one to someone who was to seeer Her that evening.

The next day I went to see one of the leaders. I was in his flat and as I was speaking about my problem the phone rang. It was Shri Mataji and She asked to speak to me, although She did not, in human terms, have any way of knowing I was there. She went through the requests I had made in the letter, one by one, as if She had it in front of Her, and said it would be good for the children if I went to live at Shudy Camps, because the schools were better there. I assumed She had received my letter. That evening I again saw the man to whom I had given it and thanked him for delivering it.

'Oh no!' he said. 'I forgot all about it!' and pulled it out of his pocket.

Linda Williams

One time Shri Mataji said that really we should not speak in Her presence, and if we knew who She truly was we would not even stand.

Linda Williams

It's not real rain, it's vibrations

One time there was a leaders' meeting in Austria, and we were all sitting in the room with Shri Mataji. It started to rain outside.

'Look at the rain,' Shri Mataji said. We looked at the rain, but we didn't hear anything. Then it started to rain more. 'It's not real rain, it's vibrations,' She explained.

We realised this, because there was no sound.

Patricia Deene

Immediately I was thoughtless

In 1988, Shri Mataji was to leave Vienna airport at 1.00 or 2.00 pm. I had to work that day, but I managed to be there at 1.00 pm exactly.

I saw a very big crowd of yogis sitting around our Holy Mother, who was talking. I knew my vibrations were too much on the right and I didn't feel so good, and all the others were in joy and peace. I just sat down and a storm of vibrations entered my body through my hands. Immediately I was thoughtless and full of joy as much as the others.

Just one simple glance of my Mother and the whole world changed.

Ingrid B

An internal relationship

I came to Sahaja Yoga in 1986 and started attending programmes. I don't know why, but while listening to Shri Mataji's talks, I got into the habit of translating Her words into German, in my head. It now seems a strange, strenuous mental activity, but it must have really helped my attention, because I had to be very alert, translating every sentence.

Eventually I had the honour of translating Shri Mataji's talks for many years in the German speaking countries: Austria, Germany and Switzerland. Translating Shri Mataji's talk on the stage was always a wonderful experience. I always tried to make sure to ask Shri Ganesha for help so that I would 'hear that which is true', that people would 'hear not my voice, but the wisdom of God', as in the translation of the Ganesha Atharva Sheersha.

In 1988 I translated several public programmes in Vienna, and also one in Graz. Shri Mataji never spoke to me directly, or even looked at me. I

really was hoping for some sort of acknowledgement, or reassurance from Her, that I was doing the right thing. On the last day in Graz, just before Shri Mataji was leaving to go to the airport we were waiting to say good–bye to Her in the ashram. By that time my heart was so full of joy, and I felt Her love so strongly inside me that it did not matter, that She went past me without acknowledging my presence. I was just grateful for everything I had experienced by Her grace, and full of gratitude in my heart. But then, to my complete surprise, as She already was seated in the back of the car, She saw me standing, and called me up, so I went to the car and She spoke to me through the window, and, to my embarrassment, thanked me, so of course I thanked Her. This incident taught me how the relationship with Shri Mataji is always an internal one, and not external.

I had similar experiences at several other times, while greeting Her and presenting a flower to Her at airports all over Europe. Every time when I felt a strong connection with Her, when I felt Her love inside me, She would greet me, smile at me, or ask me a question.

Sigrid Jones

Conducting a huge orchestra

Being on the stage with Shri Mataji, as the translator, while She was conducting public programmes was an amazing experience. Looking at the audience from the stage it felt like Shri Mataji with Her words and small gestures was conducting a huge orchestra of hearts and minds. Her talks were dramatically structured so they would touch all the issues necessary, answer all unspoken questions in the audiences, soothing emotions, preparing the people for the experience of self realisation.

Sometimes people could write down questions so She would answer them on the following night, but my experience was that Shri Mataji was responding directly to people's thoughts and feelings, even when there was no opportunity to do this. This became apparent many times. I recall one public programme in Vienna, where some of my old friends and acquaintances came to attend, and some of them had HIV, because of drug use. In this programme She responded to the silent questions in the audience, and spoke at length about AIDS, which She only did at very few occasions.

After the official part of the public programme with music, a talk and the self realisation exercise, Shri Mataji would usually stay on and people would queue up at the stage to meet Her personally. This most fascinating part of the whole evening was watching Her interacting with seekers, answering their questions and working on their problems. She never became tired or impatient with anybody, even after spending hours and hours working on people. Sometimes there were quite mad people coming up to Her, but Her patience and compassion for everybody was unlimited. She only ever focused on the Kundalini of the person, completely oblivious to their outer appearance, and even the most bizarre behaviour.

One time in Amsterdam a couple came up to Her, both dressed very inappropriately. Mother did not even flinch, and spent quite a long time with them. On occasions, for no apparent reason She would call somebody forward from the crowd. Once in Graz She noticed a very old man in the back, and asked us to bring a chair so that he could sit right at the front. Shri Mataji would never leave until everybody had been attended to, even if it was long after midnight.

Back in the hotel, or ashram, wherever She was staying She would continue working on people, and giving advice to people and yogis who had problems or questions, or people who came to Her for curing. I think it was in Graz when She worked on a woman in a wheelchair, and this woman said it was the first time she could feel her legs again, after a long time. Unfortunately I don't think she carried on with Sahaja Yoga, or adhered the advice Mother had given her. But Shri Mataji showed unlimited compassion, patience and never ending love. She only ever slept a few hours, and while we were elated but also exhausted after the few days She spent with us She went onto the next place, and did it all again for years and years, without ever having a break.

Sigrid Jones

June 1988: Austria (email report)

Shri Mataji gave a very powerful talk before the Ekadesha Rudra Puja in Mödling began, in which She touched upon many subjects. She pointed out that in past times there had only been one rakshasa at a time to be dealt with, but that in modern times, 'They are like mosquitoes', so many of them.

At one point in the puja one of the other musicians leaned over and hissed 'Phil!' and gestured to me to accompany the mantras being said, on the harmonium. At first I wasn't convinced, but then I thought, 'Why not?' and started to play. At that moment our Divine Mother looked up to see who it was and blessed me with a big smile! Songs were sung after the mantras had been finished – the puja was quite long, about three hours or so – and then Shri Mataji remained on the stage to receive the presents from the different countries.

In the evening was a public programme in Vienna, in a large and pleasant hall in the city centre. The Viennese had conceived a new way of holding programmes; first there was some music from some of Vienna's classical musicians, then a general introduction setting Sahaja Yoga in the context of modern seeking, then some more music during which Shri Mataji arrived. She spoke for quite some time, and after Her discourse most of those present received theirs self realisation. Shri Mataji left shortly afterwards to return to the Melichargasse ashram.

On Thursday evening the second Vienna public programme took place, much as the previous evening's, in front of a full audience of several hundred people. Shri Mataji stayed on to talk to the new people, remaining on the stage until 1.00 am. The bhajans group went back onto the stage and sang. Shri Mataji really enjoyed this, so did the public and the rest of us. It's the first time that bhajans have been so integrated into a programme. A team from Austrian TV was also present, and they filmed both Shri Mataji's talk and a few minutes of bhajans.

On Friday morning, we packed our things and waited for Shri Mataji to leave, after which a group of us had the great privilege to accompany Her shopping in the centre of Vienna. Shri Mataji was shopping, particularly for

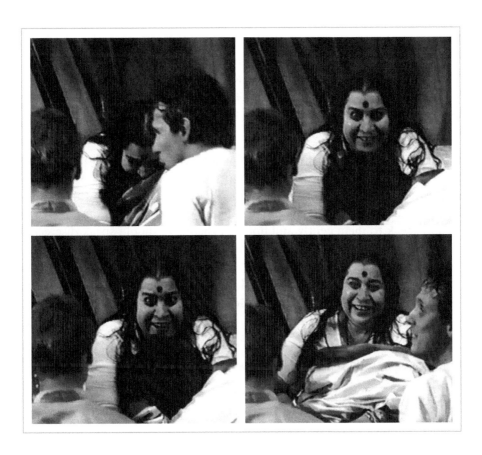

fabrics and She also bought some ties for Her husband. In fact there were so many of us accompanying Her that most of us had to wait outside the shop while She went inside with a few leaders.

Friday lunchtime it was time to leave Vienna and head south for Graz, near the Yugoslav border, where we had the privilege of lunching with Shri Mataji in a beautiful farmhouse in a village where She was entertained by the Viennese string players. She talked to them about classical music, particularly Mozart, and then about Indian music. She poured scorn on some pop music. Her husband had once pointed out to Her, on the TV, some pop star called John – 'No voice. Like a buffalo'. Shri Mataji was served Chinese food here, and enjoyed Her stay in the farmhouse so much that She decided to return there to rest all day Saturday before flying back to London.

Friday evening the public programme in Graz took place; perhaps two or three hundred new people plus a good number of Sahaja Yogis. As before the introduction was partly spoken and partly musical – we had a most receptive audience – and Shri Mataji arrived to the singing of 'Mahishasura Mardini'. She was seated regally in the centre of the stage, surrounded by flowers and saris. After Her talk and the giving of realisation we resumed the bhajans and also sang two Spanish songs, and the public loved them.

We saw Shri Mataji at the airport where She took a seat towards one end of the concourse, and the two hundred or so Sahaja Yogis – nearly all Austrian – sat around Her on the floor. She spoke to us about the need to be diplomatic with people coming to Sahaja Yoga for the first time; how we should speak to them gently and not hurt them, we should speak discreetly and sweetly and not use 'the language of chakras' too much to discuss whatever problems they might have. Then Shri Mataji listened to a few songs sung by some Sahaja Yogis, Her name was taken for the last time with a loud 'Ki jai!' and the Divine Mother left for England.

Phil Ward

Companies should make their workers' lives better

In 1988 I was writing a small thesis for my degree in Austria, and was able to ask Shri Mataji what companies should do with the profits. Shri Mataji said the companies should reinvest most of the money into the workers of the company. They should see the workers' children get education and should take over the social responsibility of the workers. Not to give them the money, but to make their lives better.

Sita Varda

Her words are truly mantras

In Vienna I was fortunate to be able to arrange an interview with a young journalist from a major newspaper, and he wrote a very nice article about Shri Mataji. After that I drove in the car with Her to the public programme.

Ever since I was a teenager I had wanted to be able to be funny, however this always came out wrong. Sometimes I used to say things that I thought were funny, but people understood them in a completely different way. In the car with Shri Mataji, we talked about that journalist.

'Shri Mataji, he said that You must be a very kind and wise person,' I jokingly said, and She laughed. I could not believe it; I had just made Shri

Adi Shakti laugh! It was one of the happiest moments in my life. And from that day on, things have changed and occasionally I have been able to make people laugh!

It shows that Her words are truly mantras, and even Her laughter can change the course of things – reverberating in the universe.

Sigrid Jones

Seminar at Shudy Camps, 18th June 1988

The leader of my area of France called one evening in the middle of the week to say that a seminar was going to take place for the English collective in Shudy Camps the following weekend, and Shri Mataji had invited Sahaja Yogis from other countries too. On the Friday night, our two cars full of yogis and yoginis were the very last allowed to board the night ferry at Calais.

On Saturday afternoon we were asked to get ready as Shri Mataji would come soon. She talked briefly and then led a guided meditation, the way we used to do in public programmes, but She gave it with specific attention to the whole world, and prayers to collectively enlighten the qualities of each chakra up to the Sahasrara. It was an extremely deep meditation for all present, a memorable experience which is available on tape.

Devarshi Abalain

You can have that one

On one occasion we were shopping for saris with Shri Mataji. She wanted to give them as gifts. One particular pale green sari had caught my attention, and later on when we took all the shopping back to Shudy Camps, Mother was sorting through the bags, She took that same green sari and threw it over to me.

'Here, you can have that one,' She said.

Danielle Lee

Annie, are you better?

In 1988, at Shudy Camps, it had not been one year since my realisation and I had a bad pain in my Left Swadishthan.

'If you get the chance, ask Shri Mataji what to do about it,' Marilyn Leate suggested.

I felt I would never dare ask Her. The day after Diwali Puja in Shudy Camps, Shri Mataji and a few of us were sitting outside Her living room. Mother asked if any of us had any questions and most yogis asked for advice or whatever. I was trying to hide behind someone as I felt shy.

'You there, ask what you want to ask,' I heard Shri Mataji say. Everyone turned to me and I knew She was talking to me. She asked me to come close to Her and I explained what was wrong, then Shri Mataji asked me a few questions and told me what to do.

A few days later She was leaving for India. We were all waiting for Her to arrive at London Airport, and I remember being in meditation with my attention on my heart. Mother arrived, walked towards the group where I was standing and stopped in front of me.

'Annie, are you better?' She said. I looked behind me, wondering, 'Who is this Annie Mother is talking to?' Then I realised it was me Mother was talking to. All I could think of was, 'How does Mother know my name?'

Annie Calvas

To express the love for the Divine through their writing or art

There was quite a large landing outside Shri Mataji's rooms at Shudy Camps, more of the size of a reception room, so a lot of work went on there, for example the packing of puja presents and other things, which on one occasion were being carefully wrapped and boxed to be shipped to India. Mother used to sit near the door to Her rooms and supervise, very informally. I was mostly downstairs in the kitchen. During that time I had one big question in my mind, which was whether I should give up with my university studies, because there were so many obstacles. I felt stuck with my thesis and did not see how I could carry on.

One day I woke up late and realised that not only I had missed morning meditation, but also that Shri Mataji was sitting on the landing and talking to all the yogis who had gathered there. I quickly got dressed and ready, but feeling quite embarrassed about having overslept, sat at the very back, and would have never dared to draw any attention to myself, thinking I had missed the one opportunity to ask the question which was burning on my mind.

Shri Mataji called me up to the front and asked me questions, so I got to discuss my problem with Her. I was working on a thesis about the German Romantics, and this caused everybody to laugh, because Shri Mataji earlier had dismissed the English Romantics, Lord Byron in particular.

She was very positive about the German Romantics. I don't recall Her exact words, but She said something like that they wanted to seek or express the love for the Divine though their writing or art. Following Her advice eventually I finished it and presented it to Her after a puja, maybe Sahasrara Day 1995.

Sigrid Jones

The Light of the Koran

I started writing The Light of the Koran, Self Knowledge through Sahaja Yoga, in 1988 and tried to get some information from Shri Mataji. She had told my husband and I to write the book and had spoken to him about it right back when we were in London in 1986. But he was so busy, and we never had time to do anything. Eventually I started, as it seemed a good thing to do for Sahaja Yoga, but did not want to make mistakes, and felt the best was to ask Mother Herself to give us some ideas. It didn't work out like that at all!

'If you want some information, ask Rustom (Burjorjee),' Shri Mataji said at the Sorrento Puja in May 1989, because in those days he was in Saudi Arabia. 'He will be able to give you some information about Islam.' So I wrote, but did not get any reply. The way Shri Mataji helped through those three years of writing was quite amazing. She would come in dreams.

'Don't put your husband's name, put a pseudonym.' Shri Mataji said when She spoke to me in a physical form.

When we started there was nothing about me in the book. But a few months before the publication Mother asked me to write an introduction, because, She said, I had to talk about my own seeking, and it would be credible.

When Shri Mataji came to Paris, which She did every year at that time, somehow every time I would be asked to cook and look after Her. I thought, 'Why me?' but later I understood, because every time She came I had a few questions about the book to ask Her.

Whenever I asked Her a question She would give me a cryptic answer. She wanted me to find the answer myself! So I stopped asking Her questions but still had them. During the three or four days She was in Paris, She Herself would come up with the subject, and give me my answer.

One particular question I had was about the houris, those ladies that men would meet when they go to heaven. Shri Mataji said that I should talk about the houris in my book. Next time She saw me She asked if I had talked about the houris and I evaded the question a bit, because I hadn't. She said I should explain that the houris are the Sahaja Yogis. But I didn't know how to express this concept. Finally, She again came to Paris and asked if I had talked about the houris.

'Well, a little bit,' I said.

'It's easy,' She replied, 'when you are realised, you become pure men and pure women. You are so pure you become like houris.' The answer was obvious.

I gave the book to Mother once it was translated into English, and She said that everything was fine. At one stage during the writing, I had got really down, and thought, 'Oh this is just a stupid woman with an ego writing'. So I asked Mother if I should continue writing the book. She looked at me, very shocked.

'Of course!' She said. After those years of work on writing the book, Mother stopped coming to France so much and I stopped seeing Her. But whenever She did come She would say just a few words about a verse in the Koran, or whatever I needed to know, and that was enough. She was giving energy for the whole year, to carry on. It was so important.

Flore Descieux

You didn't have to worry

Shri Mataji was leaving our ashram in Paris in 1988. The first car had left for the airport to check in Her luggage, and She came down the stairs, and slowly said good bye to everyone, and it took some time.

We eventually arrived at the airport and the flight was waiting for Shri Mataji to leave. She went to Her seat and we left, perhaps three quarters of an hour late. The staff of Air France, and especially the captain, were not happy. When we arrived in Munich, Shri Mataji left Her seat last and smiled at the captain.

'You see, you didn't have to worry,' She said.

The captain had announced that the flight, which lasted two hours, had arrived a quarter of an hour early.

Patrick Lantoin

Chapter 10

1988: July
Europe and America

The dog knew the protocol of the Devi

Shri Mataji came to Munich in 1988 for the Hamsa Chakra Puja. At that time we had a dog called Remo in our ashram there. He was the first puppy of Shri Mataji's dog from Rome. When Shri Mataji arrived for the puja and was coming into the tent, Remo walked slowly in front of Her to the stage as if to make a way for Her and lead Her to the place of the puja. Shri Mataji looked at him and laughed, and smiled at him.

'He knows the protocol of the Devi better than some Sahaja Yogis,' She said.

The following year, when Shri Mataji again came to our ashram, Remo was there to greet Her at the front gate. She greeted him, and patted him and made a fuss of him for some minutes.

'In your next lifetime you will be born as a human and will be a Sahaja Yogi,' She said.

He always came to the pujas and havans in our centre, and died some time later. At the last puja he came to, he ate some of the prasad, somehow.

Mara-Madhuri Corazzari

Shri Hamsa Chakra Puja, 8th - 10th July 1988

About two hundred Sahaja Yogis from several countries were at Munich Airport. Shri Mataji's plane arrived slightly late, at around 8 pm and She finally emerged from the baggage claim at about 8.20 pm to the strains of 'Swagata Agata', which was changed after a few minutes to 'Kundalini Kundalini' which everyone knew and could sing along with. Shri Mataji kindly received flowers from everyone present, speaking to each individual – 'Hello!' 'How are you?' At one point Shri Mataji said how surprised She was to see so many people and how overjoyed She was.

Eventually She drove off to the Castle of Grafenaschau where the puja was to take place. It is a big, old–fashioned country house, with white walls and little painted statues of saints and the Virgin at the corners of the building. It is surrounded by large lawns with flowers and trees, a beautiful spot to receive our Divine Mother. A marquee had been erected for the weekend's activities.

On Friday evening there was a fabulous concert by a santoor player, in Shri Mataji's presence. Before starting to play he gave us a talk about his instrument. He said that at last the great moment had come for him, as he was to play for Shri Mataji. About ten minutes into the piece, a south Indian raga, the electricity failed for a few minutes.

Before the puja, Shri Mataji spoke to us for about an hour about discrimination and discretion. She touched every aspect; from the physical onwards. She told us how the name Hamsa comes from the bija mantras Ham and Sa, Ham meaning 'I am' which brings under control the activity of the left side, and 'Sa', 'You are', addressed to the Deity, which brings down the excesses of the right side.

A beautiful present had been bought for the puja by all the countries, which was shown around to everyone on Shri Mataji's instructions at the end of the puja, a little ornament depicting a swan, carved and encased in glass. She was very insistent that everyone should attend the Guru Puja in Andorra, that no–one should suppose that since they had attended this puja they were 'OK' and 'excused' from coming to Andorra. After all, She said, it's only for a weekend, and see how much you all benefit from each Guru Puja.

In the evening the majority of people who attended the puja left, but about a hundred of us stayed on, to be rewarded with a fabulous evening at the Lotus Feet of our Divine Mother, who kindly came to join us at about 9 o'clock. Some bhajans were sung by different musicians, but the highlight of the evening was listening to some cassettes of songs recorded by the Nagpur musicians and other artistes. Not only was the music wonderful, but it was enhanced even further by the frequent comments of Shri Mataji, which blended in perfectly with the music, and She sang along with some of the songs, as did we.

Phil Ward

Hearing through our Sahasraras

The musician was playing a santoor, rather a quiet instrument. There must have been three or four hundred of us in the tent, and I was right in the back row. At a certain point the electricity broke down and the sound system stopped working. The musician went on playing, and I noticed after a few minutes that I could still hear the beautiful music just as well as when the sound system was all right. I couldn't understand how, from the right at the back.

It came to me that this man was like Tansen, the great Indian musician at the court of the Mughal emperor Akbar in the sixteenth century, who had power over the elements through his music. At that moment the electricity came back on, and a little while later the musician finished his piece.

After he had done so, Shri Mataji spoke. She firstly asked us if those of us at the back had been able to hear when the power was off, and a whole row of us put our hands up, to say we could. Shri Mataji explained that we had been hearing through our Sahasraras. Then She said exactly what had been in my mind, that his playing was so beautiful that he was like Tansen, and She spoke a bit about this famous musician.

Linda Williams

They were all very grateful

When I lived in Munich I used to translate for Shri Mataji sometimes. One time She came to stay in the ashram, we were a very small collective and there were only ten of us in the whole of Germany at that time. One afternoon a man phoned up.

'I would like to come and meet Shri Mataji because I have a group of seekers here. I have seen the posters of Her, so can we come?' he asked. We didn't know who they were, but our leader said as long as they all brought a flower they could come. We asked Shri Mataji, who agreed. So in the afternoon before we went to the public programme, this whole bus full of young seekers from all over Germany arrived.

They got out of the bus, sat down in the living room and Shri Mataji came downstairs to talk to them. They all gave Her a flower, listened very carefully and She explained a lot of things. I had to translate it for Her. At some point somebody asked a question about the left and the right side and Shri Mataji went into a very long explanation. She took about twenty minutes and didn't stop at all. After this explanation about the left and right side – things which I had never heard before – She stopped, and everybody laughed when they looked at me because I had to translate.

'She can do it,' Shri Mataji said. I relied on Her, just not thinking but relying on Her to tell me everything I had to say. It was amazing, I managed to remember most things and explain it all.

Then all these people came to Her and got worked on, and said thank You very much. After that they went out, got in the bus, and we never saw them again. They loved it and they were all very grateful to Shri Mataji, and all got realisation.

Maggie Keet

She was asking me to prepare myself

During July 1988 Shri Mataji did a tour of Europe. A number of us followed Her everywhere She was giving public programmes and having pujas. At some point, in Germany, Shri Mataji had just got off the train and She was on the platform. I was opening the way for Her, even though there were not that many people there. I was accompanying Her and She told me I should listen to the bhajans tapes and note them down, and practice them. I said I would, and later thought to myself, 'How does Shri Mataji know I am a musician, and can transcribe music from just hearing it?' So I transcribed maybe five bhajans, like Namostute, Ughade Sahasrara Mate, all composed by the Saundankar family from Nasik.

One day, some months later, in Sangamner all these Sahaja Yogis were out of town, we were at a big public programme in the open air and there was no one to sing the bhajans. I spontaneously came to the stage, sat in front of the microphone and we sang a number of bhajans, including the ones I had learnt. This was always done before Shri Mataji arrived and I had to be the lead singer for more than an hour. Then Shri Mataji came and She was happy to see me, and when She had seen me six months before, She was asking me to prepare myself for this particular occasion. I have never sung bhajans on the microphone again.

Siddheshvara Barbier

Shri Shiva wanted to witness Himself

This was in Frankfurt in 1988. Shri Mataji was there for the first visit. We had an embarrassingly small ashram, and She went into a small room in the evening after the public programme, when She returned to the ashram.

'Bring Me a piece of paper and a pen,' Shri Mataji said. 'I want to show you something.' Then She started drawing. She started off with a dot.

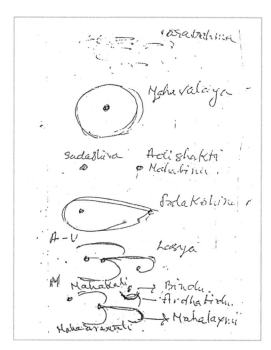

'See, this is Shri Shiva,' She began. 'When there is one, it is just a dot. There is nothing else existing. But then Shri Shiva wanted to witness Himself, in the sense that there needed to be another. So there can be a mirror and He separated Himself from His Shakti. But because the love between Shri Shiva and Shri Shakti is so deep, the Shakti kept coming back when She was pushed out.' So Shri Mataji then drew a circle around the dot, and went a few more times round and made the circle like an ellipse. The ellipse is there because the Shakti wants to come back to Shri Shiva, and He pushes Her out again.

'Go create!' He said.

So that is why all the circular movements in the universe are not perfect circles but ellipses; that is one of the manifestations of the love between Shri Shiva and Shri Shakti. Once She had accepted what She had to do, She separated Herself into three: Shri Mahakali, Shri Mahasaraswati, Shri Mahalakshmi. They started manifesting on the subtle level. There was not yet any material creation. The causal bodies for anything that exists are these three powers, and then Shri Adi Shakti created Shri Ganesha, the fourth one.

Shri Mataji explained the Om. The one line is Shri Mahakali, the bottom one is Shri Mahasaraswati, and the other is Shri Mahalakshmi.

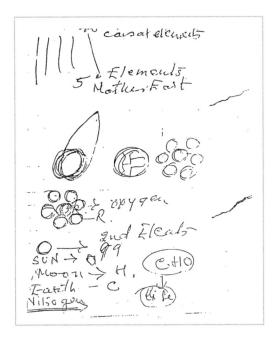

Then there is the bindu (dot) of Shri Shiva. She said that the creation went into the material creation also, you see that on the left side is hydrogen, and on the right side is oxygen and in the central channel is nitrogen, and in the Mooladhara is carbon. With these four atoms you can create amino acids, and these are the basic building blocks of life.

Shri Mataji wrote this down on the paper.

Herbert Reininger

I know that this is your rug

Being so close to Shri Mataji during so many public programmes was a great blessing. Usually there would be some music, or bhajans, and an introductory talk by one of the leaders or senior yogis. Then at some time Shri Mataji would arrive and give Her talk, pausing after every few sentences so I could translate. There were a few times when I did not understand what She meant, or did not know a word. Once I had an embarrassing experience. I did not know the word 'keep' as in 'mistress' and had to ask Shri Mataji several times to repeat the word. When I finally realised what She meant I must have blushed scarlet red!

Usually She would not interact with me on a personal level, with a few exceptions. At one public programme in Frankfurt we put a Chinese rug for Her on the stage, which had been a wedding present to my husband and myself. Shri Mataji was explaining thoughtless awareness, and how in thoughtless awareness one just looks at things, and enjoys things, without thinking. She then talked about enjoying a beautiful carpet without having to own it, or worrying about it getting spoilt, and while She was saying that She turned Her head and looked straight in my eyes, with a smile and twinkle in Hers, as if She was saying, 'I know this is your rug under My Feet!' It showed me, again, that She knew everything.

Sigrid Jones

A meeting at the airport in Frankfurt

In the late 1980's, Shri Mataji was to arrive for a public programme and puja in Frankfurt, and She was coming from Austria. The yogis in Frankfurt and all of Germany were working hard to complete the preparations for these events, and on the morning of Her arrival we were all assembled with great excitement to welcome Her at the airport.

I don't know how I managed it, but after some insisting and pleading to customs officials I found myself inside the restricted area of the airport, looking anxiously for the gate where Shri Mataji should emerge and at that moment She came! Smiling and looking very relaxed, She walked towards me. I rushed forward, my heart beating with joy, and welcomed Shri Adi Shakti to this auspicious occasion. I offered flowers and mentioned that all the yogis were waiting for Her outside the customs area and Shri Mataji said She was very much looking forward to meeting all of them. I saw some yogis who were travelling with Shri Mataji and we continued walking through the endless walkways of Frankfurt Airport.

We had just crossed a large hall about halfway through, when I looked sideways and noticed in the distance a well known Indian classical musician, who played for Shri Mataji many times and recognized and respected Her. He was walking in our direction with his wife and his son and had not seen us yet. I told Shri Mataji, and She asked me to go over and ask him to come and meet Her, So I did.

He was overjoyed to hear that Shri Mataji was here and immediately rushed to meet Her. She welcomed him like a child coming home after a long time, chairs were brought for them and his family went to Her Lotus Feet right in the middle of the busy airport. Shri Mataji asked him where he was travelling to he told Her that he was on his way from Amsterdam back to India. She asked him what he was doing there and he said he was teaching music at the music academy of a well–known (false) guru.

Hearing this, Shri Mataji's face became very stern and She started scolding him like a child, asking why he was doing this. She told him this was so dangerous and if he would not stop he might become blind. The musician was almost crying, saying that he had to support a family and needed the money, but Shri Mataji did not accept this excuse.

'What use is all this money if you go blind?' She said. She started giving him vibrations right there and then, working with Her hands directly on his body, the musician on his knees on the floor in front of Her. What a moment of divine compassion, when Shri Mataji kept telling him to be very careful with these things and that She did not want him to get hurt.

A curious crowd of onlookers were standing in a circle around us, but no one disturbed. After some time She stopped working on him, and it felt we all were coming back from a distant place to the noisy airport. We said good–bye to the musician and his family, they had their photo taken with Shri Mataji, and we continued on towards the customs and the waiting yogis.

Herbert Reininger

Shri Mataji came to me

In 1988, I was in the acting business, and could only take leave when there were no performances. During the summer I was to play in a small town near Frankfurt, but was extremely sad that I would not be able to join the wonderful tour Shri Mataji was embarking on for the whole summer. I headed for Germany and after three weeks or so got a call from the Frankfurt collective, saying Shri Mataji would make a stopover at the airport there. Nobody knew if there was any possibility for Her to come out of the transit area, but we drove to the airport.

I stood with three Yogis, looking with longing eyes at the entrance of the transit area, which was heavily guarded by control posts and policemen with weapons. I was sad again, that we were so close, when we suddenly took the decision just to walk through. We had no passports or tickets, but we went straight through the control. Nobody stopped us or asked for tickets as they did with everyone else, they simply seemed not to see us!

So we were in the transit lounge, lost again but more than happy, and as we gazed around, a door at the other end of the big hall opened and Shri Mataji, with a few yogis accompanying Her, came out. She saw us, hesitated for a moment, then smiled broadly, waved in recognition, and came over to us.

The yogis accompanying Her had to sort something out, and Shri Mataji lightly invited us to the coffee house for a Coke. So we four ended up sitting at a small round table with the Goddess having a Coke and chatting about films, drinks and whatever else.

I knew that She had known about my deep sadness and great desire to see Her. As I had not been able to come to Her, She came to me.

Andrea Wicke

Shri Mataji started laughing

It was 14th of July 1988 and we were new Sahaja Yogis. We were allowed to meet Shri Mataji after the programme. At that time She would receive all the seekers, so we went up on the stage. She looked at me and saw I had just a shirt and no vest under it.

'Why don't you wear a vest?' She asked and I replied that it was because it was hot, but She said that in Sahaja Yoga it is compulsory. She started laughing a lot!

Bernard Cuvellier

Suddenly we saw Shri Mataji

It was a Saturday morning in the summer of 1988. We had heard that Shri Mataji and Sir CP would be arriving at Heathrow, but we only learned that we could go and meet Her about two hours before the plane was due to land. It takes two hours to drive from Birmingham to Heathrow. We had to go via Bromsgrove to pick up the car which would take us, and this was in a different direction from Heathrow, so the journey would take even longer.

At the time the plane was landing we were still an hour's journey from Heathrow. The vibrations felt hot and heavy, but we kept going. We thought that we might still see some of the other Sahaja Yogis even though we knew we would be much too late to see Mother. Then as we were driving into Heathrow the vibrations became cool. As we drove towards the car park suddenly we saw Shri Mataji and Sir CP standing together, alone, waiting for their car. The Sahaja Yogis were on another pavement some distance away. Our driver stopped the car in the middle of the road, we leapt out and namaskared to Shri Mataji and offered Her flowers. She smiled at us. Then the car came, and they got in and were driven away.

Maggie Burns

Do you want more questions, or realisation?

Shri Mataji came to Colombia for the first time, officially for Sahaja Yoga, in July 1988. On July the 20th we celebrate the country's independence and about that, Mother said that the true independence is that of the spirit. She offered a public programme in a hotel room, with capacity for about two hundred people, but even before the scheduled hour it was full, with people standing or sitting on the floor. At the end of Her explanation on the subtle system She gave time for questions and answered several.

'Do you want more questions or realisation?' She then asked.

'Realisation, realisation!' most of the people repeated, like in a chorus.

Shri Mataji spent two or three days in Bogotá and during that time She gave the few yogis a chance to have a puja. During the puja She said they were now responsible for the new people, and had to help them to establish in Sahaja Yoga. The small collectivity did not have silver plates for the puja, so it was arranged with copper ones, and Shri Mataji said it was very propitious to use copper plates on that occasion.

Edgar Patarroyo

What a place, it's beautiful!

Shri Mataji came to Colombia again in 1988 – Her first visit had been in 1978. She was invited by Brigitte Nicod from Switzerland to give public programmes in Bogotá. There was also the celebration of a puja. These are the words when Shri Mataji arrived in Brigitte's house, taken from the video:

'Now you have done here. All your pure desire has worked, so full of love, so much of it. May God bless you. You are going to do something great here, I am sure. So wonderful to come here, so nice, you are already there, beautiful. So nice to come here, so wonderful, beautiful.

'It's a wonderful place I must say. I had to come here, spiritual, so spiritual, beautiful. There must have been lot of seekers in this country. Nice to call Me here. I am very happy. I could also manage with My husband.

We were travelling with the sun two hours, there were two clouds, the light started spreading and you could see the colour of Shri Ganesha, absolutely that colour, and in between it was lightning, just for announcing, so very beautiful.

'I think it's very good place. What a place, it's beautiful! The vibrations are so good, it's so full of vibration,' Shri Mataji said.

Marie-Laure Cernay

Every day we should read something

After the Shri Buddha Puja gathering in San Diego in July 1988, Shri Mataji arrived very early the next morning at Kennedy Airport, and we all followed Her back to New Rochelle, where She kindly allowed us to join Her in the sitting room as She talked about different topics. New people were introduced to Her, notably someone who was able to tell Shri Mataji about the computer network and how by Her Grace we had been able to find out some seekers in this particularly 20th–century way. Shri Mataji seemed very amused and quite pleased by this.

'Very subtle!' She said. Shri Mataji also mentioned how important it was for us to read and acquire spiritual and other useful knowledge; every day we should read something. Then She went to rest.

After a while we set off to prepare for the evening's programme. This took place in an art gallery in Manhattan, attendance was by invitation only and about fifty or so people attended. The following day there was a lunch–time programme at the United Nations, again by invitation. The attendance was disappointing, but some good questions from those that did come gave our Divine Mother the opportunity to give some brilliant answers, particularly regarding human organisations and their weaknesses.

Phil Ward

This photo was taken during Shri Mataji's first visit to Columbia. She is asking about the sari I am wearing and the leela was that She had actually given it to me.

Antoinette Wells

A delicious meal

At the end of July 1988, Shri Mataji arrived on Thursday evening at Los Angeles airport to be met by a hundred or so yogis, come from all over North America and some from farther afield. For half an hour or so our Divine Mother sat simply on a bench outside the terminal and spoke to us about Her time in Colombia, then She was driven to Dr Worlikar's house in a part of the endless suburbs of Los Angeles where She was to stay the night. We were all invited to a delicious Indian meal.

Phil Ward

I am so grateful

I was born in Brazil. The first time I met Shri Mataji was at the Shri Vishnumaya Puja in 1987 in America. At that time I was married to a man who was involved with black magic. I spoke to Shri Mataji about this and She showed great concern, but regrettably he later died.

I saw Shri Mataji again at the Shri Buddha Puja in San Diego in 1988 and there I asked Her to help his spirit. I introduced Her to my two little children: one was a baby and the other just two years old.

'I surrender my life to You,' I said. 'I am so grateful for what You have done for me and my children, and if it is Your desire I will put my name for marriage.'

'Absolutely,' said Shri Mataji, 'do that.' Just eight months later Shri Mataji found me a husband in Austria who loved children. The idea of having a ready–made family with little children who could grow up with him as their father was a blessing to him.

Angela Reininger

Thirty million good people

The following day, at the end of July 1988, Shri Mataji drove down from Los Angeles to the ashram in San Diego, where She was received with songs and flowers by the Sahaja Yogis, including your correspondent who had the privilege of being amongst the musicians. Shri Mataji sat down talked quite seriously and at times sternly about the challenge facing the yogis of North America. She was very concerned. She estimated that the ego of the Americans and its power to obscure for them the truth was so great that probably only about ten per cent of them would ever come round to Sahaja Yoga.

The Shri Buddha Puja that was to be celebrated the next day would help but there was still a lot for us to do. She appointed Gregoire as the leader of America.

'You can handle them,' She said. He thanked our Divine Mother and said that by Her calculations there would still be some thirty million good people in America, which promised a very exciting and rewarding time ahead.

Phil Ward

A spontaneous bhajans session

The programme that evening, before the Shri Buddha Puja, took place in the splendid setting of the Organ Pavilion in Balboa Park, San Diego, a huge arc–shaped building surrounding an oval open–air seating area and housing a huge organ. The outline of the building was decorated with lights, rather like in India, in fact being out of doors the atmosphere was quite Indian at times. There was a good attendance of several hundred people. A local maestro played classical organ music for half an hour before the programme began. A Sahaja Yogi gave a long introduction, and Shri Mataji arrived quite late to give Her talk and to give realisation. After the programme was over and the last of the many newcomers had been able to meet Shri Mataji, very spontaneously, we all, at our Divine Mother's bidding found ourselves on the stage and bringing out musical instruments and songbooks for a session of bhajans, at about two in the morning.

Phil Ward

The puja was very joyful

The Shri Buddha Puja took place in a simple tent erected just off the beach, with the hundred or so yogis present, seated before the dais of Shri Mataji which had been covered with turf, and Her throne was formed in front of the sculpture of the Bodhi tree, simple but effective. Shri Mataji arrived to music and we followed Her through the dunes for a few yards to the tent. The puja was very joyful. In the evening was another public programme at the Organ Pavilion, again a great success, and the following day Shri Mataji left for Los Angeles and subsequently for New York.

Phil Ward

A new name

This picture was taken at the Shri Buddha Puja in 1988, on July 23rd. The exact spot was the YMCA Surf Camp, on the beach right at the Mexico–USA border. The grass you see as a stage was all trucked in as the whole puja and camp were on the white sand of the beach. The tree was artificial – a stage prop, and was an imitation banyan or Bodhi tree, like the one under which Shri Buddha received his enlightenment.

I remember this puja well because our son, who was five at the time, disappeared at the end. We turned to see him on the stage with Shri Mataji. It was then that Michael became Gautama. He went to ask for a new name and Shri Mataji gave him one.

Richard Payment

Shri Mataji is both Shri Sita and Shri Rama

Although I was eighteen years old when I received my realisation in November 1985 and came to Sahaja Yoga, I was in many ways still a child.

Shri Mataji under the Bodhi tree at the Shri Buddha Puja 1988

In 1987 I moved from Ohio to San Diego, California to live in the ashram there, and I enjoyed the pampering love of all of my elder brothers and sisters.

In the summer of 1988 Shri Mataji blessed us by holding Shri Buddha Puja. The puja site was on a quiet stretch of beach near Coronado. We had a huge pendal for the puja, and tents set up on the sand. It was a beautiful setting.

We gathered for puja and Shri Mataji spoke to us. Then to my surprise, a dear elder brother called me up to the stage with several other young girls for the Shri Gauri Puja. Little did I realise that I would be married later that year and this would be my only chance to worship Shri Mataji as an unmarried girl. I was in complete amazement and wonder as I approached Shri Mataji's throne to bow at Her Holy Lotus Feet.

My forehead pressed against the cloth covering the sweet Mother Earth, cushioned by the sand underneath. I savoured the moment in deep joy and love for my Mother. Then, as I lifted my head and opened my eyes to gaze upon Her, I found that I was gazing instead upon Shri Rama and Shri Sita, seated in their throne, and for an instant I was in their palace, kneeling at their Holy Feet. I blinked in wonder, and the moment was gone. I was again before our beloved Holy Mother. It was in that instant that I fully understood for the first time that Shri Mataji is both Shri Sita and Shri Rama.

As my finger painted the kumkum on Her beautiful Lotus Feet, I realised my limited ability to even begin to comprehend Her form.

Amy Ahluwalia

What more could you need?

In July of 1988, I began final preparations for my move from the United States to Spain to a new life with my new husband, Josè Luis. Shri Mataji had married us in India the preceding January on the India tour. I decided that it was important to go to Shri Buddha Puja in San Diego and to arrive in Spain for Guru Puja in Andorra. After a lot of running around, I finally found the only flight available. A few days later, I found out that Shri Mataji had changed Her plane and was now on the same flight I was on.

At Kennedy Airport on July 28th, suddenly I found myself behind Shri Mataji going through security. We began walking up the ramp towards the gate and Mother turned around and waved goodbye to all Her children.

'Are you coming, too?' She turned to me and said, with a big smile and a laugh. We were all laughing and I felt the joy and love filling my being.

The plane prepared to take off finally, after a long delay due to overbooking, but there was also another delay. Suddenly, a huge thunderstorm began. Shri Vishnumaya was heralding Shri Adi Shakti, as She left the land of the Vishuddhi.

During the final hour of the flight, after sunrise, I went up to First Class to say good morning to Shri Mataji and was feeling a bit shy. She asked me to sit down for a while and began telling me about how She liked Spain and the Spanish people and the songs of the Spanish Sahaja Yogis. She spoke about marriage in general, about the upcoming European tour and the Indian musicians that were going to be on the tour as well — how Mother was shining like the Goddess! I felt so joyful and content, like a baby bird in the nest with the mother bird.

As we began to land, I began to feel a bit of butterflies–in–the–stomach nervousness about what was waiting for me – a new life in a new country where people spoke a language I didn't know, and thought to myself, 'How petty to feel such things when I'm here with the Goddess.' But immediately another thought came to me, 'She knows exactly what I'm thinking at this very moment and I can't hide it.'

'Mother, I'm feeling a bit scared,' I blurted out. She instantly took my hand with both Hers and squeezed it tight.

'Don't worry, don't worry. Adi Shakti is here with you and She is bringing you to Spain. Everything is all right. What more could you need?' She smiled radiantly.

Oh, what a beautiful, beautiful Mother! All my fear and anxiety melted into nothingness as I was filled, absolutely drenched with Her divine love. How sweetly and preciously our Divine Mother takes care of every single one of Her children.

Christina Rosi

Chapter 11

1988: July to September Europe and England

I didn't want to come until you were all here

The first puja that I attended was in Andorra, between Spain and France, in 1988. My wife had asked me to go with her. I wasn't sure, but eventually agreed, particularly if we could combine it with a family holiday. So rather than going with the UK group we went by train, with our younger daughter. By the time we arrived at the frontier station between France and Andorra in the evening, all the taxis had disappeared. Then a coach arrived to pick up a party of French students and they took us into Andorra city, about a half an hour away. It was about eight o'clock and I thought there was no point in rushing to get out to the Sahaja camp, since surely Shri Mataji would have already started the evening programme. So we had dinner and then took a cab out to the campsite.

When we finally arrived, it must have been nearly midnight and the moment we drove into the field, somebody asked us to dump our bags quickly and get into the pendal. We were aware of a car arriving behind us and a lot of noise and we had just got into the pendal before Shri Mataji Herself was ushered into Her seat.

'I didn't want to come until you were all here,' was the first thing I remember Her saying.

Ian Maitland Hume

A large smile for the policeman

Guru Puja, July 31st 1988, Andorra was a great event for France and we felt lucky that it was happening just by the French border and with France among the organizing countries. The music was by Nirmal Sangeet Sarita, with shennai, sitar, sarod and Guruji's violin concerts.

Just before the puja, I was told to indicate to car drivers the way to the entrance. When a certain car showed up I put my arms to the right hand side, moving them like a policeman regulating the traffic at a crossroads. When I was sure that the car had taken the right direction, I joined my hands and did namaskar. Shri Mataji, at the back of the car, had a large smile at the sight of this strange policeman standing in the sun in a white kurta pyjama welcoming his guru for the puja!

Devarshi Abalain

All My love, all My powers, all My wisdom

In 1988 there was a tour of Europe and Shri Mataji went first to Andorra, then Italy. Guru Puja in Andorra was at a camping site. After the puja was over, Mother told us we could go and get food. Some of us decided not to rush and then just have to wait in a line, so we continued to sit in front of Mother. Mother stayed on the stage, but the microphones and video were turned off. Those of us left behind went a bit closer and sat down, then Mother got up to leave and, as She did so, She said the following. I may not have remembered them exactly word for word, but this was the sense:

'All My love, all My powers, all My wisdom must be transferred to you people in this lifetime or My incarnation will have been a waste of time.'

Linda Williams

The vibrated sari

It was in 1988, at the Guru Puja in the Principality of Andorra, I was very anxious to attend the musical evening because Shri Mataji's brother, Baba Mama, was there with his group, Nirmal Sangeet Sarita. But a yogi from my area, for whom this was his first puja, did not feel good. As we looked for someone to make a dessert for Shri Mataji and Her family, I proposed that this yogi, who is an excellent pastry cook to do it.

'Alright, but you must stay with me,' he said.

Guru Puja Andorra, 1988

Herve, the pastry cook, decided on a dessert consisting of custard with floating masses of whipped whites of egg. I told myself that this would be quick to prepare and then I would be able to listen to my 'preferred singers'. The bhajans began and we were nearby but strangely did not hear anything. We got ready the desert, but so slowly! I asked the cook if I could go and listen, just for five minutes, but at that moment there was a pause in the bhajans.

I returned to help my Sahaja brother and in the end it was magnificent. We found some bowls and the cook presented his dessert in a very refined way. But when everything was ready, a yogini arrived and said, 'There is a change of plan. The bhajans evening is finished, and Shri Mataji has decided to take Her meal at Her hotel.' The yogini took the bowls and poured them into a pressure cooker. I wanted to cry. All the work of Herve was destroyed and I had missed the bhajans.

I went to the pendal, closed my eyes and meditated on the lesson that Shri Mataji had given me (to have more desire for the bhajans than Her divine presence) and when I opened my eyes saw two armchairs: one very beautiful and the other smaller, with my sari that I had lent, draped over it. Everyone was bowing down to that armchair.

'Shri Mataji left the most beautiful armchair to Her husband, and sat on the other one,' the people around me said, and it was the one on which my sari was placed. I felt so much such love and gratitude. Shri Mataji knows everything and always takes care of us.

Despite the floating islands having been put in the cooking pot, the dessert was served and presented to Shri Mataji in a very delicate manner by other yogis.

Editor's note: once Shri Mataji has touched something, it is permanently imbued with Her divine vibrations. Many people have been healed and com-

forted by objects She has touched in this way, so by sitting in the armchair which was covered with Joelle's sari, She gave a great and lasting gift to her.
Marie-Joelle Coeuru

An incredible day

The day of my marriage was at an ashram at Garlate near Milan, on the shore of Lake Como, in 1988. There was a huge lawn going to the lake, beautiful. I had put my name down but I had no money so assumed I would get married later, in India.

I was watching the day unfold, and Shri Mataji was up on the balcony conducting events. There was a stick dance and She was telling the ladies circling around what to do. I was watching, and felt a hand on my shoulder, and the leader said I should go with him. I knew at that moment I was going to get married. I went in front of Mother and there was Sigrid, standing in front of Mother, who was high up on the balcony.

'You two,' She said. At that moment my Kundalini shot up like a rocket.

'Englishmen make good husbands,' She said. I had met Sigrid, who is Austrian, a few times before, and had got to know quite a lot of the Austrians. One Austrian lady I had got to know came up and hugged Sigrid, and I noticed Mother looked down and smiled and Her eyes were full of tears of joy. She was human but at the same time divine, divine mother-hood, the love of the Mother on both levels.

After matching us, Mother matched a lot of other people. I had to get a kurta, and did the haldi, and dived into the lake, and felt totally cleared out. Then we had a rest and in the evening all the men lined up to touch Shri Mataji's Feet. I was feeling very nice and completely thoughtless. As I bent down She called me.

'God bless you, Steve.'

I had such a deep experience as I stood up after touching Her Feet, that I was touching the Feet of God. When I stood up everyone was singing Mataji Jai! After that I sat in the bus which was to take us to the other side of the lake. They were calling the numbers and I was in such bliss that they had to call out my number again. We were driven to the other side of the lake, put into boats and we grooms, all dressed up, sailed over the lake in the evening of the wedding. It was a beautiful evening, the stars were in the sky and you could hear Baba Mama's Nirmal Sangeet music. I felt I was not on the same planet and was in heaven. When we got to the other side and climbed off the boat there was Shri Mataji to welcome us. It was one blessing after the other!

At these weddings Shri Mataji sang the wedding shlokas personally. I walked round the fire hearing the vows, feeling the presence of the deities and how auspicious this event was. Afterwards we received a present from Shri Mataji, a cutlery set. At the end Baba Mama was there and we did the rhyming couplets in front of Shri Mataji. An incredible day.

Steve Jones

Shri Mataji appeared at the time of the Sahasrara mantras

In August 1988 there was a European tour, and after the Guru Puja in Andorra, the next event was the Krishna Puja in Milan with marriages. There was a public programme in Milan followed by a concert by Guruji, while people were lining to get the darshan of Shri Mataji. The marriages and the puja took place in the Garlate ashram's garden, by a lake, but we were sleeping in a camping ground some distance from there and we had to share our morning meditation with sun bathers, next to the swimming pool. Then we went to the ashram where Shri Mataji was staying. People were meditating in the garden and we joined them, happy to find a more suitable place.

My eyes were closed as I meditated deeply for a long time. When it was time to end, I opened my eyes to say the three great mantras and just as I did so the shutters of a window were opened by – guess who? – Shri Mataji Herself! I just did namaste. She had appeared exactly at the time of the Sahasrara mantras.

Devarshi Abalain

I will cure you

Before I came to Sahaja Yoga I suffered from depression and this continued for two or three years after getting realisation. After the puja in Italy on the Lago di Como, I was standing on the shore. I didn't realise how it happened, but Shri Mataji approached me.

'I will cure you,' She said. The next evening Her car passed by the place where I was. It stopped, the window was wound down and Shri Mataji held my hand and asked me how I was feeling. Then She left. The change didn't come immediately, but without even realising it I did get cured and since that time I have never suffered from depression.

Spanish Sahaja Yogi

This is the desire

After the 1988 Shri Krishna Puja in Garlate, north Italy, we were supposed to go up to Switzerland, where the next puja was to be, one week later. It seemed as if everybody was on their way, but our car broke down. So Helga, a German yogini, was so nice and offered me a place in her car. She had to drive way down to Tuscany first but she promised we would be heading back up north as soon as possible, and in time for the puja.

Although I was very grateful for the offer, I felt that we were heading in the wrong direction; the collective were driving north and we were heading south. After a short while I developed an overwhelming desire to be with Shri Mataji; this was so strong that I had no interest in anything else. The journey was nice, but this wonderful desire remained.

We reached Volterra, a beautiful medieval town and did some sightseeing before finally sitting down outside a restaurant for a drink. We believed that Shri Mataji would be nearing Switzerland at this time, but to our amazement, a big black car drove slowly past us – with our Holy Mother sitting in it. We left the restaurant immediately and tried to follow the car which drove slowly and carefully through the small streets of the old town. It was not difficult to follow and we were so excited.

Suddenly, we found ourselves standing at the entrance to a small but lovely square which had a statue of Shri Mary adorning one of its walls. Shri Mataji stood there surrounded by Baba Mama, the Indian musicians and two Italian yogis. As She looked towards us we made namaskar and were then asked to come nearer. Someone was massaging Shri Mataji's Feet.

'How is it possible you found us?' She asked with Her most loving smile, and Baba Mama asked the same question, which we weren't able to answer. We namaskared again and at that moment everything was so wonderful and joyful at the same time. Everybody was beaming with joy.

'You come shopping with us,' Shri Mataji said. Her Holiness went to a popular place for shopping, which dealt in semi–precious stones and white horses carved out of stone, and that sort of thing. Shri Mataji was sitting in a chair, buying and ordering things. It felt like we were in a completely different world. After nearly four hours, She stood up to leave the shop and walked towards Helga.

'What did you buy?' She asked. Helga answered that she had bought an egg made of semi–precious stone. Shri Mataji said the egg was very auspicious then walked towards me and took both my hands in Hers and pressed them.

'This is the desire,' She said. When Shri Mataji pressed my hands within Hers something so beautiful happened, I don't know how to describe it!

Christina Sweet

Don't be nervous about catching planes

My father had to take Shri Mataji to Malpensa, which is the main airport for Milan, about one hour from the city. She was staying at our house in Milan.

'OK, I am ready,' Shri Mataji said but She kept speaking to the people. Finally She was ready to go, and She said, 'but did we give any gift to your children?'

'No, but they are fine,' my father replied.

'How can I go without giving them a gift?' said Shri Mataji, and said She wanted to go and buy something, but he was worried that She might miss the plane. Mother went out of the house to a shop nearby and purchased some gifts for my brother and me, then came back, and by that time it was really becoming very late. She sat and gave us the gifts, and then said, 'Now we can go.'

My father had something like half an hour to get there, a road which would normally take one hour and Shri Mataji missed the plane. He was feeling bad, and when we all reached the airport Shri Mataji just laughed. She told him not to be nervous about catching planes and then She invited all the Sahaja Yogis to lunch in the airport and we enjoyed it a lot. She took a later flight.

Anita Gadkary

Looking after the liver

We were all invited to go to Heathrow Airport to see Shri Mataji, sometime in 1988. I had given birth recently and had developed a brown mark on my face. Shri Mataji enquired about this. I told Her I had neglected taking iron pills during pregnancy and had to take them afterwards, but the treatment had not succeeded. Shri Mataji told me that my explanation of this medical condition was not correct, and if I were to improve the state of my liver this condition would be cleared. While saying this She rubbed Her thumb on the facial mark and it faded away in a few weeks. Meanwhile I did my best to practice the techniques for improving the liver.

I was very grateful that Shri Mataji had offered to solve a problem I had not been able to fix and I didn't even have to ask Her for help, such was Mother's compassion and ability to sense what was troubling any of Her children. Later it dawned on me that Shri Mataji had rubbed Her thumb with the finger that represents the liver!

Carol Garrido

Shri Kalki's day

In the late 1980's, in London, Shri Mataji asked me about my daughter, as to when her birthday was. I said her birthday was on 5th May. Then Shri Mataji asked if it was 5th May or 6th May. I said that it was 5th May and She said that Shri Kalki's day is 6th May.

Shakuntala Tandale

For our benevolence

We were at Muswell Hill ashram in the late eighties, and Shri Mataji spoke to us. I don't remember Her exact words, but what I understood was that She told us that anything that happened to us was for our benevolence. At that same time She said that we were all jewels in Her crown. She said Sahaja Yoga would spread almost invisibly – like the flowers on the trees, you don't see them opening but suddenly they are there.

Rosemary Maitland Hume

Nature knows

Some years ago, I was staying in an ashram in England when Shri Mataji visited us. It had been very hot and dry and the country was having some drought conditions. During the first part of Her stay it rained and rained and rained. We were in Her bedroom and She was looking out at the rain.

'The nature knows exactly what to do,' She said simply. 'Human beings, they are a little different.'

Patricia Leydon

Defending the good name of Sahaja Yoga

While I was living at Shudy Camps I showed Shri Mataji a book entitled Begone Godmen. It was against false gurus, but went on to criticise all the religions and contained a remark against Shri Mataji. It was this that made me show the book to Her. She confirmed that She knew of this man, whose theories were similar to the philosophy of certain groups that were causing trouble to Sahaja Yoga in India. I told Shri Mataji that this writer tried to denigrate all the scriptures so She told me to write on the same subject and turn the book on its head by creating a book in favour of God.

'Do You mean me to do this myself, Shri Mataji?' I asked.

'Yes, and I want you to write an article in defence of Sahaja Yoga, based on your experience, for an Indian newspaper,' She answered.

Shri Mataji always took care to defend the good name of Sahaja Yoga, and testimonials were an effective way of doing this.

Luis Garrido

It will spread like wildfire

We were at Shudy Camps, in 1988 and Shri Mataji had just returned from one of Her many Sahaja world tours and though She was tired after a long trip, She took a moment to sit back and relax.

'Now Sahaja Yoga is working out all over the world,' She declared.

'But Shri Mataji, what about Russia and the other communist countries where it is not legally possible to spread Sahaja Yoga?'

'Don't you worry about Russia, the day Sahaja Yoga starts there, it will spread like wildfire,' Shri Mataji smiled.

In less than six months She was conducting programmes in Moscow with electrifying results that spread to the neighbouring communist nations. Later I had the privilege of being invited by Her to go to Moscow and saw with my own eyes how the Russian people were coming in large numbers to the Sahaja Yoga events and how humble, attentive and thankful they were in receiving it.

When Sahaja Yoga first went to the Soviet Union, just after the Perestroika had started, it was still against the law to preach about God. Shri Mataji instructed Sahaja Yogis there to talk about the all–pervading power of the Mother Nature as opposed to the all–pervading power of God.

Luis Garrido

A blasphemous film

In 1988 I went to see Shri Mataji at one of Her temporary London residences. She went through many different rented addresses in London and vibrated many areas by moving many times. It was Good Friday and was the year when a blasphemous film about Christ had been released, entitled The Last Temptation of Christ. The fact that it was Good Friday already justified Shri Mataji being pensive, introspective and saddened, and She was disturbed because England was so indifferent to the blasphemous film.

'Don't you feel hurt that Christ is being insulted through this film?' She asked.

Shri Mataji dictated a letter of protest for publication in the English newspapers, and now and again closed Her eyes and looked as if She was going into a deep meditation, so it took a long time. The atmosphere was a bit tense and to relax us Shri Mataji told us not to feel apprehensive, and to watch TV. We put it on, without any sound, and the programme was golf. She commented that watching the green lawns was good for our Agnyas, and to try to remain relaxed.

She was dismayed by the suggestion that Mary Magdalene could have had any relationship with Christ except as a disciple. For Shri Mataji the suggestion of a liaison between them, as was suggested in this film, was a great insult, a blasphemy to Christ and totally false.

Luis Garrido

Pizza prasad

One day we went shopping with Shri Mataji in Cambridge, for crockery. There were only myself and another Sahaja Yogi who was a prosperous professional.

'Shri Mataji, today is a very auspicious day because at last I have a chance to buy You lunch,' he said. 'All these years I have been eating food cooked by You at Your home, and I've lost count of how many times You've fed us. I'll be very disappointed if You don't allow me this privilege, so please allow me to buy You lunch as we are far from home and it's well past lunch time.'

'The shopping is not yet finished,' Shri Mataji replied. The shopping continued for a while and then She smilingly said, 'Now you can buy us lunch.'

We walked some way until this senior Sahaja Yogi found a restaurant that looked impressive. He asked Shri Mataji to order anything She liked, but She told him to choose. This restaurant specialised in pizzas so he ordered three extra–large ones. When they arrived we couldn't help laughing, each one was truly gigantic.

We were slightly embarrassed to be sitting at table with Shri Mataji in such an informal setting, but we attacked the pizzas with courage. From time to time She pointed at our gigantic glasses of Coca Cola and reminded us to drink plenty of it, so we carried on until we had cleaned up our plates. Shri Mataji was pleased to see us eat and hardly any words were said. She only ate a very small amount from Her own gigantic pizza.

'Shri Mataji, it looks like You were not very hungry after all,' I said.

She replied that She was feeling very satisfied seeing us eat, then broke up Her pizza into large chunks and passed them onto us.

'Thank You Mother, but we just couldn't manage any more,' we both said.

'Now it has become prasad, so you have to eat it,' Shri Mataji said, laughing, and kept handing us large chunks until it was finished.

She was smiling lovingly and we realised this was prasad and Shri Mataji was revealing something very deep about Her nature. Prasad is food that is offered to the Deity, then distributed back to the devotees and it becomes prasad. It was a lot, but we ate it all and truly enjoyed it. Mother was giving us pizza but love was pouring out from Her.

Luis Garrido

Fridges, a TV, jam and Marmite

Around 1988 Shri Mataji invited a large group of Indian musicians and their families to Shudy Camps. Baba Mama also came, and Shri Mataji's daughters, granddaughters, grandson and other relatives. There were about twenty Sahaja Yogis living there.

One day Shri Mataji came to the kitchen and told us She noticed that we went food shopping quite often which was not convenient since there were no shops nearby.

'Why haven't you used the large fridges I bought in America?' She asked.

We replied that the electric current in the US was different from the UK and some adaptation would be needed before we could use them.

'That's an easy problem to solve – ask any Sahaja Yogi with a background in engineering or electrics,' She replied. 'I told you to use those fridges, and now I understand why you didn't. When I move back to India I must take appliances that have been used, not unused items in their original packaging. Since I've lived in this country for many years I'm entitled to benefit from this tax concession.'

Later on a TV was being packed to ship back to India and Shri Mataji noticed that there was a film of food on the screen.

'What's that?' She asked.

Someone explained that a Sahaja Yogi had seen that the TV looked new, so he smeared jam and Marmite on it. Shri Mataji told us to phone him and tell him She would not resort to this to avoid import duty, and to explain to him the difference between benefiting from a legitimate tax loophole and stooping to immoral strategies.

'It's important that he understands the difference,' Shri Mataji told us.

Luis Garrido

The protective bandhan

One day while I was staying at Shudy Camps, I was about to enter the car to drive to London. I heard a sound and looking up noticed Shri

Mataji waving at me from Her apartment upstairs. Then I saw Her bringing down my ego channel from left to right several times. She also indicated that I should calm down and get into the centre. While going to London I remembered Her advice and had no problem, but on the way back completely forgot to keep my ego in check, and had a minor car accident. Then I remembered Her advice, brought down the ego and returned home safely.

So many accidents could be avoided if we put ourselves into bandhan before going out. Two Sahaja Yogis hurt themselves on the Indian tour while travelling and this was reported to Shri Mataji.

'Did they remember to put themselves into bandhan first thing in the morning before going out?' She asked, and the Yogis had not.

Luis Garrido

Colours

In Shudy Camps entrance hall there were several large square supporting columns and at the bottom they had been finished with wooden skirting boards. They had been painted, a light blue on the skirting, then a slightly darker blue in the middle section, and at the top, where they joined the ceiling the blue was darker still.

'Tell the person who created the colour scheme that usually one would have the darker tones of blue at the bottom and then gone gradually lighter towards the top,' Shri Mataji explained, because the opposite had been done. She explained that in decorating a room this is a general principle for colour schemes.

We were driving Shri Mataji through the countryside in Cambridgeshire, in May, and there were many yellow fields of rape seed in flower. She told us to look at these as they clear our Swadishthans.

In Portugal there was a Sahaja Yogi who had the habit of walking with his neck bent down and Shri Mataji told him to look at the blue sky to clear his Vishuddhi.

Luis Garrido

Chapter 12

1988: October India

Pratishthan during construction

Derek Ferguson diary entries, mostly Pratishthan

Saturday: Spoke to Shri Mataji about plastering at Pratishthan and about getting a plasterer to work with me. Maybe most of the walls will have to be done again. I gave the plasterer some lessons in technique and he is coming on well.

There is a special ceremony of Shri Krishna that is done every year in Maharashtra, where you form a pyramid to reach a clay pot filled with milk. I watched it, and one of the boys came over and said Shri Mataji said I should join in. They attempted the pyramid several times without success, meanwhile other people were throwing water over us. Then a small boy broke the clay pot and coconut milk poured out over everyone and the boys ran round trying to soak everyone who had not already been soaked. Shri Mataji watched for some time from the balcony then went in. Later She sent some sweets down as prasad. The Shri Krishna Puja is tomorrow morning.

Sunday: Shri Mataji was very disappointed with the Sahaja Yogi ladies from Delhi because they have become very Westernised. I showed Her photos of the Birmingham ashram to be. She said the English Sahaja Yogis should buy it immediately and showed Her a book about Caribbean family life. She said someone should write to the author and tell him/her about the negativity that is their main problem, and that the young West Indians should learn about Sahaja Yoga. They would not need to be told about Shri Mataji to begin with; the recognition could come afterwards.

She spoke about AIDS. She said it was not good to swim in public swimming baths and said someone caught it from the swimming pool at the Blue Diamond Hotel in Pune. They had tested negative before coming to India. It is OK to swim in a pool only used by Sahaja Yogis. She mentioned that seven more people had been diagnosed with AIDS in Pune, and it was not good to swim in some seas, e.g. England's.

We talked about the Book of Revelations in the Bible. Shri Mataji said that at least Paul had not touched it.

Shri Mataji has tried to make the Indian Sahaja Yogis live collectively, even the retired yogis, but they are very fond of their food and do not like the collective kitchen idea – but they will change. She said that India is like an elephant which is chained up but once it breaks free it will be a very different country.

I was floating in vibrations

In 1988, I came to Mumbai for the Ganesha Puja. One day before there was a music programme and I was sitting there. Shri Mataji indicated to me, like calling, but I was next to many people. I did feel She was calling me, but said to myself, 'She doesn't know me. Why should She call me?' and thought maybe She was calling someone else. After the programme, the committee leader was sitting there.

'Shri Mataji was calling you. Why didn't you go?' he said.

'I did feel that, but She doesn't know me. Why should She call me? I have never met Her.'

The next day, after the puja, I was standing in the queue to offer a flower and garlands to Shri Mataji and She called me, and then I understood. In my hand I had some poetry which I had written that was wrapped in paper and I offered it to Her. I was so happy inside and so joyous.

'What is it? Is it poetry?' She asked me, but She knew — because it could have been anything. Someone was there offering Her a sari.

'No, don't bring a sari. See, this poetry is the best gift,' She said.

She patted my face and I was floating in vibrations for at least three or four days after that. So my one strong desire was fulfilled, to go near Her and be with Her. Just that touch on my face was more than anything else.

Nirmal Gupta

Derek Ferguson diary entries, Pratishthan

Sunday: At the hall Shri Mataji spoke about how we should behave with people, and not force Sahaja Yoga onto new people, and to speak nicely to them.

Tuesday: I went to Pune to register with the police at the Foreigners Department, on Shri Mataji's instructions, with another Western Sahaja Yogi, and they said we did not need to register until we had been there for two weeks, 27th of November 1988.

Monday: Wanted to see Shri Mataji so went with a very strong desire. Usually a lot of people are there, but it was quite late, about nine in the evening. The place was empty and Shri Mataji came out and called me and it was great. We spoke about the plaster, and that She was trying to reduce the work I had to do, and how when She was away lots of things that She did not want done were done, for example the ceilings were plastered.

Shri Mataji talked about AIDS and said it came from Zambia, where they have a lot of copper in the soil. The copper affected the green monkeys, then it went to the Westerners that way. She also said the way to cure it was to give the patients injections of platinum or gold.

(To someone else present at that conversation, the following was reported: the green monkeys had had HIV/AIDS for centuries, but unlike humans they are not so immoral so it was not serious. Shri Mataji explained that the AIDS virus needs the copper molecule to reproduce, and the virus attaches itself to copper in the body. One has to introduce platinum or gold into the body – so the AIDS virus attaches itself to the platinum or gold and destroys itself)

She spoke about a politician who had recently started a centrist party in the UK and this lady came to see Shri Mataji, but only for herself. The lady told Her that she wanted to form a centre party to stop the politics moving from right to left all the time, but Shri Mataji told her that at least there was some movement. We asked if there is anything that could be done to lift the curse that is on England. Shri Mataji said that the English Sahaja Yogis take things for granted, mainly because She is there, and it was wrong, and that is why it is not lifting. She talked about the English royal family. She was expected to curtsey before the queen, but politely refused, and did namaskar instead.

We also talked about the possibility of my coming to live in India and starting a school to teach the children how to plaster. Shri Mataji said it would not be allowed for me to buy a flat because of the laws of the country, but we could invest the money we earned and live off the interest and live in an ashram in Pune, which the Sahaja Yogis are going to start building. There are two plots of land, one that is ready now and one which will be in two years' time. Shri Mataji also spoke about the possibility of buying a house with someone in England and using the money to live on.

She mentioned that England will go bankrupt mainly because of allowing people to borrow so much money on credit and they do not have an industry to fall back on like America, and that factories are closing all over England.

In the evening Shri Mataji spoke to the Indian Sahaja Yogis about forming a political party and calling it the Old Congress and getting some Sahaja Yogis to stand. She spoke about how the English politicians do not take bribes, and that the Indians do, but you cannot get anything done.

She also told some jokes – one about a king who sent a man to the sea to count all the waves coming on to the shore. So the man sat down and some merchants came along and said he was blocking their way and he would have to move. He explained that he could not unless they paid him some money first. They made an agreement to pay him, and he got a lot of money and built a palace with it.

Shri Mataji also spoke about a leading Indian politician and said he was stealing money from the country and putting it in a Swiss bank account, and due to Sahaja Yoga and the Sahaja Yogis She knows the name of the bank. Before it was thought that it was 60 crores of rupees, but now it was known that it was about 400 crores, (about 25 million pounds in 1988). She said She had high hopes for him in the beginning. She said when a community goes down, a good person always rises, like a lotus in mud.

Today was my best day – everything went like a dream.

Tuesday: Got up early and went to the flat, the part of the house which is finished enough to live in. Shri Mataji was already up, and She mentioned that the trouble I had getting the plaster mix right was necessary and now something else had worked out. She was now going to tile a lot of the wall areas to decrease the amount of plastering.

In the evening I was called again, to say my work would be reduced even more by having the ceilings wallpapered, and getting the Sahaja Yogis to bring wallpaper from London. I was also asked to supervise the workers doing the tiling. Shri Mataji mentioned to the architect that She wanted to reduce the plastering because of the effect of the dust on me.

Wednesday: Shri Mataji said I should go to the puja in Bombay, and then on the tour, as I am already in India. In the evening we were all called to watch an Indian TV programme with Her, about someone trying to get their own back on someone else.

Thursday: Shri Mataji asked me to remove some tiles from Her bathroom, but it was not possible. The Indian plasterer has picked up the English method of plastering very well.

Yesterday Shri Mataji asked me to make sure I had my train tickets as the last time the Sahaja Yogis missed the puja. She explained that today was the day of the puja to Shri Ganesha but because of convenience, i.e. people having to go to work, we have to have the puja on Sunday. Also when the Indians celebrate it nowadays, some unruly elements have crept in causing trouble. In the evening there was a TV programme about the celebrations and Shri Mataji said they get drunk and do the Samba dance, which is not auspicious, and also start looting. People on the TV were saying that Shri Ganesha should not be worshipped in such a bad way.

Shri Mataji said Baba Mama liked the way that I moved my shoulders when playing the bells. She said the Indians do not do this; they move the

Shri Mataji and Baba Mama at Pratishthan

lower part of their bodies, which is represented by the Kundalini. She said I should teach the Indians how the shoulders move, and also should learn to play bigger bells.

Derek Ferguson diary entries, when in India and working at Pratishthan

Friday: Shri Mataji asked me to read the details of the tour, which was very well planned. She spoke to the Indians about the house saying She wanted the work speeded up. She saw the plasterer doing some different work and said he should work with me all the time. She also spoke in English, saying that when the Adi Shakti separated from God, there was an explosion or eruption of sound like a volcano, without any percussion.

Saturday: I woke up early, because Shri Mataji was to leave at 6.00 am to catch the 7.30 train to Bombay. After the ladies did the aarti we bowed down and Shri Mataji asked me to put my hands wide apart, away from my head, to receive the vibrations better, and to cup my hands upwards to receive the grace from the divine. She gave another English Sahaja Yogi some money, and said, 'Take this, you will need it,' then left for Pune railway station.

Took the bus to Pune and the train to Bombay with my friend Anil, an Indian Sahaja Yogi. We reached Bombay at 8.30 pm, and arrived at the programme ten minutes after Shri Mataji. We listened to a lady singing and then Shri Mataji spoke to the Indians about Indian culture, saying that Hindi should be spoken by the Indians in preference to English. They should not take the example from the West, and the Westerners have now come full circle and are coming back to Eastern ways.

Shri Mataji also spoke about memory. She said that the lady was singing without any notebook, and so we should also learn the songs by heart. We should have a good memory, and then we would be able to be more spontaneous, and sing better. She said that the level of Sahaja Yoga had gone up.

Shri Mataji also said that we should teach the children classical music from a young age, otherwise they will have no joy, and seek outside excitement. They might laugh at you and ask, 'Why are we learning this type of music?' if you teach them later. Finally She said this was the first time that Shri Mataji had separated from God and come on this earth.

Sunday: I left the house and caught a rickshaw to the puja hall. Reached there about 12.30 and Shri Mataji arrived about 1.30. She spoke in Hindi, about the attention, saying that at the moment She is releasing a lot of energy – like the space rockets, one stage pushes the next upwards even faster. If our attention is alright and is on our Sahaja goals, we will rise very fast, but if our attention is not on the right thing then there will be problems. She also spoke about innocence, saying that some Sahaja Yogis appear very innocent on the outside, but inside they are not, so we should try to be on the inside how we appear on the outside.

Monday: Arrived back at Pratishthan and about 9.30 pm Shri Mataji returned from Bombay and we watched TV with Her. As She was going to Her room, She said She had seen many people and cured a lot of them.

Tuesday: Went to the flat earlier than usual, at about 6.45 am, because Shri Mataji was already up. She spoke about the ceilings, and I was shown a book about a marble palace in Calcutta. She worked on one of the architects, saying that his Nabhis were catching, then he mentioned that he had had cancer and they had taken out some bone marrow for testing. Shri Mataji worked on him and he said that there was always a pain at the base of his neck, so She explained that the Kundalini was trying to clear the way and was being obstructed. She gave him some mantras while working on him, and suddenly he began to catch on his right Agnya. Shri Mataji explained that the ego starts to operate when we are told that there is a problem but said it is like being told that there is a spot on Her sari – She is not the sari and we just have to clean it. If we are attached to our body, then we start to catch on the right Agnya etc.

She also mentioned that as well as having good vibrations, we should have a healthy body and after realisation that becomes easier, because the Kundalini clears things. She said I had lots of problems when I first came, but had cured myself, and asked me how I did it. She said that my spine and sitting position were fine now. Last night, while we were watching TV, water was dripping on me from above, and Shri Mataji read my mind.

'Yes, Fergy' She said, 'there is a problem there, the roof is leaking and needs fixing – so if we do think, think things that are good!' Later on I discovered that all we foreigners might have to leave the house and commute there daily from Pune, because the house was going to be inspected by the authorities, but She said I could stay because I looked Indian.

Wednesday: I went to the flat late today because Shri Mataji slept late. She said that She was going to stay at Her house until about the 16th November and not go to Australia because She wants to hurry up the work, also because a lot of money had been wasted by the Sahaja Yogis. As compensation for not going to Australia, about fifty extra people could come to India on the tour. She said people's luggage would have to be much less this year – about 20 lbs weight, even 10 lbs, because otherwise it takes about three hours to unload the buses.

Shri Mataji spoke about a hurricane, Hurricane Gilbert, which went around the Caribbean and then on to Mexico, saying it was nature that was working but people do not connect the two things together – when they don't realise what they are doing wrong, nature tries to stop them doing negative things through flooding, lightning etc.

She spoke about my grandmother, saying that instead of my mother going to Jamaica, we could pay for my grandmother to come to the UK, because the English authorities would not mind. Shri Mataji also asked if my mother was realised, and I said she was. Shri Mataji said that she should not go to Jamaica.

Shri Mataji asked about the high price of saris in England, and said that the Indians overcharged people.

'Necessity is the mother of invention,' was one of Her quotes.

Thursday: Shri Mataji spoke this morning about the greenhouse effect, saying it was caused by the behaviour of the people, and the droughts in America were caused by them allowing drugs into the country.

She mentioned that at the time of the Ganesha festivals, there is an elephant constellation in the sky, which has the effect of making the rain pour. This year the rain is even more, because of the behaviour of the people. I mentioned that the vibrations were very strong this morning, and Shri Mataji said it was Her desire, which was working things out.

The younger architect was being worked on and She mentioned that his overactive right side was making his heart catch, and he should try to have some emotional feelings, especially towards Her, like gratitude for what She has done for him. She said it should be an emotional, not a mental feeling, otherwise the chakra would not clear. He also had to ask Shri Mataji to come into his heart.

Friday: Shri Mataji said I should take more carbohydrates in food, and less protein, because the liver was in need of them. She said that bean sprouts and rice in the morning were very good. There are some Punjabi people who eat this, and they are very strong.

Shri Mataji showed me some plain marble pieces which had been coated with wood varnish, which had changed them completely. She also had some of Her furniture and some tiles coated with this, and it gave a very rich effect.

She mentioned that She may employ a cook to give the Sahaja Yogis a chance to do something else. She also said I should move upstairs to start plastering there now.

Mr Patankar, the senior architect, came today with his son.

Another saying of Shri Mataji is '19/20'. When trying to match things they should not be too close together, like two reds – but pink and red would be alright, also cloth and wood on the walls, but not cloth and tiles.

There were two stories about water. When they first started building, there was no water, but there was a farmer next door who had a well which gave water for only two days a year, during the monsoon. He would take water from it and by the next day it would be dry, so the Sahaja Yogis asked him if they could use it. He said yes, but there is no water in it. A Sahaja Yogi then attached a hand pump to it and started pumping, and it has not stopped giving water ever since. The farmer was amazed.

Secondly, Shri Mataji asked the contractors to drill for water. They had been asked to dig as far as 180 feet, so when they struck water at 30 feet, they carried on drilling, and the water which was there disappeared. Shri Mataji was very angry, so the well was left for a while.

'Why don't you put some vibrated water down the well?' She said one day. They did, and when they lowered a container down, they struck sweet water at 33 feet.

Saturday: Started work on the bathroom near my room. The ceiling has to be done before the fittings are put in. Shri Mataji came round the house with Sir CP and Her daughter, and came into the room.

Monday: Got some more instructions from Shri Mataji about the work and She went to a Marathi play with the Indian Sahaja Yogis.

Friday: Went to see Shri Mataji and She worked on me for a while and gave me some breathing exercises – breathe in, hold my breath for a while, then breathe out. She mentioned that it was the liver causing the chest problem, as I had caught a chill in my chest after going to the play and that the liver was very hot. She raised my Kundalini a few times and the vibrations started to flow much stronger and said there must be a badha in my heart chakra which has not yet gone. She also said we should not drink tap water because it was contaminated, and arranged for some purified water to be given to us.

Saturday: Woke up feeling much better, and went to see Shri Mataji. She spoke about various treatments – basil tea, breathing exercise, ice on the liver, liver diet and taking Liv 52. She said that both channels had been affected, but the chest problem was because of the liver.

Monday: Mr Patankar told Shri Mataji that I still wasn't well so She asked to see me immediately. She asked someone to get an ice pack to put on my liver and some radish leaf tea, which cooled everything down straight away. She smiled and told me to have just radish leaf tea, rice, dal and chapattis for the next three days.

Later I saw the plasterer, he also had liver problems and had not come to work that day. We managed to show him to Shri Mataji, as She was on Her rounds, and She said that a Sahaja Yogi who was there should move his left to the right, and take him to be worked on. Then Shri Mataji came and worked on him, and the fever went away. She told him to take B complex, tulsi (basil) tea, and to go to sleep, which he did. Different people, different treatments.

Wednesday: Feeling much better. Spoke with Shri Mataji and She said I should let the poisons pass through my system and She did not want to give me anything to stop it happening, and said I was alright now.

She gave a good suggestion for the bathrooms – to have smooth cement ceilings instead of plaster of Paris, because of the steam. We also gave a bandhan to get more plaster of Paris, because we were told supplies in Pune were finished. However, I sowever, I spoke to a man in Pune who had a plaster factory and managed to order some.

Thursday: Went to see Shri Mataji this morning and She told me to use more ice on the liver. She explained that radish leaf tea was a more long term thing, but ice was instantaneous. She asked me not to think, and spoke about the liver, saying that when it is out, you get a lot of heat in the body and as a reaction your body feels the outside cold even more and you have to put a lot of clothes on to keep warm. She also said heat from the liver makes the chest inflamed, and heated up. She spoke about the dust in the house, saying it is too much and that I should wear a mask or cloth to cover the mouth, and try not to mix the plaster too much myself, because it affects the chest and the Swadishthans also get affected if the liver is out.

Shri Mataji mentioned earlier that She does not like to live in cities any more and prefers to live outside, especially in Her old age.

Friday: Watched a Hindi movie in the evening, very violent. Shri Mataji said that there were a lot of true life things happening in it, that She was glad to see it, so She could put Her attention on them.

Saturday: A few Sahaja Yogis came in the evening, and Shri Mataji spoke about an eminent Maharashtran politician, saying he was trying to start a casino and an alcohol factory in Bombay.

Monday: Went to see Shri Mataji this morning and spoke about bringing some ceiling roses to India, and She said I was looking better than in England, and that She had told the cooks not to prepare so much oily food, because She was 'looking after our livers'.

I mentioned that sometimes people don't like it if you say you are happy, so Shri Mataji said you should say to them, 'Don't you want to be happy?' and you should say you are in joy and that everything is alright with you.

Tuesday: Shri Mataji spoke to us again about food, saying that the ladies should feed us certain types of food which are not hot on the liver and that all the Sahaja Yogis should go on a liver diet for a month, no meat, no oily food. They should give us things made with coconut milk, not cow's milk, and should give us milk without cream. They should give Her some sugar to vibrate, for us.

She said I should learn to drive when I got back to England, and could do that as a job sometimes. She also liked it that I had started to do some molding work, and said they pay a lot for that. She said I should put more attention on other things, and less on myself.

Today was the first day of the nine day Navaratri festival of the Goddess, so there was a small puja in the evening at about 8.30, with Shri Mataji. They did aarti, then we said some mantras and bowed down. After that we received some prasad.

'The vibrations were too much; they were very strong,' Shri Mataji said. She also said we should treat the house like an ashram, and there is a puja on the 16th, so we should do our meditation in the mornings.

The food has improved a lot since She has changed the diet to a liver one. When I asked if I should have some vitamins, being as we were not eating meat, She said it would not be necessary. I asked why my liver was not good, and Shri Mataji asked if I had taken drugs. I said no, and then She said it was because I was a seeker before realisation, and that had damaged it, so 'what to do?' She said I should take a shower which was as cold as possible.

We had a puja at about 8.30 pm, the Pune Sahaja Yogis turned up at 10.00 and Shri Mataji asked why they were so late. They said it was because they were doing puja at the main centre. She told them off, saying why were they doing puja in Pune when She was here in person? She told them they were catching on left Sahasrara, which was very serious for a Sahaja Yogi.

One Mahabharata was enough

In 1988, Shri Mataji stayed in Pune for Navaratri and blessed the Sahaja Yogis by receiving pujas on all nine days.

'When you look down, you should be able to see My photograph in your heart,' She said in one of the puja talks.

On the sixth day there was a puja in a big hall attended by many Sahaja Yogis. At that time there was a television serial of the Mahabharata every Sunday, which the Sahaja Yogis liked to watch.

'I have not seen this Mahabharata. The one that I have seen is enough,' Shri Mataji said.

Raman Kulkarni

Derek Ferguson diary entries, when in India and working at Pratishthan

Wednesday: We had another Navaratri Puja in the evening, at about 6.00 pm, and Shri Mataji said that for the next ten days we will have pujas. At this one someone read an extract from the American newsletter, praise of the Goddess by Markandeya from the Devi Mahatmyam. Shri Mataji mentioned that while he was reading them, when we worship Her, we get the benefits, not Her. It is for us to benefit from these pujas. She said things like health and wealth were right side powers. We then tried to have some music, but there was no electricity, due to the main power feed breaking down and the harmonium was broken, so we gave up. We'll be better prepared tomorrow. This is the Shri Durga Puja, and on the last day Shri Rama kills the demons.

Thursday: We had a very strong puja in the evening and they read out the Kavach of the Devi. Shri Mataji explained what the different sayings meant, for example 'May the Goddess protect me from the West', means from the Western ways of life, and not the physical direction, as in north, south, east and west. She said that when we are surrendered to Her properly, then everything works out, but when we are not, we are not protected, we can have problems, but are not to blame Her. She said the Western life style was a joke. She said the vibrations were so much that Her body was shaking, and that the pujas were needed to help the vibrations spread.

Friday: Finished reading the Kavach of the Devi, and Shri Mataji said the Sahaja Yogis should ask for a boon that they get a good chief minister who will help them spread Sahaja Yoga. She emphasised that Sahaja Yogis should put a bandhan on more regularly to protect themselves, otherwise not to blame Her if bad things happen. They gave Her a sword to hold after the puja.

Saturday: Shri Mataji went out for Diwali shopping and other things in the afternoon, and came back about 7.30.

The Delhi leader, who is a doctor, and some Delhi Sahaja Yogis came to the house and spoke about some experiments done in Delhi University and at the army hospital in Delhi. They do all the tests on the new Sahaja Yogis, and those who have been doing it for some time – blood tests, ECG, brain tests etc. It has all been passed, and they are now doing tests on hypertension and epilepsy.

We had a continuation of the puja and Shri Mataji explained the meaning of a song. There were very strong vibrations, and She said we all had to fulfill our destiny.

Sunday: Stayed at Pratishthan for a while until Mr and Mrs Naik came to invite Shri Mataji to the puja. They offered Her fruits and flowers and then did the aarti, and when She was leaving got Her to vibrate a coconut which they broke in front of the car. The puja was in Hindi. Then there was a havan, without Shri Mataji. She came back at about 9.30 pm for a music programme with a singer, a young girl who was very good, and other musicians were with her.

Monday: Lots of people came to see the house and also to see Shri Mataji if they could. She did see them, and then got ready for the puja. Mr Kulkarni, the Pune leader, read out some more pages and Shri Mataji explained some more things for us. The Pune Sahaja Yogis sang some songs, then Shri Mataji left.

Tuesday: Went to see Shri Mataji this morning with Mr Patankar, the chief architect, about some plaster plates made from a design on glass. She mentioned it would be better to stick the glass directly on to the ceiling instead of the plates, so less maintenance will be needed. I gave Her some flowers, and a copy of an Indian design magazine.

The room for today's puja has been changed to a bigger one to hold all the people. Shri Mataji spoke about the Agnya chakra, saying that heaven was not our destiny. We have to rise higher and get over our ego, super ego and comforts etc. A Sahaja Yogi was asking Shri Mataji some questions, and She told him off, saying you should not ask questions during the puja. Mr Kulkarni read out some more praises of the Devi, and Shri Mataji translated them.

Thursday: Shri Mataji came to where I was working, and said She wanted some more plaster ceiling roses put up.

They made an effigy, outside, of the brothers of Ravana, out of sackcloth and straw. When Shri Mataji came down they set it alight, and it was filled with big bangers, which were very loud. When it was finished, She went back inside, and mentioned that She wanted it to rain today, and I felt a few drops. When Shri Mataji went to Her room they did the aarti. I showed Her some photos, which She liked. She called us and gave shirts to all of us, and also a lunghi for each of us, for sleeping in.

Friday: This morning Shri Mataji spoke about the English, saying that even though they conquered India, they have not yet conquered themselves. She also spoke about Shudy Camps, about selling it, and about the good weather that they have had there. She talked about the need to include music in the tapes that are sent abroad.

The Pune Sahaja Yogis came to see Shri Mataji with some books by realised souls, to start a library – a very good collection, some Hindi, some English.

Monday: Found out about 10.30 pm that there is going to be an event on the terrace because it is a full moon night. Shri Mataji came out briefly at about 1.15am, then we all went downstairs for some prasad, a sweet milky drink.

Thursday: Somebody broke one of the marble staircase pieces and Shri Mataji said that someone was making mischief against the marble man, who was a Muslim. There are two contractors here today, and Shri Mataji told everyone off, which was good, because now they will watch each other.

Twice the staircase marble was broken. There was a lot of shouting.

Shri Mataji wanted to tape a message for the Australian Sahaja Yogis as Hamid was going to Australia. The tape was stamped Sony but it was a fake tape and twisted in the machine so they could not get it done yesterday. There is a factory in India making fake everything, and putting false labels on things like tapes. We watched a video of the TV series, the Mahabharata, and the Sahaja Yogis record it and play it to Shri Mataji when She is ready to watch it.

Friday: Shri Mataji spoke about cement and how expensive it is in India, so we are going to find out about the Feb Company's products. We talked about what needs to be done in the house, then I showed Her some of my songs and She said I should teach the Indians, so that the English can be surprised.

Left the house and tried to avoid seeing Shri Mataji because I was going to Pune. Quickly walked past Her door to go down the stairs, and She was there talking to the Muslim contractor.

'Where are you going?' She said.

'To Pune.'

'What for?'

'To do some shopping.'

She said (very humbly – it was embarrassing) She was only asking me because She wanted some buckets, and I could get a lift with one of the Pune Sahaja Yogis. She is always looking after us.

Saturday: One of the Western Sahaja Yogis had to go to Bombay, so we were awake early, about 5.30 am. Mumbai is the real name of Bombay – it means the bay of the Mother.

Sunday: I was given a bucket and jug for our bathroom. There is one for every bathroom, from Shri Mataji. There were hundreds of saris in the big room in Her flat; for the tour group.

A Sahaja Yogi had asked Shri Mataji for a favour, and She had said 'Yes' to that person. Later on, I found out that She had said 'Yes' so as not to hurt his ego, but he should not have asked in the first place, so as not to put Her under any pressure.

Monday: There was a lot of commotion today because the plaster masons were quarrelling. One got drunk and started to fight with another, and they said they would not work with each other. Shri Mataji had to reprimand the drunk one, because he had promised to give up drinking a month before. She told him that the Sahaja Yogis had given up bad habits, and now these people were taking to them.

Ravi the labourer went to a doctor, who told him he had jaundice, so he was very worried. I told him only Sahaja Yoga can cure him, because the doctor said he could not do anything. I told him some remedies, and in the evening he got a shirt from Shri Mataji, as a Diwali present. All the workers got a present and some got shawls.

Later on I was invited, with some other Sahaja Yogis, to have a Chinese meal at a restaurant, then came back with a meal that had been brought for Shri Mataji by Anil, a Pune Sahaja Yogi, but She said She did not take anything fried at the moment. We watched a programme of Indian music on the TV – mainly bhajans, with Shri Mataji, and saw a man playing the bells. He had an assortment of bells set up and She said this was the new modern way.

Tuesday: Went to see Shri Mataji this morning about Sunil, the worker. She said She would cure him and that She had invented a new medicine for the liver that only needed a drop in a cup to be effective, it was made with the cooling effect of the full moon.

Shri Mataji talked about Australia, saying that a certain lady from the UK had gone there and all the Australians were adversely affected by her. She said that when they come to India She is going to give them all lemons and chillies to put under their pillows. She also mentioned that they should stay longer, after the tour, to get the full effect of India.

She asked me how I was feeling and I said that since going to the pujas in the house every day for ten days, I felt very light. She said that She had arranged for there to be eight pujas on the tour, so that people can clear out and feel much better. Shri Mataji showed me the saris She had chosen for the ladies on the tour. They were a new design, very nice, of cotton but with silk sari designs on them.

Shri Mataji said that the Indian race of Aryans even ruled Britain once.

Shri Mataji's granddaughter Aradhana was there, and innocently started to play some pop music, and She told her to stop it. Later Shri Mataji explained that pop music numbs the limbic area, and that is why people go wild when they listen to rock music. Also your sensitivity gets less. She mentioned that you cannot reason with these young people because they do not read the newspapers etc. She said that people at Aradhana's college had even started taking drugs and doing all the things that the West is trying to get rid of and when the Indians take to anything bad they do it worse than the people in the West.

Sunil was called but Shri Mataji was eating, so She told him his complaint was not that bad and he should ask Chanda, the Sahaja doctor, for some Sahaja treatments. He had to get a bottle from the kitchen, so while he was there She worked on him for some time and told him to do the treatments. Then She blessed him with a long life and he left very happy!

Shri Mataji spoke about all the arranging She is doing for the saris, how She has to arrange for some tailors to sew everything. She said She is still waiting for the money and sizes from the English and some people had still not paid for the tour, but She has managed to keep the cost of the tour the same for the fourth year running. Shri Mataji said She was trying to finish certain jobs before She went on the tour, for example the front stonework.

She talked about mosquitoes, saying that although there are about 2,500 types, there are only two sorts that cause malaria, and the rest are just parasites. They even bite Her, and the cure is plain water, rubbed into the sting. The Sahaja Yogis who had caught malaria on the tour were frantic for water, and had drunk water which was not clean. She was going to tell people to bring water containers for the tour.

Shri Mataji said the plastering was going alright, and She is still trying to reduce my workload. She asked what fruit I like, and told the ladies to get pineapples, chikkus, guavas and papayas for us, but no fried food. She is going to take the medicine She has made to England, but people could come to India and have it instead.

Shri Mataji mentioned that tomorrow She will be busy – Aradhana is going to Riyadh for a month. Earlier in the morning She said the Australians should not feel so patriotic about their country now they had come to Sahaja Yoga. They wanted Her to come to Australia especially, because their bicentennial was being celebrated.

Friday: Went to see Shri Mataji about going to Bombay on Sunday, for my visa. She said that Her car would be going so I could go with it. She talked about the Pune rakshasa – a false guru, saying that a very important politician here was supporting him and taking money from him and allowing him to stay here. There are thousands of his disciples in the town, all paying him a lot of money. He gives off so much heat but Shri Mataji is the complete opposite; Her body temperature is very low, which is, She said, what a divine person's should be.

She talked about South Africa, saying She feels very bad about the situation there and She is doing so much to help the Africans, indirectly. She mentioned that when India got independence, they did it in a different way than the Africans. Even though thousands of Indians got killed, before independence they did not even know how to make needles – everything was made in the UK. All the gold, diamonds and precious metals were taken from India.

She spoke about the Olympic Games, and said that 1948 was the first time they did things like high jump and long jump, and it would take the Indians a long time to develop. They were very good at sports like wrestling, and after Sahaja Yoga was fully established, the games would probably stop anyway.

Shri Mataji said that it needed an English MP of either party to say something about South Africa before things could work out. What they are doing there was very bad, because they are all human beings like us. She told us that an English politician had come to see Her only for her own gain and not to help others, and that some Sahaja Yogis were like that, coming for what they could gain for themselves: power, money, possessions etc.

She mentioned that in Chile and Argentina, the European people who had gone there had wiped out nearly all the native people. Some had escaped and had gone to Bolivia and Colombia. Before Shri Mataji went to the public programme in Colombia this year, She had gone before, in 1978, with Sir CP, and someone had asked Her, if She was a very spiritual person, whether something could be done for their country, as America was giving them so much trouble, so She blessed the country. When Shri Mataji first went the place was full of shanty towns, but when She went back in 1988, it was fully modernised, with a new airport, escalator complexes, and the people travelled First Class, a big change.

Shri Mataji said that a very wealthy Sahaja Yogi had left Her in the lurch by withdrawing the support he was giving without prior notice, so She had to pay out of Her own pocket, which was wrong. But the Sahaja Yogis had spoken to him and now he had changed.

Later, after work I had dinner then went to see Shri Mataji. After some time She came, and when She saw me said there was an article about Jamaica in the paper. Found the article, but it was about what the Fiji people were doing to the Indians, and also what was happening to people in Guyana.

She said that people were invited there, but when they got there they were treated like slaves. The people from Guyana had invited Her to speak, but She had told them 'next year.'

She spoke about the English, saying the word English came from a word in Marathi or Hindi meaning the little finger, so there was no need for them to consider themselves so highly. Even the Channel tunnel would not change them, because they had lived in India for over three hundred years, and it had not changed them.

She spoke about a cult who do sacrifices to Kali, and the leader of the Calcutta centre had been a follower until one day he was in their temple and Shri Mataji appeared to him, and he immediately knew that what he was doing was wrong, so he collected all the people together and told them, then drove all the way to Lucknow, because he knew the leader of the cult would try to kill him. He went to Shri Mataji with two policemen as body-guards, and told Her the story. She said he should not worry and She would protect him. They then arrested the leader of the cult, and while he was in prison lots of politicians were killed, so they released him. Now the man who escaped is a Sahaja Yogi, so he is ok. He had personally seen the leader kill twenty–eight people – because he was the leader's right hand man – they were 'Kali sacrifices', and are attacking Indians all over the world.

Shri Mataji said that some things that the Prime Minister, Mrs Thatcher, is doing are bad for the country, like copying America, but the English cannot, because they do not make enough goods. She mentioned this morning that even if people say it is wrong for the Africans to fight, who are they to say anything? The South African (apartheid) government is being supported by the British, who should not do so. They have to fight for their freedom.

Was feeling good this morning so when I bowed down to Shri Mataji, it was nice to hear Her say that I was ok. She mentioned that Sahaja Yogis should wear Her badge when they come to India so they do not get confused with being followers of the Pune rakshasa. She told the Indians to take certain examples from the English, various technical things and certain ways of life etc, but one of the Indians said that the English don't even respect their parents, so how can we follow their ways?

Saturday: Yesterday I asked Sunil to bring a sugar cane stalk for me to give to Shri Mataji. He brought it today, but the opportunity did not arise. A Sahaja Yogi was in Shri Mataji's presence, and She noticed that his hand was shaking slightly. She told him it was a sign of nervousness, from the right side. He agreed, and a few moments later he was fine.

Sunday: Tried to offer the sugar cane again, but still no success. Later on in the evening, with Shri Mataji's permission, I got ready to go to Bombay to sort out my visa.

One of the Sahaja Yogis told Shri Mataji that Delhi University wanted some more information on how the vibrations work, to be able to sanction money for studying the effects of vibrations. Shri Mataji explained that they are a living process and contain electromagnetic force, our emotional force, and our evolutionary power, so how can they be measured or explained? You can only see the effect, She said, because science is a limited thing and the vibrations are beyond science. The Sahaja Yogi mentioned that the Delhi University Chancellor believes in Sahaja Yoga because he has seen it himself and when he is with Sahaja Yogis he feels much better. Shri Mataji said he has to decide whether he wants to go ahead because She cannot explain to him how it works. Plus the human mind is very limited.

Went to get ready and came back, then managed to offer the sugar cane to Shri Mataji. She asked who it was for and I said it was for Her. She said She would eat it Herself, but it was about nine feet tall!

I went to sort out a few things and when I came back discovered there was a puja going on. We said the mantras to Shri Gruha Lakshmi and Shri Anapurna. While the placing of the flowers was going on, someone had left the TV on, and there was a quiz programme on. There was a question about a piece of music, and Shri Mataji asked me what it was. I said it was Bonanza, but I was wrong, it was a tune from the film, The Magnificent Seven. While we were sitting down Shri Mataji said we should absorb the vibrations.

Wednesday: Waiting for Shri Mataji to arrive from shopping. She arrived at 4.25 pm to sort out the saris – some very nice silk designs. Some ladies washed Her Feet with soap and put ice in the water.

'You see what I have to do for you people,' She said. She did not go to the music programme which had been arranged for Her because She had to sort out so many saris. She mentioned that the English have still not sent their money or their sizes yet.

Thursday: Went to the programme. The music was good and they had fireworks and it finished at about 3 o'clock in the morning. Shri Mataji talked about the liver, saying that most Indian food is very heavy, and in the north they also have ghee in their food but their livers are not bad because they do not think a lot. The only people who get diabetes and jaundice in India are those who think a lot – planners, architects etc.

Shri Mataji said it is the concentrated milk in the chocolate that gives you a bad liver. She mentioned that Her mother was a very strict dietician and did not feed them any food which was bad for the liver. Shri Mataji did not start drinking tea until She was 45 years old. If babies are born with jaundice, it is because their mothers are worrying about what will happen at the birth.

The programme and the puja were very full – about a 1000 Sahaja Yogis in Mumbai, and about 300 in Pune. Not all came to the puja because of the expense, it was the equivalent of 2.65 pounds, but the wages are low. In the puja talk Shri Mataji spoke about Shri Lakshmi, saying we should be very generous, like a door which is open so the wealth can flow through it, but if it is closed the flow will stop. There should be ventilation, otherwise there can be no flow from Shri Lakshmi. We should be like a lotus, or a rose petal – very soft towards other people. The joy of giving is greater than the joy of music, which we experience in Sahaja Yoga. We have to be like a lotus because not even water sticks to a lotus.

Shri Mataji's plane leaves at 2.00 am on Friday and arrives in London at 6.30 am. She said that She does not want all the young babies to be brought to the airport so early, but some still want to come to see Her. Helped pack all the things that She is taking to England.

I have held on to that experience ever since that day

It was Diwali Puja 1988 at Shudy Camps in England, my first puja. I'd previously talked to the Yogi who'd been helping me to come into Sahaj, and asked him if I would be able to meet Shri Mataji at the puja, and he said it might be possible. The puja was held in a large marquee in the grounds of Shudy Camps.

When the puja was finished we gathered outside and Shri Mataji came out and walked between us all. My mentor had spent a lot of time with Shri Mataji from the early days in Sahaja Yoga in England and he was able to speak to Her and introduce me. I didn't know how to greet Her, so I held my hand out to shake Hers. She stood directly in front of me – She didn't smile, She held my hand very firmly and looked into me. We stood there together, Shri Mataji holding my right hand. She just stood looking at me intensely. I couldn't think anything. I didn't know how long we stood there like that; it could have been five minutes or it could have been an hour. Other Yogis also told me they didn't know how long we had stood like that with Shri Mataji holding my hand. She was raising my Kundalini in a very strong way, and I went completely thoughtless, but the other Yogis told me they also had gone thoughtless in a deep way.

I'll never forget it and I have held onto that experience ever since that day.

Rosalyn Tildesley

Presents for everyone

Shri Mataji used to give presents to all the Sahaja Yogis at Diwali Puja. In the mid –eighties most of the Sahaja Yogis who attended puja when Shri Mataji was there, used to get presents. I was standing in the puja hall and She saw me and called me, and gave me a hand bag as a Diwali present, which I have still got with me.

At another puja Shri Mataji gave most of the English Sahaja Yoginis some silver rings. When She gave me my ring, She told me to get it gold plated as otherwise the ring would give rashes. She had tremendous concern about small things.

Shakuntala Tandale

The maya of being physically close to Shri Mataji

I had a Chemistry degree, but had been doing a bit of gardening and wanted to ask Shri Mataji what I should do with my life, but the words didn't come out and I didn't want to impose.

'Tell me about yourself, I don't know much about you,' Shri Mataji said at one point.

I told Her what I was doing and She had obviously picked up my thoughts and desires, and said I should go to Germany. It was quite a surprise because I was married to an Austrian and I thought I would go to Austria.

'Austria?' I said.

'No, Germany,' She corrected me. As She said that I felt really cool vibrations on my hands. About a week later we moved to Germany so that was definitely a life changing experience. The other key thing I remember from those days was the maya of being physically close to Shri Mataji as opposed to being close to Her in your meditation.

'Mother is outside,' someone would say when we were at Shudy Camps, and one would rush out and bow down. Some days I was not that clear and felt uncomfortable being close to Mother. One morning Dr Bohdan took us all out onto the grass early about 5.30 am and I felt really good. We went to meet Mother and Her eyes went big, She gave me a smile and I knew She could see I was in a good state. All day my connection with Her was so much better, meaning the Goddess could be three feet away or a million miles away. If you are connected it doesn't matter how near or far you are, and if you are not in a good state it doesn't matter how close you are to Her. It gave me an insight into the maya of being physically around Her. You can slip into the illusion that She is a human being, but if you can go to Sahasrara you can be more aware of the subtleties of what She is doing.

Other nice moments were when Dr Bohdan's son Lenin, who was about two, would come in and Mother would play with him. Once I was alone with Shri Mataji and Lenin.

'Who's that? It's Steve!' She said, and I felt my Centre Heart opened up when Shri Mataji called my name like that.

Steve Jones

Shri Mataji working on a yogi at Pratishthan

Derek Ferguson, diary entries, Pratishthan

Sunday 10th November: Shri Mataji was to arrive at Bombay Airport from England at about 11.40 pm but She only came out at about 1.30 am. She was going to speak, but the PA system was not very good, so She took flowers and garlands and only spoke to a few people. I had come to Bombay for my visa, so had a good excuse to go to the flat where Shri Mataji was staying.

'I did not see you there,' She said, referring to the

airport, so we brought up the luggage and sat down, and She was speaking about politics.

Monday: Slept for a few hours then went upstairs to Shri Mataji's flat. She was still sleeping so I went to the visa office and they told me I could only have a one month extension. I went back to the flat and Shri Mataji was sorting out saris.

'They've arrived,' She said, told me to sit down.

Tuesday: I went upstairs and Shri Mataji was talking to Baba Mama about the arrangements for the tour – what food, fruit etc to have, and even the Christmas arrangements. I took a bus to Pune from Bombay, and Shri Mataji arrived at about 12.00 o'clock, and made more arrangements for the tour via the leader in London.

Wednesday: It was a full moon, and Guru Nanak's birthday. Shri Mataji had a small puja and spoke in Hindi about money, saying we should be satisfied with what we have.

She told a story about Her saris, saying that some people had not paid for the saris that She had bought for them and lot of bad things had happened as a result. For instance, an English Sahaja Yogi went abroad – he used to collect the money for the pujas, but he started to pocket it and now he has gone mad and is in an asylum. Then there was a Sahaja Yogini who accidentally did not pay for one, and she lost the job she had held for eighteen years. However, she realised she had not paid for it, and even before she actually did she was given an even better job than before. Just by paying or not paying for Shri Mataji's saris, so many things happen.

She said when the incarnations came they spoke about things the others had missed, but did not know that people would stick on to each religion separately, like Mohammed told people not to drink, so the Muslims tend not to drink alcohol, but they smoke, and Guru Nanak said don't smoke so the Sikhs, who follow him, may not smoke but some of them drink like fishes.

Thursday: Now that Shri Mataji is back a lot of people come to see Her, some unofficially. She has only been having orange juice recently. She came out this morning, and then not until 11.00 pm. Harsh Mehra, Anil, Anil's fiancée, Sita from Austria and Harsh's wife were there. Shri Mataji said that Anil's fiancée should go on a liver diet and should take some iron because she was looking very pale. Anil's fiancée said the doctors had told her she was very anaemic. Shri Mataji explained that when you have a bad liver, you

Shri Mataji at Pratishthan during the building work

do not feel like eating, so you lose weight and lack appetite, then you get anaemia. As She was about to leave Shri Mataji saw me.

'What is all this I hear about you having half a cup of milk in your tea?' She said. I told Her it was not me. Then She called one of the ladies and asked her and she said I wasn't drinking much tea. Shri Mataji said it had to be another Sahaja Yogi from England who is working here, and he should stop drinking so much tea. She said we can drink mint, basil (tulsi) and radish leaf tea. She said She is still working on us, and all the good will be gone if we are not careful. Just a few drops of milk are all we can have because milk is very bad for the liver. Also we can have kokum drink.

Friday: Shri Mataji told me to do the ground floor hall next, because She wants to invite the Sahaja Yogis here on December 15th, so the walls have to be plastered and the floors polished. While we were in the hall Shri Mataji mentioned that She was walking barefoot because the house was, at that point, horrible, because a lot of the work has not been done properly, so She has to tear things down and put a lot of things right. She said even the house needs vibrations.

When Shri Mataji finished in the hall, She went upstairs and a few of us went into Her living room with Her. She had Her hand on Her liver and asked for some water to put Her Feet in. She also drank lots of water and then one of the ladies dried Her Feet and massaged them. (In the leader's house in Bombay they had even put ice in the water then massaged Her Feet with a homeopathic cream and eucalyptus oil.)

After this Shri Mataji started to talk about London, saying that the Hampstead meetings were going very well. When She met the young people in London She saw from their eyes that they were seekers but were lost. Anywhere there were steps they would hang around with nothing to do, such as in Shaftesbury Avenue. One thing which had affected them was punk rock, which was no more, and drinking alcohol. She said that now they were break dancing. She felt very sorry for them and had given them bandhans. She said that the rich were getting very rich but the poor were getting worse off, the country was going down and the only thing going up was the pound, which enabled Her to keep the India Tour the same price for the last few years. There are forty English people coming this year, which was good, She said.

Derek Ferguson diary entries – Pratishthan, November and December

Saturday: In the evening we all watched the news with Shri Mataji, then there was a short film on about before Independence, and how badly the Indians were treated by the British.

She spoke about some people who wanted to get married and said there were a lot of older ladies but not older men. A lot of the ladies who wanted to get married were over fifty, which was unheard of in India. She spoke about Germany and said it is going well and they are getting a lot of Sahaja Yogis. She mentioned the different plots of land She has here, which are being held up by technicalities, including the land for the school.

Sunday: We watched the TV version of the Mahabharata with Shri Mataji. The time of the episodes was brought forward from 11.00 am to 8.30 am. Even the Sahaja Yogis were not going to the Sunday programmes so they could watch and Shri Mataji told them off. She mentioned that She was taking some tea and Sita fruit and was even doing a footsoak.

After everyone had gone Shri Mataji spoke to me about England and said that She had visited so many places in that country but the response has not been good even after all these years. She said that She has now lost interest in Shudy Camps, because the English were treating it like a holiday resort, and She wants to sell it. Shri Mataji mentioned that the English were very dry and a leading politician was a racist, even in her heart. She spoke about the people at the Customs in London and said they cannot detect the guilty people well, and often catch the wrong ones. They were even going to cut open the Indian Sahaja Yoga musicians' tablas and they opened up the harmonium to see what was inside. The musicians had explained that it had to be hollow to sound right, so the Customs people made them play the tabla just to check.

There is a lady who has been coming for the past week to massage Shri Mataji, and her husband is a barber, so Shri Mataji has arranged for him to come and cut the Sahaja Yogis' hair, including mine. I told Her that the Indians keep asking where I get my hair from and I say it comes from God. Shri Mataji laughed at this and said it is because people here would like to have this kind of hair, they regarded it as royal hair.

She told us that people should work spontaneously and not do too many drawings and plans, and gave the example of a French Sahaja Yogi who was not very good at anything, so tried marble work, but was too much into drawing and planning and the workers could not get on well with him. Then he changed to plumbing and was still making mistakes, but he is much better now. Less planning and more work, Shri Mataji said.

Monday: Went to Anil's house and Harsh was there – he had a present for Anil's wife from Shri Mataji – a photo frame, so she could have a photo of her husband to see when he was away.

Wednesday: Today I had to go to Bombay to renew my visa – Shri Mataji said I should go straight away – so I took the bus into Pune and the train to Bombay.

Thursday: The leader gave me the name and address of a Sahaja Yogi who could help me with my visa. I went to his office, near VT Station, and he told me to go to the visa office and say I had come for a puja, and to give him a ring if there were any problems. I went to the police office but the man there wanted some money. I told him I did not have any. He told me my papers had disappeared and to come back the next day, but then another man came and saw Shri Mataji's badge that I was wearing, and said he would help me.

I phoned the Sahaja Yogi who said he would help me, and we found a friend of his. When we told them I was from Jamaica, and part of the Commonwealth, he said there would be no charge and no problems with the visa. When the Sahaja Yogi told them I was with Shri Mataji and doing Sahaja Yoga, my papers suddenly turned up, they signed and stamped them and my passport. I thanked the Sahaja Yogi, after which I returned to Pune.

I saw Shri Mataji and told Her the story, which She liked very much, and said we should wear Her badge all the time, even in Pune.

Chapter 13

1988: December India

Derek Ferguson diary entries

Friday: Worked on plastering the barrel ceiling and saw Shri Mataji leave for Vaitarna, where the tour is at present.

Monday: Spoke to an Australian Sahaja Yogi who had just come from Vaitarna. Shri Mataji had arranged most of the marriages but some people who had put their names down had not come, so there had to be some changes. She said that Sahaja Yoga is the only group where you can get married four times in succession, one at a time, but if people try to stick together it would be better.

Tuesday: Shri Mataji has gone to Nasik for a puja. About 180 Sahaja Yogis have arrived from abroad, and in all 354 are expected. About 80% are new.

Every leaf that was moving was full of Her love

It was the India tour of the years 1988/9. I was in charge of the French collective that year. One day we had a camp outside Aurangabad on a hill and Shri Mataji called the leaders to have a meeting about marriages. The feeling was great, and I arrived a bit late. We were sitting round a big table and Shri Mataji invited me to come and sit next to Her. She took a couple of cushions and arranged them so I would sit comfortably. I felt spoiled, and felt Her love in every aspect.

She passed me the people's forms and asked me what I thought of this one, and that one, and asked me questions even though I had no idea what to say, but it was a question of being part of it, and being so protected by Her. She invited me to feel part of the meeting and I felt so much bliss and security. On that tour I felt Shri Mataji everywhere, every leaf that was moving was full of Her love and I was part of it, sitting next to Her. When She showed me the forms, I had no idea what was going on, but She showed them to me to make me feel good – She was managing the whole thing.

Siddheshvara Barbier

India tour 1988/9 (diary entry)

We are in the mountains near Aurangabad, on the 9th December, 1988. We have already had a puja on this large flat topped mountain, typical of the interior of Maharashtra. Shri Mataji has been with us. We saw Her on the first evening that we arrived here from Bombay, to Nasik, and the buses deposited us at a place where She was just finishing a public programme. The public programmes are very different now, and there seems to be more music than words. Shri Mataji gave a short talk, and the rest was bhajans and instrumental music; and also at times people were dancing and singing for joy. The vibrations were less heavy, perhaps because we are clearer, and the Kundalini of the universe can rise more strongly through the Sushumna Nadi. The peace and the depth of this vibrated land were like manna for us.

Yesterday morning at breakfast time Shri Mataji came out of Her cottage and had a short talk with us. She asked us what was the value and significance of this journey around Maharashtra, for us Westerners. She said this land has been especially vibrated by all the incarnations, Shri Rama and Shri Sita even walked here without shoes – and there are so many swayambhus of Shri Ganesha and the other deities in this area. She said that we must meditate every day, because to meditate on this land clears all the problems of the left side, from the Mooladhara to the Agnya, and we should put our left hand towards the photo and the right one on the earth. This land helps us to find peace and silence within us, which is difficult in our countries where life is so frantic and there is always so much to do.

Later, someone said that the point of this tour was to enjoy tapasya, but Shri Mataji pretended not to hear, and replied, 'How? Chapattis?' and everyone laughed. Then She said that this tour is not supposed to be tapasya.

Alessandra Pallini

Derek Ferguson diary entries - Pratishthan, December

Wednesday: Someone mentioned that I had a certain newspaper – I didn't but went to Pune to get it because Shri Mataji wanted to see it. She said I should go to the camp in the car with the barber.

Thursday: Left the house at 6.00 am for the camp, a nice setup and I saw all the Sahaja Yogis. Went to the programme in Pune and Shri Mataji spoke in Marathi and before She gave Her talk some Sahaja Yogis sang songs.

Saturday: A van came from the camp and picked us up for the puja. We had bhajans before Shri Mataji arrived, then She gave a talk about the mariadas and punyas of each chakra, then we had bhajans again. After that Shri Mataji gave out presents to a lot of people and we had food and went to Pune for a Marathi play. The play was about Shri Krishna winning Shri Rukmini as his bride.

Rahuri, 11th December, 1988 (diary entry)

We arrived here last night, at this wonderful place which is Mr Dhumal's farm. Today we had a puja, the second of the tour. Shri Mataji came from Her house at about midday. Her talk was beautiful and maternal, and was mostly about marriage and its significance in Sahaja Yoga, which is that it is an instrument for our ascent.

At the end of the puja every Sahaja Yogi could offer a garland to Shri Mataji's Feet and experience incredible joy. The music, and Shri Mataji's words, took us to the Sahasrara and it was like waves, drops of water resounding to infinity, producing a joy which was indescribable.

One day recently Shri Mataji mentioned our transformation, and how we are changed, and how much joy there is on our faces. She said She was so proud of us, and so loved us, but has also made some remarks to the leaders, that we eat too much and we are not punctual. Another thing Shri Mataji said was that when we are in the buses, travelling from place to place, we should always try to sit next to different people and not with people of our own country.

Alessandra Pallini

Sangamner, 12th December 1988 (diary entry)

We are sitting under the palm trees in this delightful place near a river. There was a programme at Sangamner this evening in a big hall and it was rather heavy. Shri Mataji spoke for a long time, gave realisation and then invited everyone to have Her darshan. When She gave realisation She did not say the affirmations for each chakra, and did not have us put our hands on the different chakras, but just asked people to put their hands towards Her, and then on their Sahasrara, then to put their hands up to feel the chaitanya. It was like a puja, the Sahasrara open and joyous. At the end She was very happy and said, 'Namaskar, Shrirampur, namaskar.'

Shri Mataji commented on the performance of the sitarist. She said he had exceptional attention and concentration, the fruit of his dedication to this discipline, the principle of his guru. She said that we Sahaja Yogis should be the same in order to achieve our spiritual ascent. Besides, She said that the speed and skill of the sitarist would have been impossible without the presence of the Sahaja Yogis, and that their vibrations had been the vehicle for the perfection of the playing.

Alessandra Pallini

Pink and green

In 1988, my friend was in Pune. We were talking about sari colours and I said I would like a strong pink but would never buy that for myself. The next day we were in Pratishthan, and Shri Mataji gave us saris. She told the lady to bring a certain sari. She looked at me.

'This sari is bright pink,' She said. 'I know you would like this colour, but open it.' The palau was green, and She said, 'See, this is matching your eyes.'

Sita Wadhwa

Pune, 17th December 1988 (diary entry)

We are all together in a multicoloured pendal on the bank of the River Mutanwadi, waiting for Shri Mataji, to celebrate the third puja of the tour. There are about three hundred and fifty foreigners and many Indians from Pune. There is a pleasant breeze which refreshes us, because it is a bit hot at this hour. The puja was marvellous and Shri Mataji said that Pune is the city of punyas – good deeds. After the puja She stayed with us for some time. She ate food with us and then continued to arrange the weddings, until there were seventy couples. She arranged for ladies to buy saris and have the blouses made, and also arranged for the distribution of saris to be presented at the pujas in the West – we were given two for Italy, meaning we would be blessed with two pujas this year. Then She gave presents to the men – shawls and dhotis of many colours. To the Italian leader She gave a violet coloured one, saying that would be good for the left Vishuddhi, (the religion practised in Italy gives a bad left Vishuddhi) and another Italian lady and I also got violet coloured sari as gifts.

We have been in Pune for three days and there have been two public programmes which were full of people, including some Westerners. Both programmes began with bhajans, a group of both Western Sahaja Yogis and the Pune music group. Shri Mataji was very pleased with the result.

Last night another Sahaja Yogini and I were honoured to present the garland to Shri Mataji, and to do the aarti to Her. We were a little late, and the lights did not want to light, because of the wind, and Shri Mataji entered very fast.

In Pune we went shopping, and among other places, we went to the shop where Shri Mataji had bought a lot of saris for the weddings. In the evening we went to see a musical comedy in classical Marathi, about Shri Krishna and Shri Rukmini. At the end the curtain closed to a lot of applause, and when it reopened, there was Shri Mataji. She explained to everyone in the theatre how important and how good the actors were, the whole cast. She said they would have a great future in the West.

While at Pune, Shri Mataji said that we gain good punyas on the Swadisthan chakra through loving and admiring nature and art. It is impossible not to admire the ancient and changeless places we have visited, and where the saints and incarnations have taken their births. And as our procession of seven buses wends its way through the countryside and villages it invites curiosity, surprise and admiration, according to Shri Mataji.

Alessandra Pallini

Divine cooking

I remember the day Shri Mataji cooked for us at Pratishthan in 1988. It was so delicious! It is like it happened yesterday. She went to the back of the house, they had made a fire and there was a big pot and Shri Mataji was tasting the food sometimes. She said that when She was cooking She always tasted it so She knew if it was good and could control the taste better.

Bruno Descaves

A visit to Pratishthan, 18th December 1988 (diary entry)

Yesterday Shri Mataji invited us to spend the day at Her new house, Pratishthan, this temple to the living God, but also Her home. Many of us

Shri Mataji cooking at Pratishthan

felt we were out of time, and the three hundred and fifty of us were guests here, and able to admire it with the most extraordinary guide – Shri Mataji Herself. When we entered She was sitting outside the kitchen, busy preparing food for all of us, with Her daughter Kalpana.

After some time She led us and showed us this extraordinary building. It is large and the outer walls are of white marble. There were sections of inlaid and sculptured stone from a palace that Shri Mataji had bought and reassembled here. There was an internal colonnade of a form invented by Shri Mataji, antique carved doors, decorations and a fountain of carved marble, terraces and balconies, a divine palace never seen before, absolutely regal.

'What do you think of My architecture?' Shri Mataji asked one of the yogis who is an architect, at the end of the visit. She laughed and went on walking, followed by all the Sahaja Yogis.

Then She went and sat in the large living room, and all the saris that were still for sale were there. They were for people getting married, some were bought by husbands for their wives, and some ladies bought them too. After this Shri Mataji went to the kitchen, for cooking. When the meal was ready She came to where everyone was seated in long rows, ready to be served.

'Your food is ready now, come and get it,' She said. It was a chicken biryani with salads, and Shri Mataji ate with us.

Alessandra Pallini

Something you can't forget

We were invited to visit Pratishthan, then under construction, on the India Tour of 1988/9 and Shri Mataji Herself led the visit. It is huge and we were possibly two hundred people trying to keep as near to Mother as possible. Sometimes you thought you had lost touch with the head of the line and suddenly Shri Mataji appeared in front of you, coming with a large smile from another corridor, another door, and you were near Her for a few minutes. It turned into a hide and seek situation, with the Adi Shakti leading the game, smiling at our surprise, something you can't forget. Shri Mataji cooked for us, and we all had dinner with Her in the main hall that evening.

Devarshi Abalain

The beginnings of Sahaja Yoga in Brazil

In 1987, I went to live in Salvador, Brazil, with my wife Tereza. I wrote a letter to Shri Mataji, and She said I should begin to do something about

The Western Sahaja Yogis visiting Pratishthan

Sahaja Yoga there. In September 1988 we did the first public programme in Salvador.

During the India Tour of 1988, at Shri Mataji's house of Pratishthan, She asked how things were going in Brazil. She said it would be better for me to live there than return to Italy, because She wanted to go there, so we did: we made contacts, translated texts, prepared posters – everything for organising public programmes.

Duilio Cartocci

We longed for this day

On the 18th of December 1988, we had the privilege to visit our Divine Mother's home – Pratishthan. We longed for this day to come because Mother also promised to cook a meal for us, around three hundred and fifty yogis and yoginis!

When we arrived, Shri Mataji led everyone on a tour in Her house. It is huge and well designed. Actually, we should not use the word 'house' because it is so grand. In a sense, it is a temple of the Goddess. It had been under construction for more than two years. A Sahaja Yogi from Pune told me that he used to come to help when the school was off. Every yogi from Pune liked to come to work because you felt so many vibrations while working around the house. After the house tour, Mother excused Herself to prepare the big meal.

Our Holy Mother was in the midst of kitchen smokes and hot stoves. She tasted every pot and added spices as necessary for this special meal. When it was finally served, everyone ate with such gratitude. Who else in the world could be as lucky as us to have a meal prepared by Goddess Herself! Shri Mataji told us that the rice we were eating was from the seeds vibrated by Her before planting.

Before She started to cook, I requested Shri Mataji to give me a new name, and She gave me the name Sarvesh. It means the great one God we serve, or the primordial power.

Sarvesh Su

Derek Ferguson, diary entries, Pratishthan, December

Sunday: The Sahaja Yogis on the tour all came here at about 11.00 am to view Pratishthan. Shri Mataji said they had arrived early but could come in and have the free run of the house. They all piled in and wandered round while Shri Mataji started to cook and supervise the cooking with Her daughters. People were standing there, amazed at what was happening, and the meal was mutton biryani, chicken salad, chapattis and a very nice sweet dish. When it came to serving Shri Mataji told everyone it was self–service, and in Her house men and women were the same and there was no reason for the men to be served by the women.

Shri Mataji also did a tour of the house and told everyone what the different areas were for, and said She was trying to make the people hungry by walking around. Then we ate, the food was fantastic, and She gave some presents to Her daughter from the Sahaja Yogis. We also had some of Her medicine, added to water for the sick people. Eventually it was time to go and She told people not to cry, because if they did She would cry and we would be washed away by Her tears.

Last week Shri Mataji gave me a wool jacket and wool jumper, both very nice.

Monday: Waited all day to speak to Shri Mataji and just before She left at 4.00 pm, I asked Her about the work, and there is not much left to be done.

Wednesday: Went to Pune about my ticket for Ganapatipule and when I got back Shri Mataji was already there. She said I looked well, but when

I returned to England I should not eat too much cheese, butter and other dairy products.

She spoke about solar energy for Her house, to a Spanish Sahaja Yogi. He has to prepare things for heating a secondary water tank on the roof. Shri Mataji spoke about my plane ticket and said there was a man in Air India in Bombay who would help me to go back to England.

Thursday: Had to see Shri Mataji again and She spoke about England, saying the Derby Sahaja Yogis said they were having 'revelations' and She asked the main person behind it to leave Sahaja Yoga. She mentioned that they need someone with a knowledge of vibrations to lead them. She said She is going to sell Shudy Camps and it just needs some work finishing off first.

Someone wanted to go to the Taj Mahal, and wanted to stay with the Delhi Sahaja Yogis but Shri Mataji said it would be better to stay in the ashram, and She would give him a letter of introduction, because not all the Indian Sahaja Yogis were genuine and some of them might ask him for cameras etc.

Shri Mataji has not been well these last few weeks and has cancelled some of Her India Tour. She had caught flu in Saudi Arabia.

An experience out of time

In Pune I was working on stained glass in Shri Mataji's house, Pratishthan. Shri Mataji arrived and we did namaskar and She looked at various people and asked how their families were and that sort of thing. Then She invited us up to Her apartment because when the building was at a certain stage She lived there, not in the main house. She sat down and started talking. There were about twenty people in the room. First of all, She scolded the woman who was looking after Her at the time. Then She progressed to every person in the room.

'You've got a liver. The livers are dreadful.'

'Your vibrations are shocking.'

'Your Swadishthan needs clearing out.'

'You need to shoebeat this. Shoebeat that.' She went right round the room and then She looked at me. So I gave a big smile. I was waiting for my turn.

'And what do you think of this house?' She said to me.

'I think it is quite fantastic. It's one of the most imaginative things I have seen in my life.'

I teach art and architecture and so on. Then She sat there and there was no other comment. We were there, I calculated later, from about 12:30 in the afternoon until about seven in the evening, sitting in meditation. I thought, 'It must be afternoon by now.' When I went down to get a cup of tea, everything was dark. It was seven hours roughly and the sense of time was totally cut through. So I guess it was some level of existence. Maybe in the future we will experience more of this and the concern about time — nothing so tightly bound. It felt like the whole day, you were out of time. I have never felt an experience out of time like that.

John Henshaw

The 'gana'

In about 1988, Shri Mataji taught us to look at the ridiculous and laugh at it rather than get angry. There was a gentleman with Her who was like a gana around Her. He had a very stern look and a very nasty tongue. We all used to wonder how he was close to our Mother. When he spoke to Her he would become all soft and polite. He was only devoted to Her and didn't care for anyone else.

One day the Sahaja Yogis went to Shri Mataji and complained to Her that he would not let them come anywhere near Her. He was almost like a guard dog.

'That's why I keep him near Me, to keep him out of harm's way,' She laughed and said.

Deepa Mahajan

We never felt tired

In about 1988, when we were working in Prathisthan every evening I would go home and have a bath, change out of my working clothes and come back to Prathisthan to sit with Shri Mataji and enjoy the evening. We would gather around Shri Mataji and chitchat with Her. She would explain many aspects, about Sahaja Yoga, or clearing out or look into any problem of Sahaja Yogis. People would present their poems or songs. We would then meditate with Her and this would go on till about 2–3.00 am in the morning.

One amazing thing was that even if we did not have enough sleep we never felt tired.

Deepa Mahajan

Ah, Buddha, how beautiful!

During the 1988 India tour, we visited a handicraft exhibition in Pune. There were many stalls with clothes, jewellery, leather articles, carvings and other things from all over India. Shri Mataji was also there for some time to look at the exhibition and do a little shopping.

Like everyone else, I strolled from one kiosk to the other and stopped at some nice wooden carvings. I liked some of them very much, specially a Shri Buddha statue. I took it in my hand to look at it closer. As I was standing there, I realised that Shri Mataji was standing next to me and looking at some carvings which the kiosk holder was showing Her. As usual, She was surrounded by a large crowd of people.

Being so close to Mother was too much for me and I went two steps backwards, so I was standing behind Her. I was thinking that I would not keep all the things bought in India, although I liked them very much, but would use them as presents for those who stayed back in Austria. I was also thinking that if Shri Mataji would touch one of these statues, I would keep it and place it on my altar at home. Lost in this thought, I did not realise that all the people had left and as I looked up, only Shri Mataji was there. She looked at me and came towards me. Everything was so bright all of a sudden. She greeted me and asked if I had already purchased something. I was so perplexed that I couldn't answer, then She saw the Buddha statue in my hand.

'Ah, Buddha, how beautiful,' She said. She took it in Her hand to look at it, then She gave it to me in a very friendly and gentle way.

Edwin Tobias

Just enjoy

In 1988, my wife Ruth went on the India tour. One day, there was a visit to a craft market in Pune. As Shri Mataji toured the stalls, She was – as so often – surrounded by a large crowd of people. Ruth held back. She wasn't feeling particularly good about herself and at this moment did not want to put herself into Mother's attention. After a while she became involved in buying some silk paintings. When she next looked about her, she realised that the market had more or less emptied and Shri Mataji was nowhere to be seen. Supposing that Mother had left, she continued wandering around. Suddenly she saw Shri Mataji walking towards her and there was no–one with Her. Ruth bowed.

'How are you, Ruth?' Shri Mataji asked.

'Very well, Mother,' Ruth replied politely.

'Just enjoy, just enjoy,' said Shri Mataji, and walked on.

Yet when Ruth returned to the camp, she was told that such an encounter could not possibly have happened – Shri Mataji had been with people all the time.

Chris Greaves

Shri Mataji was praising the work of the craftsmen

On the 1988/9 India trip we visited an arts and crafts fair in Pune and Shri Mataji was there too. Wandering around between the stands, you would sometimes cross Mother's way, take Her darshan for a while and then continue your visit. I was near a stand selling carved conches and there was an American yogi next to me. Suddenly Shri Mataji was there, praising the work of the craftsmen. She took one of the conchs in Her hand, and then put it back on the table before leaving for another stand. The American yogi and I remained kind of spaced out for a while, but he was the quickest to get back to his senses and immediately asked for the conch that Shri Mataji had taken.

Devarshi Abalain

Brahmapuri, 20th December 1988 (diary entry)

At Brahmapuri Shri Mataji spoke to us, when we were in the river, and here are a few of the things She said. Ramdas, who was an incarnation of Shri Hanumana, found the statues of Shri Rama, Shri Sita, Shri Lakshmana and Shri Hanumana and took them to a temple. At the age of fifteen, Shri Mahadeva said he should die, but above all the gods is Shri Adi Shakti. He became Her bhakta and She appeared to him, and stayed there as a swayambhu.

Ramdas was the guru of King Shivaji. He was fed up with all the administration and wanted to give Ramdas his kingdom, but Ramdas said no, you be detached. Most of the incarnations in India were kings: Shri Mahavira, Shri Buddha, Shri Rama and Shri Krishna. Christ had the qualities of Shri Ganesha, humility, and was pure chaitanya, but He was the King of Kings.

She also said that the gurus, Abraham, Confucius etc, tried to free people from poverty.

Sahaja Yogis have to know what is happening in the world and should work out, through their attention, international people. We should be alert and take a vow to be responsible for Sahaja Yoga. At times funny people have come to Sahaja Yoga and have occasionally even become leaders, but we should not worry about them, because they go out, and it is a warning for us not to become like them.

Alessandra Pallini

The highest of heights is the heart of Her disciple

During the India tour of 1988, Shri Mataji gathered us at Her Feet for a concert on the banks of the Krishna River. I felt that Shri Mataji was very much working on all of us. She was beating time throughout on Her left knee, probably to cure our Left Nabhis. At the end of the concert Shri Mataji said to us that the Devi resides in the Himalayas and that She is surrounded by tigers. She resides there because She loves the heights and, for Her, the highest of heights is the heart of Her disciple. As we were all surrounding Her with an infinite stream of love and devotion, I felt that this allegory depicted that we Sahaja Yogis were Her tigers.

Gwennael Verez

Written at Sangli, 21st December 1988 (diary entry)

At Brahmapuri yesterday there was a puja in the garden of a little house, near where, four years ago, Shri Mataji had sat with Her Feet in the river. This year we again all bathed in the cool fresh water, and felt the peace and silence. There were not many Indians at the puja, only those from Sangli who helped in the organisation. Brahmapuri is a long way from a big town, and yesterday, at Atita, Shri Mataji said that the people's vibrations were very innocent and pure. The evening before there had been two public programmes in other places, and again the vibrations were good and the Kundalinis rose easily.

Here at Sangli we had a puja to Shri Mahalakshmi, the third or fourth in this area, near Kolhapur. We were all ready for the puja at eleven o'clock in the morning, but Shri Mataji did not come until much later. She sent a message that She was tired after so many public programmes and the puja the day before at Brahmapuri. We spent the day in meditation and singing bhajans, and the day seemed like a puja even without Her presence.

It was almost seven o'clock in the evening when Shri Mataji came, and we did not get to bed until about three in the morning, but despite that we got up at about seven, because Shri Mataji has asked to get up early and meditate, every day.

Alessandra Pallini

Ganapatipule, 23rd December 1988 (diary entry)

We were waiting for Shri Mataji in the pendal, here in this earthly paradise of Ganapatipule. She arrived about half past eight, from Kolhapur. She said She had not been well on the previous day, and asked how many of us were sick. Many of us had coughs, upset stomachs and fever. Shri Mataji said that the reason for Her illness was us. When She asked the doctor how high Her fever was, he told Her.

'That is not a fever, I thought it was at least 104 degrees – 41 degrees centigrade. I can go to the college with this!' She said. She advised us to not dwell on the fact we were ill, or we would be worse. She gave us some hints to help us.

Wash in cold water.

When we have a fever we should not drink cold water without first eating a bit of sugar or a biscuit.

Dust irritates the throat, so it is a good thing to gargle with salt and water in the evening after a journey.

Wear enough clothes, when the evening is cool.

Alessandra Pallini

Ganapatipule, 24th December 1988 (diary entry)

We had been buying jewellery and silver for the weddings in the pendal, and Shri Mataji, came after we had finished our meal. She was welcomed with a carpet of flowers and Her entrance was preceded by two lines of girls who went in front of Her, scattering flowers at Her Feet.

There are about three thousand people here, and Indian people have come from all parts of the country. Music is the most important aspect of this seminar. There are not so many talks or meditation sessions, although Shri Mataji has instructed that we all meditate together every morning, but so much music! Groups of musicians from every part of India, and the

West, instrumentalists and vocalists, every night until very late, we never sleep more than three or four hours, and it is important to try to stay alert during the evening programmes.

On Christmas night, Shri Mataji explained that while the other incarnations were born in royal families, Christ, who was innocence and humility personified, took His birth in a very simple family. We had bhajans until four in the morning, and Baba Mama led the programme, with joy, enthusiasm, and jokes.

On the night of the 26th there was a tremendous concert by Debu Chauderi, and Shri Mataji began distributing an endless amount of gifts. She did this until ten o'clock the following morning. They were given first to the foreigners and then to the Indians, and everyone thanked Her from their hearts.

Alessandra Pallini

Ganapatipule, 28th December 1988 (diary entry)

This was the day of the weddings. In the morning we met on the beach at the place chosen by Shri Mataji for the haldi. She was on the veranda in front of Her cottage, presiding over events. When everyone was covered in the yellow paste we had a bathe in the ocean.

The weddings were in the evening and first the ladies, looking beautiful in their saris and golden ornaments, went in front of Shri Mataji for the Gauri Puja. Then they lined up behind the cloth and their husbands–to–be arrived with a band. The celebrations went on until four in the morning, with music and dancing. The next morning we all went to pay our respects to the swayambhu of Shri Mahaganesha here.

Throughout the tour, whether in the presence of Shri Mataji at the pujas, or whether for some other reason, I was in direct contact with Her on an interior level, for instance at Pune during the aarti, or at the public programme at Rahuri when I offered Her the garland, or during the Gauri Puja at Ganapatipule when I was near Her throne to take a photo of the newlyweds, or when I was called, with great joy, to offer the saris, one from the West and the other from India, and was able to also offer fruit on Shri Mataji's lap.

In such moments, due to the profound presence of Shri Mataji, I felt only the desire to thank Her – a great sense of gratitude towards the Divine Mother who has given me so many blessings, most of all this bliss, this joy of the Sahasrara, which overtakes and sweeps away every thought, every desire and gives total fulfilment and joy, the presence of God in our consciousness. All differences of sex, culture, age, role in life, are annulled in the true collectivity of Sahaja Yogis in the Sahasrara of Shri Mataji, the heart of the universal being. This enables us to know who we really are, away from the illusion of corporal appearances, so we can permanently become one with this profound love, this deep sense of peace, which emanates from being close to Her.

Alessandra Pallini

Please Shri Mataji, allow me to recognize You fully

It was during India Tour 1988/89, I was twenty–two years old and new in the Sahaj Sangham. I had indeed just got my realisation three months earlier. At that time we could offer a flower garland to Shri Mataji at the end of the puja. We would line up and offer it on the stage where She was still sitting and talking to various people. As I was a new Sahaja Yogini, my ego was sometimes still annoying me with doubts, though I was convinced through meditative experiences that Sahaja Yoga was the way and the method.

'Please Shri Mataji, allow me to recognise You fully,' I therefore prayed in my heart while giving the flowers and doing namaskar.

Then I looked at Her, and to my astonishment She stopped talking and had turned Her face towards me. She nodded Her head, saying, 'Yes!' I was so surprised and so touched. She had heard my prayer and answered me.

I went back to the end of the pendal with a light and blissful heart. Suddenly I felt a lot of vibrations flowing down through my Sahasrara and filling my whole body. It was so strong that I felt dizzy and lay down on the ground. I remained peaceful and thoughtless for a while. Then I had a vision: the beautiful feeling of a harmonious family, a father, a mother, children, happy and peaceful, a house. Shri Mataji made me feel the peace and the deep satisfaction of an open Nabhi and the beauty of the Lakshmi tattwa.

I noticed that this vision had cleansed me from my feminist conditionings and later another vision occurred to me: the picture of a very disciplined, serious and austere Yogi, shoebeating, grey and cold, and the contrast with Shri Ganesha, joyful, innocent, spontaneous though wise and powerful. I started to laugh, it was a relief.

Catherine Hallé

Shri Mataji called her back

One time in the late eighties I was not able to go to Ganapatipule because I was pregnant, and was a little bit depressed. All my family went to Ganapatipule. When Shri Mataji was giving gifts to the Calcutta Sahaja Yogis, my mother–in–law went up. Shri Mataji gave a sari to her, and she was about to leave the stage. Shri Mataji called her back and gave her another sari, for me, even though I wasn't there. When they came back it was so amazing that Shri Mataji had remembered me! She only saw me two or three times before that.

Mahua Sarkar

Giving gifts for fourteen hours

At Ganapatipule, Shri Mataji was on the stage and gifts were being given out to everyone. I did not want to go up, but eventually someone said I should because it was prasad. Shri Mataji had been there, overseeing the giving of gifts, for a very long time, and at one point She just closed Her eyes for a very short time, and when She opened them again She was quite fresh once more. In all She sat on the stage giving gifts for fourteen hours.

'Why are you so late? Now, what to give you?' Shri Mataji said when I did go up, and She took a badge with Her photo on it and put it on Her heart. Then She gave it to me.

Once Shri Mataji had a fever and after ten minutes the fever had gone. We asked Shri Mataji about this.

'I only said, "This fever is not Mine," and the fever has to go away,' She said.

Videh Saundankar

The experience of recognition I had asked for

I had only gained recognition of Shri Mataji for a fairly short time, when I went on my first India Tour in the late 1980's. I had some wonderful experiences during the time in Maharashtra but I wanted that recognition to strengthen, so asked Shri Mataji in meditation for an experience to bring that about.

At that time I was a student of architecture and my mind had a habit of trying to mentally redesign everything around me. When we got to Ganapatipule I thought I had overcome this problem, but in the fierce midday sun the thought arose, 'These trees should be of a different species that can provide better shade. They should have more attractive leaves. I would plant some over there,' and so on.

The next day there was a puja in which Shri Mataji talked about the complication of the Western mind. At one point She said words to the effect, 'the Western mind is so critical that it sees even a tree and wants to redesign it.'

I realised at that moment that Shri Mataji, as the Supreme Self in all beings, knows our every thought. That was the experience of recognition I had asked for, and in the same moment Shri Mataji looked right at me, where I sat in the pendal, and smiled so compassionately that it dissolved all that criticizing tendency.

Graham Brown

I feel that touch

I come originally from Shillong, near Assam in north–eastern India. My first meeting with Shri Mataji was at Ganapatipule in the 1980's. I was really eager to see Her. I knew She was God on earth. From my childhood I had seen the pictures of all the deities and I always wanted to see one, and now I was going to see Her in front of me. The first time I saw Shri Mataji walk up to the stage at Ganapatipule it was like a dream fulfilled for me – this is God, this is Her.

One time my brother Rishi and I performed one or two songs for Shri Mataji. Baba Mama presented us to Mother and said we were from Shillong, very far off. He said on the mike, to everyone, that we had saved all year to buy gifts for people and to come here, and we were shocked – how did he know all these things? The first time I was in front of Mother, I bowed down to Her and She touched me on my heart.

'May God bless you', She said, and whenever I think about that moment, I feel that touch. 'Very nice,' She said.

Shoma Arcilio

You should serve your guests first

After the Ganapatipule seminar in 1988/9, it was announced that there would be a puja at Alibagh, a village near Mumbai. Many yogis from all over the world went to it. After the programme was over, we, the yogis from

Mumbai had dinner and went to the buses which had been hired to take us back to Mumbai. Before the buses left, we got a message from Shri Mataji to come back to the programme. When we arrived, She was not on the puja stage but at the entrance of the house. She was upset with us, as we had all had our food before the foreigners. She asked us how we could eat before our visitors.

'You should serve them the food first. You should be taking care of them,' She said.

We realised our mistake and felt very ashamed. Then all the foreigners were asked to sit in a row and everyone from the Mumbai collective served them their food. Shri Mataji was walking in between the rows, looking at each person to see what was missing on his or her plate. She was calling us to come and serve rice here, dal there, etc. She not only told us our mistake but made us face it and correct ourselves. At that time I was just a teenager, and hardly knew anything about the Lakshmi principle, but the example She showed us will stay with me for the rest of my life.

Maneesha Shanbhag-Cruz

The first mobile phone

In 1988 there was the first New Year Puja at Alibagh. A miracle took place in the house. Shri Mataji reached there around 7.00 pm from Ganapatipule, and many other Western yogis too. When Mother stepped out of the car She was so surprised.

'This place is so beautiful. I always wanted to come here,' She said. Mother went into the bedroom and said to the other yogis, 'I must tell Sir CP about this place and he must come and visit it.' She asked one of the yogis if somebody could get Her a phone as She wanted to call Mumbai. Since it was not a developed/ village there were no phones. Then She asked Mr Koli for a coconut. He asked Shri Mataji if She wanted to eat one and She said She did not, but She wanted a fresh one from the tree. A village boy climbed up and got one in ten minutes and gave it to Her. She went into Her room and closed the door.

Many country leaders were sitting in the hall outside, and after an hour one of the leaders came and said that Shri Mataji was using the coconut as a phone and they had heard She was speaking to Sir CP for nearly an hour. Later the yogis found out that this was the year that mobile phones first came out.

Lena Koli

Shri Adi Shakti always follows Lord Shiva

A few of us yogis were sitting around Shri Mataji and Mr Koli asked Mother if a certain story from our grandfather's time was true. The story went like this: there once came a man, very large and smart, walking on the seashore.

Puja at Alibagh, 1988

'Now you have come back from fishing, how were the waters and how much fish did you catch?' he asked the fishermen. One fisherman jokingly said that there were a lot of stones in the sea and less fish. The next day when all the fishermen wanted to go out they saw the sea was full of stones everywhere and they could not go fishing. They realised the man from the day before must have had something to do with it, and they all went searching for him. After walking for a few miles they saw him sitting under a banyan tree with closed eyes. The fisherman who had been joking the day before went running up to him and fell at his feet and asked forgiveness.

'Tathastu,' the man said, meaning 'Blessings forever', and then said, 'go, everything will be all right'. From that day everyone in the village worshiped at that tree and said it was Lord Shiva. Shri Mataji said that the story was true.

'Shri Adi Shakti always follows Lord Shiva and that is the reason I am here now,' She said. After that all the yogis and we went to the seashore with Shri Mataji, and She was barefoot.

Lena Koli

All the gods had a meeting in heaven

After coming to Sahaja Yoga Mr Koli put all the pictures of gods he had in the ocean.

'If Mother is Shri Adi Shakti,' he said, 'I don't need the other pictures', but he did not have the heart to throw the picture away of the gods dancing at the Feet of Shri Adi Shakti, which is now in the mantra book.

'Mother,' he asked Her, 'I feel You are the One who is sitting there, but what is the meaning of this picture?'

'All the gods had a meeting in heaven,' Shri Mataji said, 'because they did not know what to do with humanity. Whichever aspect of God was sent to the earth, the people troubled them, i.e. Christ, Shri Rama, Shri Krishna.

'I will go as a Mother for mankind, and I will go like a normal person with all the worries, sadness and happiness in life,' Shri Adi Shakti said. 'I will go through everything and also through all the mayas (illusions).' This announcement of Shri Adi Shakti was a blessing for the gods, and this was the joyful incident when all the gods are dancing, so Adi Shakti is there to help them.'

Anand Thandev, meaning Joyful Dance, was the name given by Shri Mataji to the picture. After this announcement Shri Mataji said Mr Koli should make thousands of copies of this picture, and give it out to yogis all over the world so each one could have one in his or her house. It brings joy and love to everyone.

Lena Koli

The gods had a meeting in heaven

Chapter 14

1989: January to March India and Nepal

You cannot force anyone

It was January 1989 and I was living in India. I was at Pratishthan and Shri Mataji started to talk about Indian culture with me, and I told Her I was reading the Mahabharata.

'You see,' She explained, 'that all happened because you cannot force anyone into marriage.'

Sita Wadhwa

I think you asked for a name

We went to Pratishthan in 1989 and we'd sit every morning with Shri Mataji and have tea and then work on Her house. I had always wanted to have a name because I had felt that my name wasn't my name. The first Ganesha Puja that we'd been to was in Los Angeles in 1986, and at one point all the children and infants were called up on stage. I really wanted to go and get a name from Mother, but I could see that no other adults were doing that and didn't know what the protocol was. But there we were in Mother's apartment in Pratishthan, so I asked if She would give me a name.

We were sitting with Shri Mataji, and we were very thoughtless. The carpet man came, with a younger man to do all the physical work. It was like being in a sari shop where they roll the saris out, then you look, then they roll out another one. So he'd roll out a carpet. Mother would look at the carpet.

'What do you think of this carpet?' She'd say, and She'd look at somebody.

'Oh, it's very beautiful, Mother,' then you'd have to say something else, so you'd say, 'Well, I see there are beautiful green patterns and white stars.' Mother would smile, and then the next carpet would get rolled out. She'd look at another yogi or yogini.

'What do you think of this carpet?'

'Oh, it's a very deep red, Mother,' then the next carpet rolled out.

'This carpet is from Pratishthan,' She said, or something like that. 'Look at the floral design, and this is telling something about the deity. Now see the thread count, this is a high quality one. See the way the knots are tied.' She started educating us about carpets; it was just so sweet.

There were more wonderful days. Then we were getting ready to leave and Mother was sleeping in Her apartment, so we all did namaskar by Her door and went out to a little twelve–seat minivan to go to Mumbai to catch our flight. Mother walked down from Her apartment to say Her goodbye to us. She knew we were leaving and came down to say goodbye so we could thank Her graciously. She thanked us for working there and then pointed at me.

'I think you asked for a name,' She said.

'Yes, Mother.'

'Dattatreya would be a good name.' That was how I got my name.

Dattatreya Haynes

Shri Hanuman's mischief

In February 1989 Shri Mataji went to Chorwad near Junagadh, the ancestral home of an old Sahaja Yogi in Gujarat, and he had arranged Dandiya. This is a Gujarati dance performed collectively with batons, around Navaratri.

The songs have a special beat and the lady who was singing the songs had a very nasal voice. We all danced and danced. Later Shri Mataji asked the lady to come and get her realisation. When Shri Mataji raised her Kundalini, she suddenly started feeling very thirsty. So a glass of water was brought for her, but try as much as she would she could not bring the glass to her lips. Shri Mataji asked her what the matter was.

'Whenever I try to lift the glass I feel someone is holding my hand and not allowing me to drink the water,' she said. Shri Mataji was smiling with a twinkle in Her eye. She asked her who she followed.

'Hanuman,' the lady said.

Shri Mataji then asked her to ask, 'Shri Mataji, are You sakshat Shri Hanuman?'

The lady started asking and suddenly her hand was freed and she could drink the water. Then Shri Mataji asked her to go and sing. Her nasal twang had vanished!

Later Shri Mataji explained to us that Shri Hanuman is a monkey and so very mischievous. He was angry that the lady could not recognise who Shri Mataji was so he created the thirst and held her hand down.

Deepa Mahajan

We were just watching

Sir CP comes from the north of India, a place near Lucknow. Shri Mataji and Sir CP lived in Lucknow for some time after their marriage and Sir CP was posted there as a civil servant. At that time Mother met quite a lot of people in the society. One of them was a very renowned doctor in Lucknow.

Later, Shri Mataji wanted to build a house in Lucknow and Her plot was next to this man's house. He wrote to Mother and Sir CP, without knowing them at that time, saying that he had heard She was going to construct a house and he'd like to help and She 'would be most welcome to come and stay with us when you build this house.' So Shri Mataji came to Lucknow and stayed with this doctor for some time while She was constructing Her house. She built this whole house in the shape of a ship because Sir CP was working in the Shipping Corporation at that time.

Mother came to Lucknow in 1989 for a wedding. The daughter of this doctor, whom She regarded as a very good man, was to be married and Shri Mataji was in Delhi at the time, so this was a private visit where there were no Sahaja programmes. Mother was attending a social gathering, a wedding, and we were also going there, luckily enough. She flew from Delhi to Lucknow and, because it was Her private visit, the people who had invited Shri Mataji greeted Her. We were just watching the whole thing.

Shri Mataji stayed with the doctor. When She came for this wedding, She was like a normal family friend of the doctor and nobody there could make out that She was divine. Shri Mataji was participating in all the traditions and rituals of the marriage. In India, all the relatives and friends gather and it's a big social event.

You could see Mother getting involved in all that, as part of the family. The doctor, his wife and his whole family had such tremendous respect for Shri Mataji. She told us that this doctor recognized Her when She first came to Lucknow. He seemed to be a special person. He had a very pleasing personality and was over seventy at that time, but he didn't look it. Mother spent the day there and went to the wedding in the evening, and stayed for one more day after that. We got in touch with Shri Mataji and asked if we could have a Sahaja Yoga programme. My father spoke to Her on the phone.

'Are there some Sahaja Yogis here? Is there a centre?' She asked. 'Can we meet?'

'Yes, Shri Mataji, there is,' my father replied.

'All right, I'll come to the centre.'

Mother came to the centre. It was the initial stages of Sahaja Yoga in Lucknow and hardly ten or twenty were Sahaja Yogis at that time. She saw everybody and talked quite a lot about Lucknow. The next day She went back to Delhi.

Akshay Saxena

Sitting on Her throne

On the same evening as She was flying to Delhi from Lucknow, She had a public programme in Noida, near Delhi. We all went to the airport in Lucknow to see Her off, but the flight was delayed. There was a sofa there and Mother was relaxing on it. She closed Her eyes and someone took a photo of Her while She was relaxing. We all saw Mother on the sofa in the airport, so we thought She was sleeping. This was 7.00 pm in Lucknow.

At the same time, somebody took a photograph of the stage in Noida, at the public programme where Mother was supposed to be, but because the plane was delayed, She had not arrived. The miracle was that when the photo came out it showed that Mother was sitting on Her throne in Noida, at the public programme, watching everybody there. Mother definitely was in Lucknow at the time, sleeping on the sofa in the airport.

Akshay Saxena

Shri Mataji was there – or was She?

A very ordinary camera

Shri Mataji had gone to Lucknow to attend a marriage, in March 1989. When She came back to Delhi, the flight was delayed and we had arranged a public programme for Her in Noida. By nine o'clock Shri Mataji had still not arrived, because of the delayed flight. At nine thirty, She came and addressed the audience, and said She was happy that they had waited so long for Her, and apologised for the unavoidable delay. But Mother is never away from Her children. She is always there.

This point was proved after a few days. A few photographs were taken by Raja Chatterji's father with a very ordinary camera. When the pictures came out and were printed, Shri Mataji was visible on Her throne, present at the place of the public programme in Noida, at about seven o'clock. In human terms, at that time Shri Mataji was in Lucknow or in the plane. In the pictures Mother was on the stage at Noida, and those pictures were taken much earlier than when She, in Her human form, arrived there. In one of the photos you and see a man in blue jeans winding garlands around the column (bottom left) and two ladies preparing the aarti tray (bottom right). One lady has her back to Shri Mataji on the stage (pale blue sari), and if Mother had been visible to those people, this would not have been going on, because the Sahaja Yogis, and especially the Indian Sahaja Yogis, know the protocol of the Devi.

GK Datta

The Noida miracle photo

I remember this incident. A group of us were painting pots which were used for decorations. Suddenly we felt very strong vibrations as if Shri Mataji was there. Though She was not there physically, but we could still feel the joy and a few of us spontaneously stated singing bhajans. It was after that Chatterji Uncle took the photographs.

Shubhra Nicolai

We were still preparing for Shri Mataji to come for the public programme, and behind Mother is already sitting on the stage. At this time She was in another town and Uncle, who was addressing the programme, is sitting at Her lotus Feet, being explained something. Later that evening when Mother came to our house for dinner Uncle mentioned to Mother, 'I didn't know how I managed to speak for so long, and kept seekers interested in my talk,' and at that time. Mother smiled and we understood after seeing this miracle photo how She had guided him all through his talk.

Our father had called a cook to prepare food for all the yogis, who would eat after Mother had left. The cook prepared food for a hundred people and nearly 150 ended up coming but the food was sufficient for everyone and even the cook was surprised as to how he managed to feed 150 people.

No wonder, we had added food from the plate Shri Mataji had eaten...

Simmi de Techtermann

We could still feel the joy

I remember this incident. A group of us were painting pots which were used for decorations. Suddenly we felt very strong vibrations as if Shri Mataji was there. Though She was not there physically we could still feel the joy and a few of us spontaneously started singing bhajans. It was after that Chatterji Uncle took the photographs.

Shubhra Nicolai

My Sahaja Yogi friends never had that opportunity

Enlargement of Shri Mataji on throne

Because I worked in the Customs, at Delhi, I was able to see Shri Mataji off very frequently. However, my Sahaja Yogi friends who lived in my neighbourhood never had that opportunity. So once I asked Shri Mataji if it would be possible to bring all the five or six Sahaja Yogi families together to have Her darshan. Shri Mataji readily agreed, and Dr Nigam, who was with Shri Mataji at that time, suggested I should ask if She would like to visit his house for this. This happened, and She came there with about twenty people, and we had bhajans, and She stayed until about one thirty in the night, so we had about five or six hours with Shri Mataji.

GK Datta

The flowers were the right of the ganas

When Mother used to leave for Mumbai, or maybe abroad, from Delhi, She told us something important. Concerning the flowers and bouquets which were given, as many as possible should go with Her. Once or twice people wanted to carry those flowers home for a keepsake, but Mother told us that this was not right, because those flowers were the right of the ganas. They had to be given to the ganas only.

GK Datta

All the stitches were totally cured

My wife was operated on for her gall bladder at Yamunanagar, and about twenty days later we went back to Delhi. She had a number of stitches on the right side of her stomach, and two of them got infected, and did not heal up. About two months after the operation they had still not healed. I was with Shri Mataji and She said I could bring my wife to Her. She went and sat with Shri Mataji, and I left the room. Later my wife came out, and said she had told Shri Mataji about the problem with the stitches.

Shri Mataji put Her hand on my wife's stomach, on the place of the stitches, and she felt as if snow was just melting inside her stomach. The very next day all the stitches were totally cured.

GK Datta

A strong puja

After Birthday Puja in Delhi on the 19th of March, 1989 we went to Mumbai to arrive just in the morning of the 'real' Birthday Puja, where thousands of people came. It was a very strong puja. After Mumbai, I was lucky to follow Her to Kolkata.

Sita Wadhwa

The Himalayas protect India against all negativity

This is taken from a letter sent from Sita Varda to her family in Europe in 1989.

'As there was no First Class on the plane, Shri Mataji was sitting with us flying to Kathmandu, in March 1989. What a tremendous feeling to fly with Shri Adi Shakti above Mother Earth, knowing that everything is just Her creation! During the flight Shri Mataji gave realisation to an air hostess and worked on her for about ten to fifteen minutes. One small girl came just to stand in front of our Mother and to look at Her with great eyes.

This is a born–realised one!' Shri Mataji said. Her parents came to get Shri Mataji's blessing, then their brother and his wife, et cetera. The aisle became full of kneeling people but then everybody had to go back to his or her seat as we were landing in Nepal. The landing was very hard, as if Nepal's earth wanted to give a big hug to Shri Mataji to welcome Her in the land of Sahasrara.

Lieselotte and Herbert have got a new ashram, a beautiful, very modern house with a big garden, where they had a small pendal with a big buffet of Austrian specialities prepared specially to please the Nabhi chakra of all the Sahaja Yogis during their stay in Nepal. The same evening all the Sahaja Yogis from Nepal were introduced to Shri Mataji, including two Austrian boys aged 18 and 19, who were exactly one week old in Sahaja Yoga. Shri Mataji was very pleased with them.

'What a depth – look at their Kundalinis, such great seekers. They must have been seeking for ages,' She said. Then we had bhajans. In the begin-ning nobody could be found to play the harmonium – so our Divine Mother Herself took the instrument and played! She not only played the harmonium but was even singing Herself and then teaching Lisa how to play a particular raga. It was really incredible. The whole atmosphere was so joyous.

The puja the next morning, 30th of March, was just beautiful and again very joyous. Shri Mataji spoke about Nepal, or rather the Himalayas being the Sahasrara of the world and how these big mountains protect India, the Kundalini, against all negativity. She said the Nepali people were very religious minded, but very poor people who tolerate too much. After the puja everyone was allowed to present a garland to our Mother's Lotus Feet and Shri Mataji was very happy about the vibrations of everyone.'

Sita Wadhwa

Shri Mataji playing the harmonium with Liesel Weihart in Kathmandu

Pashupatinath

In 1989, we had gone with Shri Mataji to Nepal where we stayed in the house of Herbert and Lisa. Herbert was a very good cook and he wanted to please Shri Mataji by offering Her all the non–veg delicacies, so he made a many course meal. The first one was a chicken delicacy, the next one was a pork delicacy, then came mutton, then duck, then fish etc. He would bring up each one to Her and explain its intricacies. Shri Mataji tasted all of them.

'He has presented every type of pashu that now I have really become Pashupatinath,' She quietly remarked. Nepal is famous for the Pashupatinath Temple, which is a very ancient temple of Lord Shiva who is known as the Lord of the animals.

Deepa Mahajan

The Lakshmi tattwa

The Easter Puja was at a very lovely place outside Kolkata in the grounds of the Frooti (mango drink) factory. A Sahaja Yogi owned this factory and Shri Mataji herself inaugurated the production of Frooti on the west coast of India just before the puja. It was incredible to see Shri Mataji in between all these juice preparing machines and hundreds of Frooti packs. Directly after this function She was driven two hundred metres to the puja pendal. The Kolkata people had had special florists prepare the place so it was a beautiful decoration with thousands of fresh flowers.

It was a Mahalakshmi Puja, where Shri Mataji explained, amongst many other things, the relation between Lakshmi tattwa and Mahalakshmi power; unless and until our Lakshmi tattwa is established, Mahalakshmi power will not start acting through us. Shri Mataji explained that we have to become like lotuses, fragrant, light, and tolerating even the ugly worms, which may be in the leaves. Not only the ladies – also the men have to become like this.

Shri Mataji spoke about the poverty in the Kolkata region. She said that the people are so poor because the Lakshmi tattwa is not established. People are miserly. They have to show more generosity and hospitality; they have to look after others – then the poverty problem will be solved. Factory owners, or people with money, should also start to be like fathers to their workers. Another remarkable thing about this puja was that Shri Mataji had told the Sahaja Yogi leader, the night before, that Sahaja Yogis could also bring their friends, i.e. non–Sahaja Yogis, to the puja! We were only fifty to seventy Sahaja Yogis.

Sita Wadhwa

A cruise along the River Hoogly

During one trip to Kolkata Shri Mataji went on a cruise along the River Hoogly, that is the Ganges, and most of the Sahaja Yogis of Kolkata accompanied Her. It was a trip downstream to the northern end of the Sunderbans. This is the largest mangrove forest in the world and is the Ganges delta – the home of the Royal Bengal tiger and lots of crocodiles and things like that.

Shri Mataji called the married couples to Her and talked to them and blessed them. My wife and I went to meet Her after the meeting with the couples. We were singing, and She asked my wife to sing and she sang one of Ravindranath Tagore's songs. Shri Mataji was sitting with a keyboard or harmonium, and my wife sang a song about the Adi Shakti, how the primordial energy manifests. Shri Mataji was following my wife on the keyboard even though She had never heard this song before. She also mentioned that Her father was a scholar in Bengali and how from him She had heard many Bengali songs including one popular hit of yesteryear, which translated goes like this – 'Oh my companion, please hold my hand and escort me, because I don't know the way'. It is a well–known song in Bengal, and the next year this same song was sung in front of Shri Mataji. Some other songs by Tagore were also sung before Her the following year.

Gautam Sarkar

You are already deep!

In the late eighties we were making a trip down the Hoogly River, Calcutta, with Shri Mataji, and She asked that one by one all the Sahaja Yogis went to Her. There were about a couple of dozen of us. My turn came and I was the last to go.

'Mother, I want to go deep in Sahaja Yoga,' I asked Her.

'You are already deep!' She said. So I bowed down, and She said, 'Just a little on the Nabhi,' and She gave me a tap on my back.

Shri Mataji played the harmonium for us on that trip, and a rhythmic instrument as well, a sort of bell.

T. Roy

Shri Mataji looked so affectionately at me

I knew Shri Mataji was very fond of Rabindranath Tagore's music. Whenever She came to Kolkata She wanted to listen to Tagore's songs. In the March 1989 Barasat programme I was about eight months pregnant, but I had practiced for two months and selected most of the Tagore songs which are dedicated to God. When I sang in front of Shri Mataji She was very happy and She looked so affectionately at me. After the programme She gave me a beautiful red sari. She told me that if I could sing so well at such an advanced stage of pregnancy, the soul which was coming in would be a very great soul.

Mahua Sarkar

Born from the divine

In 1989 there was a puja in Barasat on the outskirts of Kolkata, in April. My wife was singing there even though she was advanced in her second pregnancy. Shri Mataji looked at her and said she was carrying a realised soul, and my daughter was born on the 8th of May. The same year Shri Mataji gave her the name of Divya at Ganapatipule. My mother went to the stage and asked Shri Mataji for a name.

'She should be called Divya because she is born from the divine,' Shri Mataji said.

Gautam Sarkar

I am there, so don't worry

On one occasion when Mother came to Calcutta, we were all going before Her at the airport and offering our bouquets, I asked Her when She would come to Barrackpur, where I lived. We had been showing Her some photographs of a festival or fair, where we had had a stall, and She was very pleased with them. I asked Mother when She would come to Barrackpur.

'To how many places, all over the world, can I go personally? I want to go but... but I am there, so don't worry.'

It was so joy giving and sustained our efforts, when Shri Mataji said that.

T. Roy

Chapter 15

1989: April and May England and Italy

Blindness caused by prejudice

In 1989 we went to pick up Shri Mataji from Heathrow Airport, in London. She was slightly annoyed that when coming out of Customs the airport clerk denied Her access to the VIP exit route, because all the Sahaja Yogis were expecting Her to exit from there and if She came out from another exit She would have missed meeting them. The airport clerk in question did not believe Shri Mataji had VIP status, and She directed him to check the Who's Who book. He did that in front of Her and though She spelled Her surname several times he could not find it.

I asked Shri Mataji how this could be. She explained that the man was Indian and having lived in the UK for a long time, he couldn't believe that an Indian person had VIP status, and this made him blind. Luckily another clerk recognised Shri Mataji as being entitled to the VIP exit. This incident caused Shri Mataji's Feet to become very swollen, but after a few minutes of massage by a Sahaja Yogi, they went back to normal.

Luis Garrido

The European Tour 1989

Here is a short account of Shri Mataji's visits to various European countries in 1989. This does not include Her visits to other parts of the world in that same year. This type of schedule went on for many years.

The tour started with Shri Hanuman Puja in England just after Easter, and then Shri Mataji went on to visit Italy for the Sahasrara Day Puja in Sorrento, just south of the city of Naples, to be followed by programmes in Naples and Rome; then Spain, with programmes in Madrid and Barcelona and the Shri Buddha Puja in Barcelona, then on to Greece and Turkey with a puja and two programmes in each country.

July saw Shri Mataji visiting France for the Shri Devi Puja for that country, Belgium, and Holland, and for a public programme in Paris. A few days later Shri Mataji was in Munich for two programmes and the puja to Shri Paramchaitanya, followed by the journey through Germany, Austria, and Italy to Lago di Braies for the Guru Puja. Two days after the Guru Puja Shri Mataji was in Vienna for another two public programmes, then back to London for two programmes there, then Milan for two programmes and the puja to Shri Bhairavanath, then to Switzerland for the Shri Ganesha Puja and two programmes in Geneva, then to England for the Shri Krishna Puja and then to Finland and Russia.

Phil Ward

My heart jumped

I was just in Sahaja Yoga and had heard of the marriages. I had been in a relationship for six years and did not know what to do. Marry this man? Marry in Sahaj? What was the right thing to do? For some time I had been praying to Mother for an answer. I had dreams of Her I did not understand. Then Mother came to Germany and we were all sitting in front of Her Feet and She talked to every one of us. She asked me how I was, and about my parents. I just sat there and did not dare to ask the most important question for me.

'How old are you? You should get married,' Mother suddenly asked with a smile.

'Oh no!' I thought, 'Mother please don't leave me like this. Oh, please!'

'Don't worry. I will find you a nice man,' She said.

Some time later, it was at the Shri Hanuman Puja in 1989. I had got married the year before and had moved to my husband's country. The collectivity there was much smaller and I felt very alone, and did not understand the language. I felt ashamed of feeling like this, and felt far away from Mother's attention. The day after the puja I was standing outside the hotel, waiting for our group to leave. Suddenly the door opened and Shri Mataji came down the little path.

'Hello. How are you?' She said as She passed by.

'Fine,' I whispered. I was so astounded. She walked on, turned, and looked at me with a melting smile.

'By the way, thank you for the mirror,' She said.

My heart jumped. With these little words She told me that She had not forgotten me or left me alone. She knew exactly, and She wanted me to come to my senses! I laughed loudly. There was only joy. This feeling of being alone left, and never came back.

Barbara Martens

No pain at all

We were at Margate in 1989, at the Shri Hanuman Puja.

'Anyone who has any problems can come up to My room tomorrow morning,' Shri Mataji had said the day before. I decided to go as I had had a painful back problem for about a year. Initially people were going in individually, but then She said we should all go in together. I happened to be the first in so I ended up sitting right at Shri Mataji's Feet. She asked me what was the problem so I told Her. She asked me if I had had a fall – I said no, forgetting that I had in fact had a fall a year or so before. Mother then told me to turn with my back facing Her, and She put Her Foot on it. She knew exactly the spot that was painful, and I could feel Her toes moving on my back as She sat talking to other people about their problems. She also made me put both hands on the floor, and I could feel a lot of heat coming from them. After about half an hour Mother asked me how I felt.

'A bit better, Mother,' I answered, although to be truthful I couldn't feel much difference. When I got up to leave the room, though, I was amazed to feel that my whole back felt loose – whereas before it had been tight and painful. Gradually, over the next few months, my back improved until the pain completely went.

There was a girl there to see Shri Mataji at the same time because she had a problem walking which was to do with her hip – she had been in constant pain all her life because one leg was shorter than the other. Shri Mataji put Her Foot on her hip and told her to look at Her Feet and to put her hand towards a candle. I saw the girl a year or so later and asked her how her hip was. She said she was cured and now had no pain at all.

Frances Firth

Shri Hanuman Puja 1989

Namoh namoh Maria

This was Shri Hanuman Puja, 1989, Margate, England. I was with Shri Mataji upstairs, and we were coming downstairs to the puja hall. Shri Mataji was coming down the stairs and She stood at the bottom of the stairs, and Namoh, namoh Maria was going on. I was a few steps behind Shri Mataji, a little bit higher up and while the bhajan was going on I could see Her Sahasrara just throbbing – just alive – it was like a huge amount of light was coming from inside. Shri Mataji just stood there until the bhajan was finished and ever since then Namoh, namoh Maria is a bhajan that makes me completely thoughtless, because it reminds me of Shri Mataji's Sahasrara and I can be back on those stairs, totally lost in it.

Prerna Richards

Advice from Shri Mataji

At the end of 1986 I began work on a book about Christ called Sophia. My writing, which began very slowly with a few chapters, received an added impetus when my wife Ruth went to stay with Shri Mataji in Rosary Gardens, in London, in mid–November 1987. Mother had just watched a programme on TV about the Gnostics and was enthusiastic about it. She told Ruth that Thomas, the apostle, was a good man.

Later, in April 1989, after I had finished Sophia, I was traveling back in the train from Margate to London after the Shri Hanuman Puja when Mother waved for me to come into Her compartment. Another Sahaja Yogi had been telling Mother what Sophia was about just before I went in, but She had forestalled him by saying, 'I know. I know everything.'

She told me that I should mention Her directly in the book and only then would it be published. Erring on the side of discretion, I had not mentioned Her. She said that I should say I had got the knowledge in the book through my self realisation. She added reassuringly that they wouldn't get after me the way they were getting after Rushdie, in a reference to the then current fatwa on the writer Salman Rushdie, for writing a book on religious matters.

Chris Greaves

One of the most lovely days of my life

I was on that boat where that amazing series of photos were taken, on the way to Capri in May 1989. The sky was so blue and the water clear, as if I had fallen into paradise. I did not see anything of the miracles though! It was such a clear day, there was lots of sunshine and a wonderful feeling.

The boat was very crowded and I was far at the back, but we felt so happy and safe, as if Shri Mataji was taking care of us all. We were singing a lot on

the boat and there was a lovely dinner, a pizza I recall. Later we went ashore and Shri Mataji wanted to do some shopping in the little village there. All the Sahaja Yogis wanted to follow Her, but we didn't want to bother Her so we did it very discreetly, and didn't go into the shops, but stayed outside. There were flowers all over the place, growing everywhere. I only remember the emotions in my heart, one of the most beautiful weeks of my life.

Shri Mataji did a public programme on the island, and I was very close to Her, right at the front. The Sahaja Yogis were singing Jogawa! Uda bai, uda bai, ho! very loudly. I was thinking that they were perhaps singing too loudly, because the new people who wanted to talk to Shri Mataji couldn't. Sure enough Shri Mataji read my mind and looked at me.

What naughty ones they are!' She said, or something like that, but She was laughing, and I felt She wanted it to be like this and maybe didn't want to speak. She was very sweet.

Henriette Hagrasman

When we were on the boat we didn't see any light coming

I was on the boat trip when Shri Mataji was with us, near Capri. We were going round another smaller island there and when we got to Capri, Robert Hunter, who took the photos, went to the photo shop to have his pictures developed that he had taken on the boat. When he picked them up an hour or so later, I happened to be with him, and we were eager to see how they had come out. We thought they were normal photos.

We were so very surprised when we saw them with the light coming in every photo on the boat. In every successive photo there were more and more vibrations (light) coming. We were amazed and didn't understand about them at all. When we were on the boat we had not seen any light coming. It was a wonderful trip with Shri Mataji but there was nothing unusual happening. Also there was no light in the other photos on the same reel of film.

Mara-Madhuri Corazzari

Sorrento, Pompeii and Naples

In 1989 I went to the Sahasrara Puja at Sorrento, where that incredible miracle photo was taken. The puja took place in a cinema, and the backdrop was very plain, and there was just Shri Mataji sitting on a simple chair on the stage.

After the puja programme there was a public programme in Naples. Somehow, by my mistake, my son and I got left behind, alone, at the Sorrento campsite where we were staying. I wasn't worried as I had the address of the programme in the evening, and said to my son, 'Let's go and look at Pompeii.' So we took a local train there.

We entered the Ancient Roman town, buried by the volcano eruption of AD 79. We started walking, not really having any plan, because it is a very big area, and somehow I felt guided to go in a certain direction. A few streets later, who should we meet but Shri Mataji and a lot of Sahaja Yogis all sitting near Her. It was a miracle that we just spontaneously walked straight to them all. We joined them, and then Shri Mataji said we should all have lunch together, which we did, at an open air restaurant nearby.

The public programme in Naples was well attended and was in a beautiful old palazzo in the centre of the town.

Linda Williams

Shri Mataji's magic

After the public programme in Naples, in May 1989, we stayed in the old school for the little children outside Rome. Mother was there, and a lot of Sahaja Yogis from various places, as well as the children. The next day a journalist came to see Mother. I was at the back of the room with my son. Mother called me to the front as the journalist wanted to talk about the damage inflicted by false gurus, among other things.

I sat at Mother's Feet and She very graciously gave me a cup of tea. I was a bit worried as the journalist didn't speak much English. I hadn't spoken Italian for fifteen years and am not good at languages, plus it was only my fourth language. Mother encouraged me to try in Italian though, and it was amazing, after that cup of tea the Italian just flowed out. Later the journalist complimented me on my almost perfect grasp of the language. Just, and only, at that time, I was using words I did not know I knew, thanks to that magic cup of tea!

Linda Williams

Everyone was impressed by Her personality

I phoned Shri Mataji in Rome and She spoke to me very sweetly, the Great Mother, and accepted the invitation to come to Brazil. After some uncertainties, I decided to phone again, at six o'clock in the morning. She was very sweet, and I tried to explain everything about Brazil and spoke to Her of the room we had been offered by the government. She was amazed, and asked how it was possible that we had managed to do so much in a city like Brasilia, where we did not have much help. I explained that everyone was impressed by Her personality.

'But how do they know it?' She said.

I told Shri Mataji of the little biography I had made of Her. She was astonished, and asked where we had got it from, and who had written it. I explained that I had written of Her life with Gandhi, of Her mission, of Her husband etc. She confirmed Her coming to Brazil. The programme was to consist of Salvador, Brasilia and Rio. We did not ever hope for so many blessings for Brazil, in so little time.

Duilio Cartocci

We must be more relaxed

Shri Mataji came to Rome and we had a puja and a public programme, and on the day She had to leave I was the driver. The flight was at twelve o'clock and at about half past eleven, Shri Mataji came out. It was quite late and we could not possibly reach the airport, as it was at least an hour's drive. She sat in the car and we went very fast. She went to sleep and when we were ten kilometres from the airport, there was a big traffic jam. Finally, we reached the airport at half past twelve and saw all the Sahaja Yogis outside the airport and wondered, because usually they would be inside. We stopped and Shri Mataji asked what was happening.

'Shri Mataji, the flight is cancelled,' they said.

'Let's go and eat something,' She suggested. We went to a restaurant at the seaside and had a nice meal of fish. Someone had a newspaper and saw that a certain place was for sale, so he asked Shri Mataji if we could go and see it.

'Yes, why not?' She said. He phoned and made an appointment and we went to see it. It had two big buildings and the owner had divided it into two, along with the land. He had been trying to sell it for years, but no one was interested because it was too big, so the price came down and down. We went inside and the more we saw of the one half, the more we knew this was the right place. We came and told Shri Mataji.

'Go and see the other one, too,' She said. So we did and then She said we should buy both of them. Shri Mataji said that if the flight had not been cancelled, we wouldn't have found this beautiful ashram which was used for the children's school. She said we always get worried when She is leaving and we must be more relaxed about Her departures.

Akbar Samii

How can your Mother do all the work?

On May 21st, 1989, in Barcelona, I was telling the French leader how fortunate he was to have massaged the Feet of Shri Mataji. On the Friday there was a public programme and we came almost at the end. Shri Mataji was sitting down and the programme was finished but She was receiving all the new people one by one and working on them. So many Sahaja Yogis were around Shri Mataji. Then I saw Her, who didn't know me, apart from the one time I went shopping with Her, and I had never talked with Her. She looked at me and called me over.

'How can your Mother do all the work if you don't help Her?' She said to me. 'Please, come here and sit next to Me.' I sat next to Her, giving vibrations to the new people when Shri Mataji indicated treatments for them. Sometimes, there was some new person who couldn't speak English and just spoke French, and I was translating.

Pascal Shrestaputra

The beginnings in Greece

When Sahaja Yoga started in Greece in May 1989, I was lucky to be one of those who was there when we had the first public programme, which was postered in a big way by some Sahaja Yogis from Rome. There were about five hundred people at the programme and then we had a seminar at the home of a Sahaja Yogi, who had a kind of a castle. We had the first havan, and when everything was ready suddenly someone started to shoot cannons, at that auspicious moment.

Wolfgang Hackl

I trust you

I lived at Shudy Camps for a while, in 1989, after my mother had left for South Africa and some of the Sahaja Yogis there were looking after me. I think they thought that I was going through a slightly wild phase in my life, as I was fifteen and enjoyed going to parties with my friends and going to pop concerts and things like that.

I remember Shri Mataji came for a visit and I'd returned from school and I was told in very ominous tones that She wanted to see me. So I thought, 'Oh no, Mother isn't going to be happy with me.' I hadn't really done anything wrong, but from the tone I was worried.

I changed into my best outfit, an angora jersey and a navy blue kilt with green stripes on it. I went to see Shri Mataji and, as I walked through the door, She was sitting on the sofa and She looked me up and down.

'Auriol, I've told you never to wear black,' She said.

'I'm sorry, Shri Mataji,' I replied, looked down at myself and thought, 'I'm not actually wearing black. I'm wearing navy blue.' But I didn't say anything and was expecting Her to be displeased with me and get told off about my behaviour.

Instead, Shri Mataji started asking me what it was like to go to school in the West, as opposed to India, because I had lived and been to school for six years in India. She sat and talked to me for quite a long time and asked many different questions about what I thought about the different ways of schooling and whether I preferred it in India or the West.

I was telling Her my opinions on the matter. Every minute I was expecting Her to start telling me that I had not been behaving properly and then the conversation came to a close. By this time, She had been served some food and was sitting at the table and I was sitting the other side of it to Her.

'But you're not wearing black, are you? You are wearing navy blue,' Shri Mataji said eventually. Then She said to me something to me I will never forget. 'You know, Auriol, I trust you, and I will always trust you. You can go now. It's okay.'

If I had ever thought of doing anything wrong at that time, that thing She said would have stopped me because I knew She trusted me and I would never break that trust.

Auriol Purdie

Three Sahaja Yogis reminisce about laughter

In 1989 when we were helping Shri Mataji pack away tea sets in Shudy Camps, another yogi and I, at dinner, were enjoying the vibrations and cracking jokes, and both of us have quite loud and distinctive laughs. I was wondering if our jocundity would be disturbing for Shri Mataji but later heard that She had enquired as to who was laughing and had enjoyed listening to us and said laughter was a quality of the heart. Such a great Mother who enjoyed the laughter of Her children.

Steve Jones

I remember giggling blissfully outside Mother's suite in Shudy Campo along with you and others, Steve. We had sneaked upstairs one evening and were sort of eavesdropping outside Mother's door, whispering like daring children, as though She somehow wouldn't know we were there! Bogdan (Shehovych) was inside with Mother, who was watching the movie, Back to the Future. The absurd juxtaposition of this zany American film with its whacky professor, and dodgy mariadas, and the Adi Shakti actually sitting inside there watching it, was too, too much.

Marilyn Leate

I remember! And the part in Back to the Future where he is about to kiss his own mother when she was a teenager and she didn't know he was her son from the future and they stop before they kiss as they feel something is not right.

'Ah, you see, the mariadas!' Shri Mataji said.

Steve Jones

Swirling gold dust

When we were at Shudy Camps with Shri Mataji, who had just come back from a programme, probably a public programme in Cambridge and

She was walking up the stairs. She was at the end of the corridor, so I watched Her passing from the other end. I looked at Her and for a split second I saw like very fine gold dust swirling behind Her where She walked.

Sharon Vincent

Shri Mataji likes people to act naturally

I think Shri Mataji is always very happy if you are doing a little thing for Her. When She is with yogis, She doesn't like them to feel in awe of Her. She likes people to act naturally, I guess.

Once at Shudy Camps, Shri Mataji had a group of us sitting round Her and everyone was talking quite casually, almost as if She wasn't there. Of course, we were aware because She is God. But it was all happening very naturally.

Barry Humphries

A very powerful mantra

Shri Mataji called me up to Shudy Camps, to work with Sir CP to help with his book. I was very concerned about my own ascent, and was able to talk to Shri Mataji, up in Her room. We sat for a while and She talked about a number of things, none of them personal, but She looked at me and was obviously aware of my concern.

'Don't worry, you will be all right,' She said. When I went downstairs, there was a video of Mother playing, and just at the point I looked at the video, on the video She said, 'What is the problem? You live, you die, you have done it so many times, don't worry.' I realised that I was all right, because I am the spirit, no matter what happens. It was quite clear to me.

During this period Shri Mataji was at Shudy Camps for about three months, recovering from an injury. I had the opportunity to spend several moments with Her. A powerful experience was when She dealt with an Agnya catch of mine. She put Her finger on my Agnya, and told me to look at Her Agnya. I was sitting literally a foot away from Her and looking into Her Agnya.

'Say, seven times, Shri Mataji, You are the Holy Ghost, the Christ, the ascent,' She said.

After I had done this, and it was one of the most powerful mantras I have managed to retain. I have used and passed on that mantra to many people.

Guy Beavan

Good art

At Shudy Camps there was a period when we were packing all of Shri Mataji's belongings that were going to be shipped back to India. She used to come up for about two weeks at a time, mostly over one summer, and She must have come five or six times. There was a team of about seven or eight of us. Shri Mataji would come out onto the landing at about eight o'clock every morning, and we would all be there. Sometimes She would talk to us for maybe a couple of hours.

'Right, now we have got to get on with it!' Shri Mataji would say, and we would all jump up and keep bringing all the things – hundreds of tea sets, and porcelain. It was incredible – it would become like an art appreciation lesson, because we would bring something along, and She would say, 'Just look at this, look at the way the artist has expressed himself!'

One day I found a pot which was really brightly coloured and thought, 'Shri Mataji will really like this one,' and She did not like it at all and suggested we should throw it away. She would show us what was good art and what wasn't. One person would wrap everything up, in tissue paper and bubble wrap, and the rest of us would keep bringing things.

Chris Marlow

Assembling chandeliers

In 1989 Shri Mataji was away on a tour and I decided to assemble and hang some chandeliers belonging to Her that were packed away in the attic at Shudy Camps. I had been told by some Sahaja Yogis that Shri Mataji had asked for this to be done on several occasions but no one had done it. People reassured me that She would be pleased to see this done. When Shri Mataji first arrived back, I was surprised that She did not say anything about the chandeliers. A few days later She spoke to me.

'I never told you to assemble and hang the chandeliers,' She said.

'Everybody told me that You asked for the chandeliers to be hung, Shri Mataji. Did all these people lie to me?' I asked.

'I did not ask you, I asked someone else, that's My point,' She replied.

'Yes I see that now,' I answered.

'Do you know how many years ago I asked for the chandeliers to be assembled and hung?' Shri Mataji asked. 'Three years – a long time.

Circumstances have changed, we are packing everything to go back to India and you could have saved yourself the trouble of doing this. But on the other hand they look very nice, and I wanted to ask you to assemble two more chandeliers, to fill in a gap. Now we are expecting guests we could make the place look nice.'

Luis Garrido

Shudy Camps House from the back with some of the Sahaja Yogis. In the foreground is the large lawn where the marquee was pitched for pujas. The house is situated in the depths of the English countryside, near Cambridge.

Pruning roses

At Shudy Camps, around 1989, Shri Mataji asked us to prune some rose bushes in the front of the house, so we waited for a gardener to come. A week later She again suggested we prune them. We replied that we didn't know how and would rather have it done by a proper gardener.

'Just prune them, there's nothing to it,' Shri Mataji said, but we lacked confidence.

Later there was a programme on TV featuring an experiment by the Royal Agricultural Society in which ten rose bushes were pruned by an expert, another ten by a gardening amateur, and ten by a madcap with a chain saw. The conclusion, judged by experts, was that the three methods of pruning produced the same amount and quality of blooms the next season. By now we were convinced that even we could do it.

Luis Garrido

The builder with the noisy drill

Around 1989, in a temporary London flat in Buckingham Palace Road, Shri Mataji was back in London from a long tour around the world. She explained that She had developed a headache that week because every time She tried to take an afternoon rest the builder next door would start operating a pneumatic drill.

'This man needs to be stopped, he has no right to do this,' we said.

We asked Shri Mataji whether we could stop him and She replied that the man was not important, what was important was our desire to see Her welcomed by the whole country.

'In that case would You allow me to give You a head massage for the pain?' one of the Sahaja Yogis said.

'Since you suggested it, you might as well,' Shri Mataji replied.

A towel and oil was brought and later Shri Mataji explained that from then on, the builder next door no longer used the drill the moment She decided to take an afternoon rest.

Luis Garrido

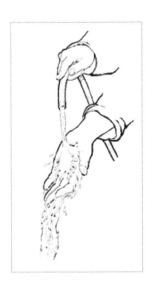

Watering the garden

This simple method of vibrating water was taught by Shri Mataji in 1989 at Pratishthan. When watering the garden with a hose, let the water fall onto the palm of the hand (the Sahasrara) and from there the water will cascade down to the plants or soil. Ideally the person using this technique would be wearing a badge or a pendant of Shri Mataji, otherwise keep the attention on Her or on the Sahasrara.

Luis Garrido

Chapter 16

1989: May Southern Europe

Go on a liver diet

When I was living in France, we went to the Shri Buddha Puja in Spain in 1989. Shri Mataji was at the airport leaving Barcelona. It was very hot and She came in and looked at me.

'You're feeling down, aren't you?' Shri Mataji said, and knew exactly how I felt. 'It's your liver. Your liver is too hot,' She said. 'Go on a liver diet.' As She walked away She turned and said, 'Three months!'

So I did it. It did me a lot of good and I never felt down again. For the next three years Shri Mataji put all the French Sahaja Yogis on a liver diet, for three months every summer, to cool down the French liver.

Leanne Huet

Shri Mataji gave Her hand

It was in Spain, and the Spanish people had made a beautiful blue seat for Shri Mataji at the puja. Mother had a public programme in Barcelona and we went there from Montpellier in France. After the programme was finished, She went out through the main aisle of the building, and everybody was standing to say goodbye. As She passed She gave Her hand to every single person on the right and left side, all the way out of the building. I too took Shri Mataji's hand, and was amazed at how soft it was, like a baby's hand, so gentle.

The next day we had a puja in a hotel on a mountain I felt a sweet feeling in my heart, and it was the same feeling I had felt from Her hand the day before.

Jean-Michel Huet

His hand had been closed for years

There was one man at the programme in Barcelona who couldn't open his hand and Shri Mataji told me to put mine on the hand of that new person, and massage it. His hand opened a bit, enough so that Shri Mataji could put Her Feet on it, which She did for a few minutes. After that She removed Her Feet and asked him to try to open it and he could open his hand much more. It had been closed for years, and Shri Mataji opened it. The whole atmosphere was divine.

'Can you remove My socks?' Shri Mataji then said, very sweetly. I did so and was touching the Feet of Shri Mataji – a dream come true. She asked me to massage Her Feet. Again, like the year before, it was my birthday. I kept on massaging for about half an hour. After everything was finished I felt completely thoughtless, as if I had no body, just ether, air and vibrations. I could not speak, just wanted to be silent and enjoy the divine vibrations, like a revelation. I knew Shri Mataji was Adi Shakti – not mental, but an experience, and I felt one with something so big. This lasted for about twenty minutes, thanks to Her power, and She had granted my wish on my birthday.

Pascal Shrestaputra

The coolness was inside my hand

I came to Sahaja Yoga in Paris. After a month or two I wanted to know who Shri Mataji was. I went to a programme She was doing in Barcelona with a friend. After the programme, my friend told me to join the queue and go up to see Shri Mataji. I must have been the last in line. I felt all my chakras turning, and when I got near Her I was thoughtless.

'I received my realisation a month ago,' I said, and She just laughed.

'That is why you are so good,' She said, took my hand, and it was as if my hand was in the fridge – but the coolness was inside, not outside. Slowly it came outside, the coolness.

Claude Ishram

Shri Buddha Puja, Barcelona (email report)

Shri Mataji arrived at the place of the Shri Buddha Puja, in 1989, a small and simple hostel on the top of a hill overlooking Barcelona. The decoration of the puja scene had been very lovingly done, particularly with a great painted frieze behind Shri Mataji in the intricate style of some of the Ajanta cave paintings. Many of the Buddha figures could be seen teaching how to give bandhan or how to raise the Kundalini, if one looked closely. Shri Mataji talked at great length about Buddha, stopping at one moment to look at Her watch.

'I hope you people are not in a hurry!' She said. It would have been a very hot day, but our Mother took care that Her children should not suffer too much. She raised Her left side to Her right twenty–one times, then wondered aloud whether She had not overdone things as the air became quite cool, seven times would have been enough.

That afternoon we had just retired for a siesta when someone came round to tell us that Shri Mataji was in the courtyard where the puja had taken place and was chatting to people, and that we should all go there. She spoke of the necessity of our promptly following any instructions She gave, and gave the example of Sorrento, two weeks earlier, where She had insisted on our looking after the children very closely. This was not done, and one of the children fell from a height of ten or twelve feet. By Mother's Grace the child was brought to Her and healed, otherwise permanent damage would have been done to him, his hip bones having gone out of line. Shri Mataji went on to talk about some miracle stories which have been experienced in Her presence, some of which were quite hilarious.

In the evening the second of the two public programmes took place, in a hall on the twenty–third floor of a conference centre in downtown Barcelona. Shri Mataji arrived after a long introduction by José Antonio. After a time he requested the singers to start singing bhajans, and the audience enjoyed them immensely. The vibrations just grew and grew.

When Shri Mataji arrived She remarked that all the people had received their realisation through the music. She gave a very short talk after which She simply asked the people to hold out their hands to see if they could feel a cool breeze; there was none of the usual holding the hands to the chakras on the Ida Nadi, as though the music had already worked that out. Then a surge of people towards the front as Shri Mataji received one by one all the newcomers, during which we continued with the bhajans. It went on for hours and we were exhausted by the end, but Mother kept us going. At one point a large choir of Spanish Sahaja Yogis sang some beautiful new Spanish songs, which Mother really enjoyed. They were very discrete, not pushing their way onto the stage but waiting until Shri Mataji asked whether they had anything to sing. The evening ended with a Spanish Sahaja Yogi and Yogini dancing some Flamenco on the stage in front of Shri Mataji, to the delight of everyone. It was a fantastic contrast to the first evening. The next morning we were able to see Shri Mataji off from the airport in Barcelona as She returned to England.

Phil Ward

It will be clearer later

I went up to the stage to take a photo of Shri Mataji in May 1989 after the Barcelona Buddha Puja, and my old Polaroid didn't have a zoom so I had to go very close to get a good photo. When it came out Shri Mataji looked surprised, and wanted to see it. But of course it was not clear at once, because you have to wait a few seconds before it is clear enough, and dry. She took it and looked at it.

'It's not clear now, it will be clearer later,' She said with a nice smile, talking about my Polaroid photo. I know She was referring to me as I left Sahaja Yoga shortly after and returned twelve years later with reinforced faith.

Colette Desigaud

A crown made for Shri Mataji

In 2007 my wife Arlene and I travelled to Nirmal Nagari, near Pune to celebrate Christmas Puja with Shri Mataji. I noticed a stone plaque on the wall which read Sangrahalaya, meaning museum. It is relatively small, but wonderful and filled with vibrations.

I entered and saw gifts that were made and offered to Mother during the spreading of Sahaja Yoga displayed in cabinets, and beautiful photos of our Mother holding flowers in Her hands. On the wall facing the entrance there were more gifts and a big frame which displayed 108 photos of Mother with different facial expressions. In another cabinet were crowns which had been offered to Shri Mataji at past pujas. To my surprise, I recognised a crown that we, the Spanish collective, had offered at the Shri Buddha Puja in Barcelona in May 1989.

I was filled with tremendous joy and gratitude towards our Mother, to see the crown displayed here. My heart only had the words, 'Thank You Mother,' and the feeling of entering history.

When Mother offered us that puja in Barcelona, a few months before, at a national meeting, I presented the idea of making a crown for Her. From my city, Zaragoza, I started working on it, a difficult and delicate task requiring lots of attention, and it was carved from birch wood. A carpenter friend of mine assisted with cutting the pieces, then I carved the shape with patience and love, and the end result was very light in weight. Whilst working I said mantras and put on my bandhan, so that all would go well. It was a collective collaboration.

At the puja, when it was time to offer the crown to Shri Mataji, I saw with surprise the yogis offering Mother a different crown, because in Madrid another one had been prepared. I felt frustrated and sad, because I had put so much love and energy into ours. I lowered my head and asked myself, 'How did I fail? Maybe my ego?' I felt rejected but slowly accepted what was happening. As I lifted my head to look toward Mother, She was wearing the crown I had made and immediately felt immense emotion and joy. The words, 'Thank You Mother,' and 'Forgive me, Mother,' were on my lips and my eyes filled with tears.

The yogis later told me that the Madrid crown was offered first because the size and fit were more appropriate. This is true, because mine lacked technique and professionalism, but not love. The experience was a miracle of appreciation, a natural manifestation of the Divine essence of Mother's love. She knows when we put love into the things we do. On leaving the museum I went away realising that Mother knows everything.

Later, I discovered that this place is historically related to Shri Rama, an episode of the Ramayana, which the yogis in India know as, 'the place where the horse of Shri Rama was stopped or detained.'

Joaquin Orus

The forgotten kettle

On the occasion of one of Shri Mataji's visits to Madrid, She had a very intensive schedule, with the first public programme on the day of the arrival, and on the next day a puja in the morning and another public programme in the evening. On the third day She was leaving.

The two crowns for the 1989 Shri Buddha Puja, left from Madrid, right from Zaragoza

On the second day of the visit, after breakfast, we went to the place where the puja was held and Shri Mataji went directly to the public programme in the evening without going back to where She was staying.

In the evening two yogis who were accompanying Shri Mataji came back and when they arrived they saw a kettle on the stove, that I had put there to boil some water in, in case Shri Mataji might want more tea in the morning before leaving. Everything was just fine, even though the stove had been on from early morning to evening!

Spanish Sahaja Yogi

Greece is a specially blessed country

In May 1989 our flight to Athens arrived in the early evening, in unusually wet weather. Just as the last of us had got into our taxis to go to the leader's flat a tremendous thunderstorm started, but stopped when we reached there. For all the other Sahaja Yogis the experience had been the same; the rain only started when they had reached their cars or their homes. Shri Mataji redirected the hot weather towards the north; Switzerland,

France, the UK and even places as far north as Norway were to enjoy exceptional sunshine for the next few days, while things cooled down on the Mediterranean.

Shri Mataji was very pleased to see that so many Sahaja Yogis had come to greet Her at the airport, and we all accompanied Her back to the flat where a radio interview took place. The interviewers seemed to enjoy it as much as we did and promised to broadcast it at prime time, so that people would know to come to the programme the next evening.

The next day everyone was summoned to the flat for puja and Shri Mataji came around half past three. She sat on Her throne in front of a mere forty or so Sahaja Yogis, under an improvised Greek arch which was decorated with flowers and leafy branches, an amazing feat by so few Sahaja Yogis. In Her puja talk Shri Mataji explained that the puja was happening on a Wednesday, for the first time ever. She had been born at midday on a Wednesday, and just as babies have to sleep after midday, She also had had to sleep for a while just then.

'And you were also tired,' She said.

She talked about how Greece, being on the right side of the centre in the Himalayas, was the place where much of the creation took place. For this reason the Greeks have a fine sense of how far to go with anything, without going to extremes. A case in point was Alexander the Great, who when he reached India was so impressed with the culture of the country that he did not stay but retreated out of respect, which Shri Mataji contrasted with the crass behaviour of the British two thousand years later.

During the puja some extracts were read from the Apology, Socrates' dialogue at His trial. Socrates explained why He was what He was and how He worked things out, and warned and denounced the ones who condemned Him. Socrates, Shri Mataji said, always spoke the truth, and was a very straightforward and courageous personality. Like Lord Jesus, who also spoke the truth, though in parables, He was condemned by those who did not wish to hear, and His followers became confused and lost the essential message that He had taught.

The first public programme took place that evening in the ballroom of one of Athens' grandest hotels. Shri Mataji received all the new people at the end of the programme, which consequently lasted until well after midnight. Quite a number had suffered from false gurus and our Mother devoted a lot of Her attention to them.

After the programme dinner had been arranged in a local club with Bouzouki music for Shri Mataji and all the Sahaja Yogis. It was quite empty apart from us. A small dance band was playing, and a few of us danced on the stage; my wife and I were persuaded to dance a slow waltz under the gaze of Shri Mataji. Then we persuaded the members of the band to stand aside and a few of us went on stage to play a little music, and have a great deal of fun.

The following day there was another interview, with a girl from one of Greece's best newspapers. She spoke very good English, was respectful, posed sensible questions, and finished by receiving her self realisation without any problem apart from the usual journalistic liver. During the interview Shri Mataji mentioned that a special diet can be followed to improve it.

In the evening there was another public programme, very successful again. Shri Mataji spoke quite a lot about Socrates and Pallas Athena. Afterwards She returned to the flat and a few of us had the privilege of being able to stay and listen to some recordings of traditional Greek music, and then some Indian classical music with Her. Shri Mataji translated some of the songs, particularly one by Kabir in which he pokes fun at death and the way humans take it so seriously.

We finally got to bed at 3.30 am, and got up again at 4.30 to go to the airport and check in for the flight to Istanbul. We were travelling on the same flight as Shri Mataji, and at the airport accompanied Her shopping and then sitting at Her Lotus Feet in the departure lounge as She ate breakfast, read the newspaper and chatted. One important point She made was that we must all have a very strong sense of discrimination about what to tell and to whom, and what not to tell.

Phil Ward

Read Homer

A good many years ago our Holy Mother was in Greece.

'Read Homer,' She said to me before departing, and then She added, 'you have the books, read them.'

Theodore Estathiou

A regal setting

In Istanbul, in May 1989, we were met at the airport by Sahaja Yogis who had been preparing for Shri Mataji's coming for the first time. Shri Mataji was staying in a large flat belonging to a Sahaja Yogini from Milan whose husband has been assigned to Istanbul for Olivetti to help set up their Turkish subsidiary. It was a beautiful flat on the banks of the Bosphorus, looking out to Asia a kilometre away over the water, with large ships sailing past.

The evening's programme took place in a large country house in a park to the north of the city, close to the Bosphorus. At first the intention was to hold the programme outside, but as the sun dropped the air started becoming cooler and the first drops started falling, so we were moved inside. Grégoire continued his introduction and Saïd Ait–Chaalal from Algiers spoke for a little while as a Muslim (it was the first programme in an Islamic country, and Shri Mataji had asked for as many Sahaja Yogis as possible from a Muslim background to go there). The room was not large, and we sang bhajans. Shri Mataji's chair was on a small dais, a very regal setting in which to receive our Divine Mother.

There were perhaps a hundred or so people; the hall was quite a way from the centre of town and rather inaccessible. The audience was quite receptive to Shri Mataji's discourse and at the end a member of the audience, who from his behaviour had some sort of official position, stood up and formally thanked Her for coming to Istanbul. Although quite a few people had come from false gurus generally people had no problem getting realisation. As Shri Mataji left at the end of the programme we saw something of the difference between the Turks and the Greeks; the Turks said much less, but glowed and radiated their enjoyment, a very humble people. Shri Mataji chatted briefly and shook hands with some new people as She left.

The next day a puja took place at the flat. We thought it would just be a small puja for Turkey but Shri Mataji gave a very important discourse, not so much about the country, but about our hearts. She talked about different types of people; some have knowledge but are lacking in compassion as their knowledge is purely mental, and some have compassion but no discrimination. We must be like the sea, She said; it touches all the countries with equanimity, does not drown any of them but stays within its limits; we must not have too much concern for any one individual at the expense of the collectivity. We must not lose ourselves in other people, but must stay within the maryadas of our compassion, and must put Mother in our brain and heart. Some people, She said, feel themselves from time to time remote from Her; but She does not move, She is what She is, a fixed quantity, and if we feel ourselves estranged it is because it is we who have moved away. Conversely, if we feel close to Her it is not because She loves us or has concern for us more than others, but because we have moved closer to Her in our hearts, not physically. So the key is not how much Mother loves us, but how much we love Her.

After Her talk, Grégoire read out a prayer in which he, on behalf of all of us, besought Shri Mataji that in future the spreading of Sahaja Yoga would depend less on Her presence and more on the work of the Sahaja Yogis. In particular, he cited Shri Mataji's forthcoming itinerary in America. Shri Mataji looked at all of us very compassionately and gently.

'Do not worry about Me,' She said. 'I may look human, but I am not. Do I look tired?' She asked us all, and we had to admit that She looked anything but tired!

The evening's programme had been arranged in the Conference Centre of the Hilton Hotel, in the business area of the town, and the hall of six hundred seats was completely full by the time that Shri Mataji arrived. After Her talk She received people on the stage, while the Sahaja Yogis gave vibrations to newcomers, who all seemed very normal and cultured; in particular there were a number of musicians, one of whom sang a traditional song to Shri Mataji, as an interlude to the bhajans.

After the programme some of us returned to the flat. My wife and I went and Shri Mataji was so kind as to give us both names. It was particularly important for my wife, as her name, Ursula, has very sad vibrations (apparently this is generally true of all names beginning with 'U'). So it was that at the Lotus Feet of our Divine Mother, we became Lakshmi and Narayana.

Phil Ward

Shri Mataji's cashmere coat

When I was a very new Sahaja Yogi in 1989 I found out that Shri Mataji was going to visit Greece and Turkey. I asked if it would be alright if I booked myself on the same flight as Mother from Heathrow to Athens, and they said that was ok, and I was in Economy Class. At the airport, the yogi who was accompanying Shri Mataji suddenly asked if anyone else was going on the flight, and my name was put forward.

He came to me and gave me Her coat, the coat that we have often seen in all the photos – a sort of cashmere cream coloured one. He asked me to go to the departure gate because Mother was delayed as She wanted to talk to the yogis, and he wanted to make sure that the plane was delayed for Her. I couldn't believe I was carrying something of Shri Mataji's, but when I got to the departure gate I was completely confident and explained the situation and they were fine and agreed to hold the aircraft. When Mother came along and walked towards me, it was the first time She spoke to me, and She just put Her hand on my arm.

'Thank you,' She said. Her face seemed so big, and it seemed as if I was a tiny child looking at Her Mother, and Her eyes seemed so big as well.

Later, I was in an aircraft with Shri Mataji, I was standing near Her, She placed something in Her mouth, and as She did that I got a very strong taste of cardamom in my own mouth. I found out later that She had been eating cardamom.

Danielle Lee

Chapter 17

1989: June
The Americas

We reached the programme thirty minutes earlier

In June 1989, we were on a New York City highway, and Shri Mataji was in the car. She was pointing the way to the Sahaja Yogi who was driving Her (he was a taxi driver at that time). Apparently he missed an exit on the highway and lost his sense of direction when trying to get to the Queens World Expo Center. Nevertheless, we actually reached the programme site faster than the other Sahaja Yogi brothers who took off thirty minutes earlier.

Another event at that time was that Shri Mataji wanted to go to China Town for dinner after the programme. I was with the different group of yogis, but ended up finding Mother in the same restaurant.

Sarvesh Su

The pain of the Native Americans

At the Virata Puja in 1989, Shri Mataji was presented with a beautiful feather crown as worn by the chiefs, but Mother requested not to circulate the photo of Her wearing it, because when She wore the crown She said She felt all the pain the American Indians had to suffer. It was an original Native American one.

Anonymous

A request from the Divine Mother

A photo with Shri Mataji in a Native American feather headdress was taken at the Virata Puja, 1989 in Northern New York. It was one of the most powerful pujas I have ever attended. At the end of the puja talk Shri Mataji asked us all to bow down and She gave us Divine vibrations in our brains for about ten to fifteen minutes.

During the time when we normally recite the names of the deities, Carolyn Vance recited a hundred and eight names of the major Native American Indian tribes. After each name we asked this, collectively.

'Shri Mataji, please have compassion on all the Native American souls who were killed and let them take their rebirths.'

After this Shri Mataji was given the headdress by the leaders. The vibrations were the strongest I have ever felt. The entire hall was full of so many vibrations. They placed it on Her head for a very short time and then She asked them to remove it. Later Gregoire relayed a message to us from our Divine Mother, that we should not circulate the photo taken then, because She felt tremendous pain from the terrible past. Even if Shri Mataji is no longer in Her Holy Body, it was Her wish not to circulate it and so we should respect this request.

Anna Mancini

That's the way you all have to be

I was about eleven or twelve and Shri Mataji came to Toronto in 1989. I was next to Shri Mataji at the airport, and She was collecting flowers from all the yogis. She was talking to the yogis from Toronto, and there were about forty or fifty of us there. There was a lot of attention on getting an ashram in Toronto. I said this to Her.

'Yes, this is a very, very good idea,' She said. Then She began describing how it should be – it should be out in the countryside, like a ranch, like India. 'See,' said Shri Mataji, 'they talk, and they love each other, and that's the way you all have to be.'

Mohan Gulati

Shri Mataji said we had to come

It was in about 1989, and we were at the airport in Toronto. My mum had asked Shri Mataji if we could go to India that year for the India tour and She said it would not be a good idea. I was completely heart broken. So two weeks before the tour was to start, Shri Mataji called the leader and said that we had to come. So we were given this message, and were enthralled. But we didn't have the money. Just about ten minutes after we were asking ourselves that, we got a call from the lawyer who said that a case that had been stuck in court for two years, had finally gone through and my father received $25,000 Canadian in cash.

Mohan Gulati

You will be above the problems

In about 1989, in Toronto, Shri Mataji was talking to us.

'I will stay on the earth until Sahaja Yoga is established,' Shri Mataji said. One Sahaja Yogi interpreted that as meaning that Shri Mataji will be with us while all the problems are still there, because when all the problems are gone, She has done Her job. She was standing next to Shri Mataji, and Shri Mataji said something about the problems.

'Shri Mataji, I don't want all the problems to go away,' she said to Shri Mataji, 'because then You will leave us.'

'That's not the point,' Shri Mataji laughed and said. 'The problems will always be there, but you will be above the problems, they will not touch you any more.'

Mohan Gulati

Shri Mataji at Keith Road ashram

In 1989 Shri Mataji came again to Vancouver for a public programme and a puja. At that time the ashram was on Keith Road in West

Shri Mataji arriving at Keith Road ashram

Shri Mataji with Her granddaughter at Vancouver Airport

Vancouver; a small two story house just two blocks from Burrard Inlet and the Pacific Ocean.

For this visit Shri Mataji was accompanied by one of Her granddaughters, Aradhana. We hadn't prepared a separate room for Her granddaughter but Shri Mataji was not concerned and simply said they could share the same room. It was on the ground floor with an entrance through French doors, with a southern exposure. When Shri Mataji was in Her room and resting at various times during Her visit, we were able to sit in close proximity, on the lawn in meditation and on one occasion in the early morning, She opened Her doors to greet the yogis and yoginis and converse with them.

Lori Wills

A timeless event

Again that year the programme was held in Robson Square Media Centre in the centre of Vancouver; by now we had more people in the collective and were able to advertise and prepare for it properly. On the way to and from the airport, as well as to and from the public programme Shri Mataji was driven through a beautiful park in the middle of the city called Stanley Park, during which She commented on the many fine old cedar trees there. The public programme was a wonderful success and about two to three hundred people attended and got their realisation.

The following day, a Sunday, Shri Mataji accepted our request to do puja to Her and we had a small Sahasrara Puja, attended by about thirty–five established yogis and yoginis. It was very lovely and Aradhana participated as well with the painting of Shri Mataji's Feet, the offering of the amrit elements and various gifts from the centre and from other parts of North America. We enjoyed a lovely meal in Shri Mataji's presence following the puja and She spent time speaking with us about Vancouver and the spreading of Sahaja Yoga, as well as responding to those who had personal questions.

It was a timeless event from start to finish and we felt so much love and divine attention being showered upon us throughout and following Her visit. She was there only two full days but so many things happened in that short time, a sorting out on so many levels.

From Vancouver Shri Mataji flew to Bogotá, Colombia to hold a public programme and the first puja for that country. By some mysterious miracle, it happened that an extra puja sari had come to Vancouver from India that year and it was destined to be taken on to Bogotá to be offered at that puja.

Lori Wills

Shri Mataji repaid me a thousand fold

Shri Mataji came to Vancouver, and She was travelling with Aradhana, Her granddaughter and Harsh Mehra. She was only there for a short period and we had a wonderful puja as well as a public programme. During that time Harsh and Aradhana decided to visit Victoria, which is about a two hour ferry ride from Vancouver just off the coast. There are some very beautiful gardens which we toured around, and we spent two or three hours there. Then we took a trip into the city and took the ferry back. When we got back the public programme was in progress and we missed a bit of it.

The following day Shri Mataji left for San Diego, for the ashram She had purchased there. A group of us got in the car and decided to drive down to San Diego. It was a twenty–four hour drive, and we got there just before Shri Mataji had a Shri Mahakali Puja. After the puja She went up to Her room. While we were in Victoria Harsh said it would be useful if we had someone with a knowledge of diamonds and jewellery, and I mentioned that I had worked at some jewellery stores. So Shri Mataji called me up after the puja. She looked so gracious, as always, and answered many questions that I had about starting a retail business in the forty–five minutes I was with Her. I was literally and figuratively in heaven!

I ended up going to India, buying a whole lot of jewellery, and starting a retail jewellery business. Shri Mataji was obviously working on me, and She was showing me Her jewellery and Her saris, and it was really a special time to be with Her. I felt it was a direct result of having taken some time to be hospitable to Harsh and Aradhana, because obviously I missed the time in Vancouver with Her.

Later during the week Shri Mataji went shopping and I was invited to go, however in the end there wasn't enough room in the car so I stayed back. Ten minutes later there was a call saying Mother had forgotten Her glasses and to send Alan (me) in a car with them to the store. My small sacrifice was repaid a thousand fold and I learned an important lesson as a result.

Alan Morrissey

Jesus was My son

The very first time I met Shri Mataji was in 1989, when She came to a public programme in Vancouver, and all the new seekers were able to wait in line and meet Her Holiness in person. I had been practising Sahaja Yoga off and on for a year before I met Shri Mataji. I was very attached to Lord Jesus, as a Christian, and wore my cross around my neck. When it was finally my turn, Mother took me by both hands, and immediately I felt a mild shaking, as my arms started to quiver and react to Her purity. She looked at my ivory cross.

'You know, Jesus was My son,' She said, 'and you shouldn't wear this. His message was the resurrection of the flesh in spirit, not the crucifixion.' I was too stunned to say anything and just stared silently, in awe of Mother's energy and eyes, which seemed to pierce right through me.

'Yes Mother,' I said finally, and bowed and left.

That night I had an astonishing dream of Shri Mataji, concerning my wearing of the cross, and I awoke to find it lying at the foot of a statue of Shri Ganesha, and Lord Jesus is the incarnation of Shri Ganesha. I never wore it again.

Brent Fidler

Driving Shri Mataji

While driving Shri Mataji from the airport to Her hotel we were stopped at a light and a person appeared to wash the windows of the car. I started wondering to myself, 'Should I tip this person or not?' It was quite a dilemma as I had heard it mentioned that Shri Mataji had suggested not to tip some of the people begging in India. So in the middle of my dilemma Shri Mataji said to me go ahead and tip the man.

Another time we were driving in Her car, I wasn't sure of the correct way to go and Shri Mataji said to me that She was never lost, because wherever She was She was there, so how could She be lost?

Alan Morrissey

Shri Mataji would explain the plot

Another incident was watching Hindi movies with Shri Mataji in Her hotel room after public programmes. I found it very difficult to remain awake, especially after a few nights with very little sleep. Hindi movies without subtitles all begin to look the same to me after a while. I could see Shri Mataji and the Indian boys all enjoying them, and here I was fighting to prevent myself from nodding off. I'm sure She knew my dilemma, and would very sweetly explain the plot to me during the show.

Alan Morrissey

Answers from the divine

Shri Mataji visited the USA just a few months after I came to Sahaja Yoga in 1989. However I was not able to manage the trip, being a single mom of three teenagers with very tight finances, and an almost crippling bad back. Shri Mataji had gone from the Midwest to California, then on to Fort Lauderdale, Florida.

I had a dear friend who worked for the airlines and she offered me a free plane ticket to Florida. Helpers were needed to assist in the house where Mother would be staying, so I called and asked if I could help.

'Yes, please join us in Florida,' the yogi answering said. Being so new in Sahaja Yoga I had no idea what an opportunity this was – about a dozen of us staying in a private home with Shri Mataji.

Off to Florida I flew, and in the airport recognized another person wearing Shri Mataji's pendant so we shared a cab to the house. I ironed Shri Mataji's saris, washed dishes, tended children and just soaked up the amazing vibrations. These little chores seemed to be cleansing me as I did them. Could I really feel these vibrations or was I just fooling myself? Would I be able to sustain these and pass them on to others as all the yogis said was possible? While standing at the sink doing dishes and pondering these questions, I suddenly felt an electric charge in the air. I looked up and there was Shri Mataji, simply walking into the solarium. I immediately bowed my head and folded my hands in namaste. She smiled at me.

'May God bless you!' She said.

Simple words but the feeling was incredible. For the rest of the day I floated around, wide–eyed. The next night we all hurried to a nearby hotel where I had my first glimpse of a public programme. Shri Mataji walked on stage, gave an introductory talk, answered questions, and then did the long form of self realisation, having everyone collectively put their hands on the chakras and say the affirmations with Her. Then She blew in the microphone and told us to watch Her without thinking. In that hot Miami evening many of us felt the incredible coolness of our own Spirit for the first time.

Afterwards She invited the newcomers up to the stage to meet Her. Even though I was staying in the house I still went up and She smiled so sweetly at me. To my complete surprise She placed Her hand above my head.

'See, she is dwijaha!' She said to the yogis on the stage. I was to find out that means twice born – realised – and my doubts were finished. If Shri Mataji Herself said it, who was I to doubt any longer?

I returned home in awe of the events that took place in those three short days but that would forever change my life. My doctor said my back was much better than it had been since he had begun treating me, so I told both him and my friend from the airlines about Sahaja Yoga. What a joy to not only get self realisation from Mother Herself, but to be able to pass it along to others. What more is there?

Betty Cooper

Shri Mataji gave advice

In 1989, Shri Mataji came to Colombia again and offered a public pro-gramme in a convention centre, in a room for about four hundred people, but as it was full even before the time the manager let the next room be opened, and again it was full, so finally the whole place was for Shri Mataji's programme.

We also had a puja on that occasion. Shri Mataji spoke about Christ and at the end the yogis offered a map of the country to Her. At that time there was an earthquake, not very strong but enough to be reported in the news.

From Colombia Shri Mataji went to Brazil, on our way to the airport at night in the car Mother was saying that people waste lots of time in the traffic jams in the big cities, although it was night and the road was empty.

On the airport Shri Mataji sat in the waiting room with the yogis sitting around Her, She let them ask questions and gave advice to them.

Edgar Patarroyo

Shri Mataji's Feet appeared completely blue

The Sahasrara Puja in 1989 in Bogotá was attended by a small number of people. By all accounts it was beautiful, and a photograph was taken in which the Lotus Feet of Shri Mataji appeared completely blue. She was extremely happy, and pleased with the seekers of Colombia. She told us that She expected that the majority of Sahaja Yogis in the future would come from such countries where the people are simple–hearted, and not from the West.

Phil Ward

Everything was just in a plan

The first Brazilian Tour: 28/06/1989 Salvador, 30/06/1989 Brasilia, 01/07/1989 to 03/07/1989 Rio de Janeiro.

Shri Mataji was so kind to come, and with Her came a man from Australia who had been born in Argentina. Some years before he had asked Her to come to Argentina, and She had said that Argentina was not yet ready, but within three years She would be in Brazil, and it was so. When Shri Mataji said that no one was in Brazil, and no one was going to invite Her. So everything was just in a plan, and She knew exactly what was to happen.

It was Wednesday the 28th of June 1989, and the great day had arrived. Shri Mataji would arrive at Salvador at twelve o'clock. I went to the airport with my little daughter Vijaya and some other new Sahaja Yogis. From the roof we saw the plane arrive and waited, our emotions rising, for Shri Mataji, Shri Adi Shakti, to appear at the door of the plane. As soon as She saw us She waved, and with Her were a number of Sahaja Yogis. I ran to the car park to get the car, to put it near the exit, while Mother collected Her baggage.

I returned to the door where the passengers came out from and a Sahaja Yogini came to me, worried, because Shri Mataji had stumbled. How could that be? Shri Mataji was there, tranquil as always, with all the Sahaja Yogis who had accompanied Her, and She greeted me warmly. The Sahaja Yogis were a bit agitated.

Duilio Cartocci

Shri Mataji at Rio Airport with the Sahaja Yogis

Divine Motherly love

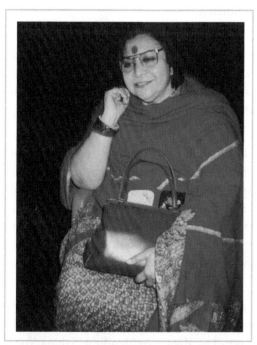

Shri Mataji at Rio Airport

In 1989, when Shri Mataji entered Brazil, She had to change planes in Rio and we boarded the plane with Her, to Salvador. The airplane landed in that old style airport and we had to walk towards the airport building. I was walking beside Mother when suddenly the Goddess stumbled. I tried to help Her, but how could a minute mortal do such an impossible task? There was something else going on that we could not see. Shri Mataji turned to me.

'Let Me do it, Bruno. I will have to stand by Myself, alone,' She said sternly, and did so. There were those eternal seconds where Mother was working out something that we could not know, but the feeling was intense. Then we walked towards the Arrivals gate and Shri Mataji was very joyous, greeting the Sahaja Yogis.

Later on She explained to us what happened. Salvador was the capital of the state of Bahia where there were many slaves during the colonial era, and many were tortured and killed. So all those souls were trapped and could not incarnate again. Their only possibility to free themselves was to touch the Feet of the Goddess. So when Shri Adi Shakti, in Her incarnated form, arrived in Salvador those unfortunate souls flocked to Her. It was an act of Divine Motherly love.

Bruno Descaves

Chaitanya

Once in Salvador in 1989 we went to have dinner in a terrace restaurant by the sea. Shri Mataji was sitting at the head of the table and we all could see the sea at night.

'Look how beautiful the chaitanya is in the sky! Can you see it?' She said.

There were like little tiny lights falling on the sea. What a magical moment – so shiny.

Bruno Descaves

This house is an ashram

We left in the car to go to the ashram and with me were Shri Mataji, Brigitte from Colombia, Bruno and his wife Misao. I drove towards the house slowly, passing by Itapoan beach, a very panoramic journey, to give enough time for the others to collect their baggage, go more quickly than us so as to get to the house to warn my wife Tereza of our arrival, and to prepare the aarti.

Despite being delayed we arrived home first, and insistently rang the bell to warn Tereza that we had arrived, and to prepare the aarti. Tereza, not suspecting anything, came, opened the door, found she was in front of Shri Adi Shakti in person and stood there without saying anything. Mother meanwhile read the big writing above the gate: 'Nirmala House' and called to Tereza.

'This house is an ashram,' She said, and made Her way to Her room on the first floor.

Meanwhile the others arrived and they brought Shri Mataji's luggage into Her room. In a short time it was full of Sahaja Yogis and us, and after

Her questions, we began to tell Her all the good and less good things about Brazil. She listened very attentively and said that is it is very good if one can see the defects of one's country.

Shri Mataji mentioned Her fall at the airport and said it was because of the spiritualism and black magic. Later someone told me She said She had thrown Herself in front to protect the Sahaja Yogis, who were behind Her, from an attack of bhuts.

I showed Her all the articles in the various papers about Her coming and She seemed happy, and said we had done a lot of work. I replied that in reality it is Shri Hanuman who does everything, and that is why everything went so easily. I gave Her a bird of silver and quartz. Then Mother tried a typical meal with carajè, vatapa et cetera. After a long conversation we left Her room but Mother called me back and gave me a magnificent silver vase, bought in the USA, the first present for the Brazil collective.

Shri Mataji rested for a bit and we saw to the final details. About six o'clock we were again in Her room to speak to Her. She wanted to know how much we had spent, so She could pay for the preparations. We refused, but She insisted, saying that for the first year the costs would be too much to be totally on our shoulders, and She would contribute from the international fund. We repeated that we had full trust in the power of Shri Lakshmi, but in the end, after Her insistence, we accepted $350, feeling that perhaps it was auspicious to allow the world collectivity to contribute. We asked Shri Mataji if She would like to phone to Sir CP, and She consented to do so.

Shri Mataji with Duilio's daughter

Later Mother went down for an interview with a journalist from the Folha de S. Paolo and with the TV Itapoan. The room was full of many of Tereza's friends.

The interview was very good and at the end we all went out on to the veranda, to take photos of Shri Mataji. As soon as the journalists had gone Shri Mataji cured a great pain in the neck of Chris, a friend of Tereza, and he began to play with and amuse Vijaya.

Duilio Cartocci

We are babies in Your presence

We decided to make a tour of the town of Salvador with two cars. I drove the car with Shri Mataji and some other Sahaja Yogis, the left side was very strong, as can be imagined, and Mother slept deeply, as if She was working on the whole area. She did not want to see the old city, so we went to eat at a restaurant called 'Escuna', by the sea, and we all sat together at a big table, with the noise of the waves, the light of the stars and the best atmosphere.

The food was not that good, but what did it matter? Everything was fantastic. Mother was at the head of the table, and I was near Her and hung on all Her words. A Sahaja Yogi went on asking stupid and useless questions, and She replied so lovingly, so humanely, and also we were able to join in the game. Shri Mahamaya! We are still babies in Your presence.

We then went home and because we arrived before the others we found the gate closed, and no one answered the bell. Not wanting to leave Shri Mataji to wait standing outside a closed gate, I agilely climbed over the gate and opened it from the inside.

She looked at me, laughing, and complimented me on my skill, and was then concerned at the lack of security in the house, if I had been able to get in so easily. I replied that I wasn't too worried, because Shri Durga was looking after me. She looked at me, somewhat abashed, and then said I should make it better and be more careful. And in fact we did have two robberies after this.

Finally everyone went to sleep after a day that had been so intense that it seemed like a whole month.

Duilio Cartocci

The fantastic, simple, deep and powerful first puja in Brazil

We got up early on Thursday the 29th of July, 1989. The interview with TV Bahia was suspended, so Mother, with two Sahaja Yoginis, went to do some shopping at the Mercato Modelo. Shri Mataji was tireless, and

Shri Mataji with Bruno the day before the puja

walked between the stalls without stopping, touching and vibrating so many objects. We spent the whole morning shopping, until finally we met a journalist and photographer from the Giornale Globo, who had come to look for us, exclusively to interview Shri Mataji. After we had bought a tablecloth and some sheets we returned to the ashram, and She showed us how to clean silver objects with lemon and salt.

About five o'clock I went to Her room to invite Her to the puja. I found the door closed and knocked but no one replied, so I opened the door and entered. I found Shri Mataji resting on a sofa, in a profound sleep. I did not have the courage to wake Her, so I remained in meditation in front of Her while She slept. The time was flying past, and everyone was waiting in the living room, and the public programme would be after that, on that same evening. Later, when She was awake, we asked that if She would like to have the puja in Rio di Janiero instead, as maybe She was tired, and would prefer to rest until the public programme. Shri Mataji said it would be good to do the puja now and while we all sang the Shri Ganesha Artharva Shersha She came down the stairs and sat in front of us in the living room.

Thus began the fantastic, simple, deep and powerful first puja in Brazil, where about eleven of us were present, and we had the great privilege of coming to the Feet of Shri Adi Shakti, sakshat Shri Mahakali. Some powerful photos were taken, especially one of Her Feet, which had just been decorated. It is very strong when used for meditation.

Duilio Cartocci

Is it time for the puja?

The puja was going to be offered before the public programme, but time was passing and Shri Mataji did not come down from Her bedroom. I was asked to go there to call Her. I knocked on the door but heard nothing, so I slowly opened it and Mother was sleeping. What to do? Gently I tried to call Her for the puja. But there was just Divine silence. There was a feeling that She was not there, her Divine body was there but Shri Adi Shakti was not. After some time She came back.

'Is it time for the puja? I will be coming down in a few minutes,' She said sweetly

Bruno Descaves

The people of Brazil were very good

The first time Shri Mataji was in Brazil, in 1989, She had been to Rio di Janiero and Salvador. In Salvador She said this name is very important, because we had to save the country, and She entered it there. She said the people of Brazil were very good, and also the native Indian people. She said we must be aware that we had to save our country. She was very content, but said Brazil was very heavy, with the black magic and other reasons, but when we did the puja She said we should not worry any more about these things.

Tereza Cartocci

The moment Shri Mataji entered the hall there was a fresh energy

The puja finished at the same time as we were supposed to start the public programme, then with the blessings of Shri Mataji we went to the Raul Chaves Auditorium, offered by the university. The room, with a capacity of five hundred people, was completely full and there were also people standing waiting. I gave a long introduction while waiting for Mother to arrive. Bruno, who was driving Shri Mataji's car, lost sight of the car in front of him that was supposed to be showing the right way. After a bit of a drive around, Shri Mataji Herself showed the way to the hall where the programme was being held, even though it was a town of three million people and She had never been there before.

The public meanwhile were waiting patiently and with interest. Shri Mataji entered from the rear door and walked up the central aisle between the rows of seated seekers to Her seat on the stage. A Sahaja Yogini who was there for the first time said that the moment Shri Mataji entered the hall, in spite of the great heat, she felt a fresh energy coming from behind, to the point that it made her turn round. Everyone received realisation and at the end could come up to Shri Mataji to meet Her personally.

While we were coming back in the car Shri Mataji said She was very pleased with everything, and at our home asked if She could go out on the veranda to be in the open air, again expressing Her joy at the programme and the seekers who were there.

Duilio Cartocci

The param chaitanya organised everything

The next morning we got up early and were somewhat agitated because we had to take the plane to Brasilia. The second car, an old Fiat, was in theory going on ahead to the airport with the luggage to do the check in, but it would not start and we could not open the boot for the baggage, so we were very late. We put all the baggage in the main car and went ahead to check in. The others would arrive by taxi with Shri Mataji.

We were supposed to leave on the 8.00 plane, but at the airport we discovered that the agency had by mistake put us on the 8.15 plane and it was delayed for an hour. As always, the param chaitanya organised everything much better than we did, down to every little detail. Some of the Yogis flew directly to Rio to do the final preparations while others, including me, flew with Shri Mataji.

Duilio Cartocci

The children sang a welcoming song

At Brasilia, on Friday 30th June 1989, we were met by Vera and her nephew Bruno. Vera offered Mother flowers. She took her hand to give Vera vibrations, and cure a little problem. Vera was involved with a cultural association called 'Cidade da Paz', situated in a marvellous park. We went directly there and were received very warmly by children, who sang a welcoming song in honour of Shri Mataji.

A TV crew was also present and Shri Mataji gave two interviews in the open. Then She took off Her shoes and allowed them to film Her while She walked barefoot in the rich nature, by the pool. Shri Mataji explained that the earth of Brazil is special, because it is red like the earth of Shri Ganesha.

Shri Mataji was offered the room of the president of the foundation, who was absent at that time, but She wanted a simpler one. We remade the bed in another room, with new sheets bought by Vera. We all ate together, with a representative from the cultural section of the Indian Embassy.

Shri Mataji meanwhile toured Brasilia with some Sahaja Yogis to do some shopping, and bought, among other things, some dried flowers. Mother arrived back at the Cidade da Paz at six o'clock, a little before me. I told Her this was because I had been trying to get the visa, and then went to prepare the last minute preparations. This room was the 'Gran Circular' offered by the governor of the Federal District, with the precious help of Vera.

Shri Mataji in the grounds of the Cidade da Paz

About seven twenty, as we had arranged, I began the introduction to about nine hundred people. Shri Mataji delayed Her arrival and I extended the introduction until eight o'clock. Finally She arrived and sat graciously on the stage, prepared in a typically Indian fashion. At the end of the talk everybody received realisation and felt the cool breeze. Shri Mataji invited everyone to greet Her personally and received everyone who wanted to meet Her, and was very sweet. They seemed to be good seekers. Towards the end a young man came up.

'How are you?' Shri Mataji asked.

'Well,' he replied.

'No, you are not,' She said. He was looking at Shri Mataji in a strange way and jumped uncontrollably like an epileptic. After one or two minutes, She gave a bandhan and said, 'Now you are free.'

Immediately he became calm, looked around and asked what had happened. After this we returned to the Foundation and while going there Shri Mataji commented that She had noticed the problem, and made it so he could not come up to Her until most of the people had come and gone.

Duilio Cartocci

Shri Mataji could see what was inside every one of us

At that period Shri Mataji used to work on people at the public pro-grammes. In Brasilia, Brazil, in 1989, when all the people came to Her at the end of the programme, to be worked on and so on, we saw that Shri Mataji was keeping one lady, who was trying to push forward, a little aside. Finally when all the public went away, Shri Mataji let this lady come close to Her. The lady turned out to be epileptic, and started having a fit. Shri Mataji said She saw this before, which was why She kept her aside until everyone had gone away. Then Shri Mataji freed her from this posses-sion. Shri Mataji could see what was inside every one of us. That night in Brasilia, there were a lot of people.

Duilio Cartocci

Mother, are we free?

When we returned home Shri Mataji went directly to Her room. Tereza told me that Shri Mataji wanted to see me so I went to Her. She advised me to tell Vera and Gill, from Brasilia, about Sahaja Yoga and asked them to be with me for at least eight days so I could explain everything. She asked me why I was so serious that night, and I told Her that I felt it was a great responsibility to have invited Her to do a public programme at Brasilia. We spoke for a long time, and She asked me many things. I took the courage to ask Her a most important question, which for a long time I had not found an answer to.

'Mother, are we free? Does it exist, free will?'

'Of course, you are free,' was Her answer. She had me sit in front of Her and asked me to repeat a number of times: 'Mother, You are the Holy Ghost.'

She asked me to go closer to Her and began to massage my Sahasrara with oil. I must admit that because of the enormous amount of administrative work I was not able to go into thoughtless awareness, and continued to think of the thousand and one things that I believed I had to prepare. I told Her this, and She began to work on my Agnya chakra, massaging the ego and super ego, my left and right temples. After about five minutes a complete silence came within me, a profound state of nirvichara samadhi. Oh sweetest Mother, source of compassion! She continued to work on me, and after having had me turn round so I had my back to Her, worked on my Vishuddhi, massaged my neck and asked me to relax.

At about one o'clock in the morning Shri Mataji finally lay down and asked me to massage Her left Foot with camphor balm. To begin with I was tired, the muscles of my hand stiff with tiredness, but then, after a time I became more relaxed and the pain went away. After about fifteen to twenty minutes Shri Mataji asked me to massage Her right Foot, for another twenty minutes.

Mother meanwhile slept and breathed deeply, as if She had come from some place far away. I massaged Her Feet very hard, then suddenly, in a low voice, as if She had come from another dimension, told me to change Feet. She also told me what type of massage, with which hand, whether with the thumb or the base of the palm, whether to massage the Vishuddhi or the Agnya on Her Feet, and whether it should be the left or right. Her ability to pass from a deep sleep to a totally conscious state was surprising, and then She would go back into a deep sleep, with deep long breathing, and all while I was massaging Her so strongly.

When I went to sleep it was about 3.30 am, and Misao was still working in the kitchen. In the morning I got up early to see her still in the kitchen, preparing breakfast. I was amazed at the way in which this Japanese lady could keep going, she was always working but was always so serene and tranquil. Shri Mataji had deep words of praise for her.

Duilio Cartocci

Only the Kundalini could do the subtle work

Today we invited Shri Mataji to the Cidade da Paz, to have a meeting with the people who work with the street children. The association had produced a translator, not a Sahaja Yogini, to translate Mother's words. I do not remember all Her magnificent discourse, but at a certain point She became very profound and the translator could not express Her vastness. I felt it was the moment to intervene, even though my English was limited, because I understood the point that Shri Mataji was making with great emphasis.

I began translating. Mother spoke of the importance of raising the Kundalini of abandoned children. Only the Kundalini could do the subtle work of inwardly curing and for this the best people to do this would be those involved in the project, so they should first get their realisation. Shri Mataji invited them to go to a programme that evening. When I had finished speaking in front of the members of the association, Shri Mataji gave me a sweet smile and nodded Her head approvingly, as if to confirm the need for my spontaneous and improvised translation. What joy to be able to be involved!

In the evening, when I was in Her room, Shri Mataji again thanked me for my translation. She smiled a lot and asked me whether I could understand or speak English, and how well I could participate in Her light and joyous game.

Tereza Cartocci

Immediately she was better

We were in Brasilia on the 1st July 1989. In the morning we got up very early to take the plane to Rio de Janiero. Shri Mataji and I had breakfast on the veranda and She met all the new members of the foundation.

I went to the airport a bit before to check in. Mother arrived after all the other Sahaja Yogis but unfortunately the plane was full so only She and I could travel. The others came on an afternoon plane. After a short wait they announced our plane, and I asked permission to go in front of the crowd so we could get on the plane more peacefully.

Near us was a lady who seemed to be in pain, and to have a bad back. Shri Mataji came close to her, and gave vibrations, and immediately she was better. Then she walked to the plane alone, and sat next to Mother. Throughout the journey Shri Mataji gave her vibrational comfort, and in the end invited her to the public programme.

Duilio Cartocci

In truth, I am

We arrived at the airport at Rio de Janeiro and discovered that there was no one to meet us. After about fifteen minutes Bruno arrived and explained that he had got stuck in an incredible traffic jam and had only miraculously managed to get out of it. When we were going back to the house, we saw the jam, kilometres long on the opposite side of the road. At Bruno's house his wife Misao received Shri Mataji with the aarti and then offered Her a wonderful meal, which She distributed to all present. Mother then rested for a bit.

The programme was organised for six o'clock and we arrived at ten past six. Some people had already left. After some music I began an introduction for about thirty seekers, some a bit strange. At a quarter past seven Shri Mataji arrived, sat down calmly, looked at me, and looked at the number of people.

'A little disappointing,' She said, then began to describe Sahaja Yoga, and it seemed that it was the best talk Shri Mataji had given in Brazil. I was particularly serene and relaxed; the great work done by Her on me the previous evening had produced effects.

Then She gave everyone realisation and allowed them all to come and meet Her personally. I remember one lady who was suffering from some form of epilepsy: Mother cured her and took her head between Her hands and went close to her ear and whispered the mantra: 'Sakshat.....' 'Sakshat......' 'In truth, I am....'

Duilio Cartocci

Kalatit

I have many nice memories with dear Mother Shri Mataji. Shall I tell one?

The one that gives me 'frisson' was before the first public programme in Rio in 1989. Duilio (Cartocci) was giving the introduction and all the yogis had left, so I stayed in the apartment to take Shri Mataji. I was waiting in the living room, when She came out of Her room. Beautiful, with powder on Her cheeks, She was just radiant. Then She comes to me and asks with a very sweet voice:

'How do I look Bruno? Am I OK?'

'Mother You look beautiful!'

'Thank you Bruno... so, shall we go?'

So we went, the two of us in the car, and the ganas, and it just felt like driving through the clouds in heaven. These are just one of those situations that are kalatit – timeless – writing it is like seeing Her again coming out of the room.

Bruno Descaves

The small Sahaja Yogis were sitting around Shri Mataji

When we entered the house, after spending some time unloading the sound equipment, we saw Shri Mataji sitting on an armchair and all the small Sahaja Yogis were sitting around Her. She was happy and immediately created a relaxed and familiar atmosphere.

She did imitations of some deranged followers of false gurus. It was all very amusing and we could not stop laughing, and were sitting on the floor laughing. Also Shri Mataji was laughing and Her laughter was contagious. We passed two hours laughing and talking, and everything was so beautiful and clean, they were incredible moments. At times I was rolling on the floor with laughter, without being able to control myself. Then we went to bed, and another day which seemed an eternity has passed.

Duilio Cartocci

Shri Mataji opened me to a subtler vision

The place where we stayed in Rio, and Shri Mataji's room, faced the Hills of the Two Twins (Morro Dos Dois Irmaos). The morning after we arrived we were sitting on front of Shri Mataji while She had Her breakfast before the open window. She was looking at the view and noticed a lot of baddhas outside in the sky, and with Her hand gave some bandhans. I asked what they looked like and She, astonished, asked me if I did not see them. I said I had not, and She asked me to look again towards the sky, outside the window. At that moment I could see clearly little dark spots which whirled in the air, like little black commas. It was as if Shri Mataji, for a moment, opened me to a subtler vision, but from then on I never again saw that.

Shri Mataji then spoke about a Brazilian person who had caught a bhut from a relation, and said he would do well to start to work actively, then he would go into the right. Bhuts do not like the right side, and would run away.

Duilio Cartocci

Shri Mataji with the Hills of
the Two Twins behind Her

Shri Mataji asked for a pen and a pad of paper

At ten o'clock in the morning of the next day, on 2nd July 1989, a journalist from the Manchette arrived and also other people, at the time arranged for the interview. Two Sahaja Yogis entertained them until twelve o'clock, when Shri Mataji came. She explained Sahaja Yoga, and then worked on Enrio's son who suffered from asthma, then She worked on all the family, and finally also the journalist.

Shri Mataji asked for a pen and a pad of paper, and explained, with a drawing, how the Kundalini and the chakras move and work. I was seated behind Her and She called me and explained everything personally. I remember that the three channels of energy, for simplicity, are drawn parallel, but in reality they coincide with the height of the various chakras, that is the left channel goes up from the Mooladhara chakra, passing on the left side, but at the level of the various chakras it re-enters the centre, and continuing to rotate, forms the left side of the chakra. The same happens on the right channel, so that in reality the chakras are formed by the overlapping, superimposition of the left and the right, while the central chakras stay in the centre, between the two side chakras, placed not horizontally but vertically, one above the other.

The Kundalini, on the other hand, rises from the Mooladhara directly to the Nabhi in a straight line through the central channel, then it descends again to the Swadishthan which revolves around the Nabhi. I understood that the distance between the Swadishthan and the Nabhi could vary and it is when the Kundalini fills the space between these two chakras, that is the Void, that the self realisation can take place. I think I understood that the soul has a movement which follows the right channel, or at the least this is how Shri Mataji had drawn it.

The bhut, when it enters the human being, works from the other side, trying to neutralise the movement of the soul and entering into every single molecule of the body. The spirit on the other hand seems to move vertically, between the two movements of the soul and the bhut.

Duilio Cartocci

Explanation of Dopamine

Shri Mataji demonstrating Her explanation

I will explain better the picture above: Shri Mataji makes a ring in the right hand joining the thumb with the Vishuddhi finger and another ring with the left hand the same way. She says that one ring is the right side activity and the other the left. If they work separated from each other the middle channel doesn't have the possibility to ascend. When one ring goes on top of the other, it means working together in a collective state, like in the picture, and it creates an opening for the centre channel to pass through, then the Sushumna nadi can ascend.

Bruno Descaves

The chakras and the Kundalini

Mother explained how the Ida Nadi and the Pingala Nadi on their own don't create a space for the Sushumna Nadi. When they work together, i.e. joining together, they form a third /channel between them so the Kundalini can rise.

Here Shri Mataji is drawing the chakras, explaining how a catch can shift from chakra to chakra. For example, if the catch is residing in the Nabhi, when we start working to get rid of it the catch shifts to another chakra; i.e., a catch can have two bases, and uses them as appropriate to stay in the subtle system of the person.

The diagram which Shri Mataji is drawing is the same one as in the explanation below.

Bruno Descaves

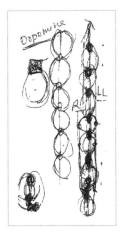

Shri Mataji's diagram

Shri Mataji drawing the diagram

The example of two ropes

Shri Mataji explained to the media in Rio, Brazil, in July 1989, about the rising of the Kundalini and also about possessions in relation to dopamine. She said when man makes his ascent, he does not do so in a straight line; he goes first to the left, then to the right, then to the left again. Kundalini ascent does this also, dividing herself into two. The reason for it can be understood if we take the example of two ropes. These two ropes together, side by side in the process of going up or coming down cross over twice, making four loops – two each in the opposite direction clockwise and anti-clockwise at every chakra.

She also said that the soul manifests on the left side in loop forms and the possessions cleverly close the loops on the other side. That is why a possessed person has at times a split personality. Sometimes the negativity or possession takes charge and sometime the person is in charge, depending on how strong he or she is. But when the person is under the influence of drugs or alcohol the possession is in full charge.

By stimulating the release of dopamine the negativity reinforces the nerve circuit and then the person becomes obsessed with a negative thought pattern. If you can get into thoughtless awareness the nerve circuits can be dissolved and the negativity will leave.

Juan Vega

Dopamine – the chemical reward

I will try to tell in my way what Shri Mataji said about Dopamine, dharma, possessions and realisation, in Rio de Janeiro, in July 1989.

Shri Mataji explained that afternoon about the importance of having the right side and the left side of our being in equilibrium. When this happens, the two holes join and, as in the picture above, the centre channel passes through and realisation takes place. She also spoke about dharma. That is the righteousness. After realisation we know what dharma is, how our actions naturally happen the right way and we stop being mental.

Then She made a picture of the seven chakras and the channels and explained how the possessions enter into us. They use a pair of chakras to trick us (for example: the Agnya chakra and the Nabhi). That is why when we try to clear one chakra it goes to the other chakra to take refuge. Then when we start clearing the other chakra it goes back to that chakra. It is a vicious circle and unless we understand that we have those two chakras caught up and work on them simultaneously, the possession won't go away!

Lastly Mother explained how the possession makes the person act in an adharmic way. Dopamine is the chemical that gives us rewards for doing good deeds. But when the possession takes over the dopamine cycle it makes the person act in an adharmic way. When this happens it makes the body of the possessed person release dopamine. That person then feels good, and the conditioning of leading an adharmic life is created because of the reward of the dopamine. Each time this happens the conditioning becomes stronger. That is how the murderers feel good in killing, the liars in lying, the corrupt people in stealing, or any adharmic persons in doing adharmic behaviour. In order to break that horrible conditioning, that person has to meditate. So instead of feeling the chemical reward of the dopamine the person will go deeper and feel the joy of the spirit.

Shri Mataji spoke about the reward mechanism of the dopamine in 1989, but only on the 1990's it was discovered.

Bruno Descaves

Shri Mataji with the diagram

Shri Mataji greatly appreciated that gesture

Today Shri Mataji was to leave for New York, but decided to stay one day longer. She said that at the end of Her trip, She had been working very hard on the Sahasrara of Rio, to open it. Our joy was enormous.

She rested until five o'clock, and while She took tea, Brigitte, Delia and another yogi came into Her room, while the others sat outside in the passage. Shri Mataji immediately began talking about a lot of different subjects. She asked me how large the hotel rooms were that I was thinking of building at Bahia, and compared them to those of Her house, Pratishthan, of which She spoke a lot, of Her large bedroom and the marvellous bathroom.

Shri Mataji told us about the influence of the Aryan Sanskrit culture. She noted the similarity of English words with those of Sanskrit, for example in the words a.m. and p.m., which are abbreviations of Sanskrit words. I asked Her how it was that according to Her, Markandeya was 13,000 years ago, while for the scientists the oldest Indian society, the Indo–Aryan, was at the most 5,000 years old. Shri Mataji replied that the intellectual scholars came up with theories to give confirmation to their preconceived ideas. The Sanskrit culture was much older and the Aryans left India then returned a second time. She said that Shri Rama was alive eight thousand years before Christ, and Shri Krishna six thousand years before Christ.

While She was speaking, the vibrations became so fresh and strong in my hands that I could not have any doubt about what She was saying, and I told Her this. She noted that the increase in the perception of vibrations improved the Vishuddhi and this happened because it was important to develop a sense of collectivity in us. She gave the example of Brigitte, who at Bogotá, during the puja, although she had been invited by Shri Mataji to put on the ornaments, had given this to another Sahaja Yogini, realising that there would not be many other occasions like this where she could have such a great joy. Clearly Shri Mataji had greatly appreciated that gesture.

Duilio Cartocci

None of us said another word

Another yogi told about the family of his uncle who followed a false guru, and this false guru had materialised a photo of Christ, in which He had a long face and hair. Shri Mataji said that the photo was obviously false; Christ, She explained, was about five foot ten, a little less than six foot tall, and was robust. Michelangelo has painted Him in the Sistine Chapel more or less as He really was, with a round face like Shri Mataji's and brownish hair.

She explained the enormous conditioning we have about Christ. We have such respect for Christ because He is already dead. Shri Mataji is a total incarnation and is in front of us now, in the present. Also, Christ had only twelve disciples and they were not cultured, without education and without realisation, but even so they did so much. What can we do with all our powers? If only we could realise who She is. She explained the confusion which Paul made and how he had destroyed the true work of Christ. None of us said another word. We remained fixed while Mother spoke and manifested before us.

Furthermore, Shri Mataji explained to the journalists that St Thomas, after the (crucifixion) death of Christ, went to India, and then returned to Egypt, where he wrote a truly Gnostic gospel. The word Gnostic comes from the Latin word gnosi and also in Sanskrit, the word for knowledge is gyan. After having worked on everyone present Shri Mataji retired to Her room.

Duilio Cartocci

There were tears in my eyes

She said we have to become dedicated to the cause of Sahaja Yoga, just as Her family, who were very well off, with seven large houses, cars and so on, sacrificed everything in the struggle against the English for the freedom of India. Her father and mother were imprisoned many times, and because of this Shri Mataji was busy in their home, where the rest of the family lived, always carrying the keys with Her. She also explained how She was tortured with ice and electric shocks, all in the quest for liberty.

There were tears in my eyes, and my Kundalini was at the Sahasrara. I thought for one moment that I was perhaps too emotional, but then I noticed that Brigitte and Delia also had tears in theirs.

Duilio Cartocci

Every word of Shri Mataji's is a mantra

Shri Mataji told us not to close our eyes in front of Her, but to look at Her Feet. Every word of Hers is a mantra.

Shri Mataji, sakshat Shri Adi Shakti, then had us say the mantra of Shri Chandra Ma seven times, with our right hand seven centimetres above the Sahasrara, to cool down the right side. Then She had us say the mantra to Shri Himalaya, also seven times, with the left hand ten centimetres above the Sahasrara. Then She asked us to say, again seven times, 'Mother, please come into my head,' to give more intensity to the request. I instinctively put my hand in front of my chest, and asked everyone to do the same.

Having done that, always with our attention on Her, She asked us to say, 'Mother, please, come into my heart', with our right hand on the heart, twelve times. To finish, She asked us to say, 'Mother, please come into my attention,' with our left hand on the liver.

Duilio Cartocci

Try to understand Who you are in front of

In Brazil in 1989 Shri Mataji made it like a family feeling – all together. We were very few of us, and we went shopping in Rio de Janiero. Once we were with Shri Mataji and we had a very old car. We were about seven ladies and myself, the only man, and also a driver. We were at the market and decided to go home but did not know how to there.

'No problem,' Shri Mataji said. Four or five of the ladies sat on the back seat, and there was the man who was driving, and Shri Mataji sat in the front with another lady. There were about eight people in the car. I took the bus!

When these things were happening it was easy to lose the protocol. The day after Shri Mataji started to talk to us in a nice way but then became stronger and stronger. She showed Herself as Shri Adi Shakti. For the first time I saw Her completely transformed. It was so powerful.

'Try to understand Who you are in front of. Try to understand Who is in front of you,' She said.

It was such a strong and powerful moment and Shri Mataji was completely transformed.

The day after that She left, and at that moment I could not look at Her any more, because She was Adi Shakti Herself, with all Her powers, with all Her deities around Her. So all things change very quickly.

Duilio Cartocci

The hair of the Goddess

Shri Mataji was staying in Rio in the apartment suite. One afternoon I decided to ask Her about the hair a yogini from Australia had given to me in an envelope.

'Shri Mataji, a yogini from Sidney gave me an envelope with Your hair.'

'Really? Let Me see... well, is this hair Mine? Let's check the vibrations! Yes, it is. See how cool it is!'

'Oh yes Mother!' It was hard for me because apart from Her hair, Shri Mataji was present in person. 'Mother, is it alright that I keep it?'

'No Bruno, it is not proper, please put it in My bag over there.'

Bruno Descaves

Chapter 18

1989: July Europe

I don't get tired at all

In July 1989 Shri Mataji went shopping in Marche St Pierre, in the Arabic area of Paris. There were about five of us with Her, and I am not a shopper – I do not like shopping for more than half an hour. This trip lasted for five hours and it was really hot, in July. Marche St. Pierre was a very cheap place with several floors and Mother was choosing a lot of fabrics. We were all very tired and I couldn't take it any more; we were all sitting on the edges of the counters, even the men. Shri Mataji was looking very dark – Shri Mahakali that day – very impressive.

'Isn't it amazing?' She said suddenly. 'I have just come back from Brazil. I don't know how I managed it, but within two days I had two pujas and a public programme and I didn't get tired at all. How could I do that?'

After a few seconds I wasn't tired any more and we carried on shopping, very fresh and active and as light as butterflies.

Guillemette Metouri

Shri Devi Puja, July 1989 (email report)

Our Divine Mother was last weekend in Melun, south–east of Paris, France, for the Devi Puja for France, Belgium, and Holland. We arrived on Friday evening after driving through hail and thunderstorms from Geneva, Switzerland, which on the one hand relieved France from the worst drought the country has had since 1976, and on the other destroyed half the wine crop in the east of the country, apart from cleansing the vibrations before Shri Mataji's arrival.

Shri Mataji arrived from London on the Sunday morning, following Her tour of North and South America. We drove to Charles de Gaulle Airport, Paris, to greet Her. She emerged into the arrivals area to be greeted by a few hundred Sahaja Yogis, all with flowers, and Shri Mother appeared very fresh. Then we went back to the camp site to prepare for the puja.

As Shri Mataji had gone up to Her room to rest, initially we did not hurry too much to prepare ourselves for the puja, until a message came round saying that our Divine Mother would be coming down in fifteen minutes. Some time after that a further message came saying that a sandwich and drink were being prepared, and we all relaxed again.

Suddenly a shout went out that Shri Mataji was arriving. We all dropped whatever we were doing and raced to our places with quite some embarrassment. However we were reassured by the divine smile as Shri Mataji took Her place on the stage, which had been decorated with many flowers and with a huge sun and moon painted behind Her throne. Shri Mataji began Her discourse by saying how overjoyed She was at seeing such a meeting of Sahaja Yogis, showing how the collectivity was attracting the Sahaja Yogis from all over. Afterwards the puja took place in a very light and joyful mood with the reading of mantras, including the hundred and eight names of Shri Krishna, and music.

On Monday evening there was a programme in Paris attended by five or six hundred people, and again on Tuesday evening, when Shri Mataji stayed on after Her talk and gave vibrations and advice to people until nearly two o'clock in the morning. She was very pleased with the programmes.

Phil Ward

Shri Mataji was deeply asleep, but She wasn't

After the Melun Puja in 1989 we were at the hotel with Mother. There was an Indian lady in the room with Her and She still had the kumkum on Her Feet. Then the Indian lady needed to go out, and I had to go in. It was quite impressive to go in alone, in the silence with Mother. She was deeply asleep, but in fact She wasn't. I started to fan Her and after about twenty minutes Mother was snoring softly, in a very relaxed way and suddenly She opened Her eyes very sweetly.

'This is very nice, thank you,' She said in a very fresh way and was smiling, but then was immediately sound asleep again. I carried on and my arm began to get tired. Later Shri Mataji woke up again and said, 'You should stop because it is going to hurt your arm.' Then She went back to sleep and I carried on and later She woke up. But to think that Mother was deep asleep, and She wasn't at all. She was more aware of me!

Guillemette Metouri

We asked for forgiveness

I am from France, and in 1989 we had a puja with Shri Mataji near Paris. It was in July, and that same year we were celebrating the two hundredth anniversary of the French Revolution. We did a play about Marie Antoinette, and at the end all the yogis asked for forgiveness for what we, as French people, did to the king and queen of France at that time, who were executed by the guillotine. It was very moving and very deep.

Genevieve Brisou

You must admit, this is fun!

In July 1989 Shri Mataji arrived at Munich airport late in the evening, to be greeted by a crowd of Sahaja Yogis from many countries. The next day was the first of two public programmes. Both evenings the hall was full, with perhaps four hundred people, and on the second evening Shri Mataji arrived after quite a long introduction and some music. She took Her place on the stage and spent a few minutes introducing the song Jogawa to the audience, talking about its writer, Saint Namdeva, and explaining how the words of the song invite the Kundalini to rise. She suggested that the audience sang the chorus and clapped their hands to the music. The vibrations were tremendous and at the end Shri Mataji beamed at Her listeners.

'You are all very serious people, but you must admit, this is fun!' She said. She spent the rest of the evening receiving the newcomers on the stage.

Before the two programmes the German national puja was held, in a hall in a village to the south of Munich. Shri Mataji kept everyone guessing until the last minute about which deity would be the subject of the puja; only during Her talk did She reveal that She wanted the worship of the Paramchaitanya, the All–pervading Divine Power, to take place.

Phil Ward

A movie

I travelled with Shri Mataji and it was after the Paramchaitanya Puja in Germany. It was a little town, in July 1989 we all gathered in Her little hotel room after the puja, a group of us sitting on the floor there with Shri Mataji on the chair. She wanted to see a movie and one person came up with a film called Always. It was about a man who was a fire–fighter and he got killed. There was one scene where he had an unresolved issue and he went back as a spirit to the place where he worked. There was a simple man sweeping and he casually, in spirit form, went up to this man and started to make fun of him.

'Oh you're so stupid, so ugly,' the spirit of the fire–fighter started saying, and so on, and the man suddenly became depressed and then the spirit of the fire–fighter said, 'Oh what did I do?'

That is exactly how bhuts work,' Shri Mataji said.

Angela Reininger

With Shri Mataji in Germany

We had a lot of very close contact with Shri Mataji as She travelled to different cities in Germany. At the time my husband Herbert was leader of Frankfurt, and he had started Sahaja Yoga there, in 1986. Shri Mataji went to Munich, Berlin, Dusseldorf, Frankfurt, and in East Germany there was a public programme in Dresden, just after the fall of the Berlin wall in 1989. My contact with Shri Mataji was cooking and ironing for Her, always such a blissful experience. I served Her, and sat at Her Feet while She ate.

Angela Reininger

Shri Mataji's throne was moved (email report)

From Munich Shri Mataji drove to Lago di Braies, in the north of Italy, for the 1989 Guru Puja. This is in a part of Italy which is culturally and ethnically Austrian, but which was ceded to Italy at the end of one of the world wars. Lago di Braies is a small lake, maybe one kilometre long, surrounded by spectacular mountains. The puja was organized by the Austrians, who had built an enormous decorated stage rising out over the lake for Shri Mataji. It was the largest collective event ever to take place outside India, with nearly a thousand Sahaja Yogis attending from around forty different countries.

On Sunday we had been told to be in the tent for the puja at 10.00 am. A little before that, the message came round that the puja would not start until after lunch; by early afternoon we were all in the marquee awaiting the arrival of the Great Goddess for the Guru Puja. The skies were darkening, and rain started falling; the elements somehow seemed angry. A wind started gusting over the lake and beating at the sides of the marquee, the thin tissue which shaded the stage from the sun began to leak drops of water over the decorations, and still Shri Mataji did not come.

At around five o'clock, the Austrian leader appeared to tell us Shri Mataji had remarked that since Shri Lakshmi emerged from the waters, Her attraction to the water might be too much for the stage supporting Her, so Shri Mataji's throne was moved under the shelter of the marquee, on a quickly-improvised podium. Shri Mataji finally arrived around nine o'clock and sat down to talk to us. The bad weather had by this time subsided.

Phil Ward

Did you enjoy your tour?

This story starts in Europe and ends in England. In 1989 we went to the Guru Puja on the frontier of Austria, Switzerland and Italy. I asked my daughter to come close to me, rather than be in the front with all the young people. She was not happy and told me that I did not have confidence in her, so I let her go back to the front. But at the end of the puja, Shri Mataji corrected the young people who were in the front. Thus I had my reply and my daughter also. I had the impression that during the tour of Europe, Shri Mataji showed me many different aspects of Sahaja Yoga.

Some days later I had to go to Brighton for the wedding of a Breton Sahaja Yogi. I missed the first boat and at the time decided by the Divine, crossed the channel, the suburbs to the south of London and thought, 'It is perhaps today that Shri Mataji will finish Her tour of Europe, and will return to London.' I called an English Sahaja Yogi and he said that Shri Mataji would arrive on that day.

I did not know where I was, but went on, and saw in front of me a car with a photo of Shri Mataji in it. I followed it and arrived at the airport. We were only about twenty yogis, all of them English except me. To greet Shri Mataji at an airport is always a special moment, and She arrived and spoke to all the English yogis whom She knew well. I was very shy, and as Shri Mataji did not speak to me I thought She was angry with me and my daughter because of the incident at the Guru Puja. But just at the moment when She was getting in Her car, She looked at me.

'Do you enjoy your tour?' She asked. With Her special insight She resolved everything and filled me with joy.

Marie-Joelle Coeuru

A symbol of Shri Ganesha

In 1989 we went for the Shri Mahakali Puja in Milan and the Shri Ganesha Puja in Switzerland. Before going to the puja, my son and I went everywhere in Mantua, Italy to find the proper gift we could give to Shri Mataji. Although we didn't have that much money, we searched for a nice gift appropriate for Her and found a glass perfume holder. I noticed that it had four points on all of its areas and was very beautiful. We offered it to Shri Mataji on behalf of the state of Ohio, USA, because at that time that is where we were living.

When we offered it to Her, She told everyone that the bottle was a symbol of Shri Ganesha and I remember all the yogis applauding.

Anna Mancini

1989 Shri Ganesha Puja (email report)

After the puja and programmes in Milan, Shri Mataji arrived in the mountain village of Les Diablerets, Switzerland, for a Shri Ganesha Puja. This took place in the Salle des Congrès in the village, where the stage had been decorated with a huge mosaic of Shri Ganesha behind the throne. Shri Mataji liked it very much and said that mosaic was a western art form, which the Indians do not have but which they would very much like, and asked us to take it to India.

In the evening there was another musical programme. This started with a Swiss gentleman who played the alphorn and yodeled, then the Indian musicians returned; Shri Mataji had suggested to them that they play something a little more 'popular', some film music. They played and sang until well into the small hours. Shri Mataji arrived and Baba Mama asked our Mother what She would like to hear. Qawwali, suggested Shri Mataji.

'Qawwali, Shri Mataji?' replied Baba Mama, and they rose to the occasion for another twenty minutes or so of joyful dancing and singing before Shri Mataji gave us Her final blessings and we left the room.

Phil Ward

It is perfectly possible

It was Shri Krishna Puja in 1989 in Saffron Waldon. I went up to Shri Mataji towards the end of the puja, and because I am an actor, I asked Her about drama and whether it was possible to give realisation through drama.

Shri Ganesha Puja,1989

'Yes, yes,' She said, 'it is perfectly possible. Don't worry, I'll write you a drama. There will be false gurus, and things like this in it, and people would come to see how they are false, and would come to the truth through their seeking and they would get their realisation and get to the spirit, through this kind of drama.'

So it is possible!

Tim Bruce

A gift from Shri Mataji

I can remember a wonderful Shri Krishna Puja in England. During the puja I looked up at Shri Mataji and She was blue – Shri Krishna blue – and I thought, 'I am dreaming!' So I closed my eyes. Then I opened them again and She was still blue. I nudged the lady sitting next to me.

'She's blue,' I said. The lady smiled at me in a very puzzled way and then continued with her meditation. It was then that I realised that this was a gift from Mother, for me to see – very humbling

Mary Heaton

Editor's note: In a number of miracle photos Shri Mataji's Feet have appeared blue. Traditionally Lord Krishna's skin had a bluish tinge.

Shri Mataji had been singing along with us

The 1989 Shri Krishna Puja took place in a large secondary school just outside Saffron Walden, some ten miles from Shri Mataji's house in Shudy Camps and fifteen miles south of Cambridge. On the day of the puja, we gathered shortly after breakfast to be told that our Divine Mother would not be arriving until the evening, and the puja might last until a record time.

Shri Mataji at the Shri Krishna Puja 1989

Shri Mataji arrived around nine o'clock. Food was served around half past ten, and the puja proper started some time after one o'clock in the morning. Your correspondent, pulling his ears, admits that he finds it difficult to remember many details of our Divine Mother's discourse, and suspects that others had the same difficulty keeping alert. However, there was a sudden miraculous arousal when, shortly after the talk, the song Bhaiya kaya taya was sung. This song was composed by an uncle of Shri Mataji, and is a sublime statement in words and music of the power of the spirit, in particular in driving away fear. We did not all immediately understand why this song was so strong, but Shri Mataji said afterwards that we all woke up because She had been singing along with us! The puja ended with our Divine Mother's departure around seven o'clock, long after the sunrise.

Phil Ward

I would save the kumkum

In the late 1980's and early '90's the young girls between the ages of about eight and sixteen used to put the kumkum and the perfumed oil on Shri Mataji's Feet at pujas. Now it is the married ladies, but it used to be the young girls. I was just the right age to do this quite a few times, with my friends, because we were very few. This was in England and Europe, and it was amazing to have this opportunity to hold Shri Mataji's Feet in your hand. I used to go back to school in England after the puja and my friends would ask what I had been doing, and I would say I had been hand painting, and I would save the kumkum as long as possible, to the last bit under the nail.

Alexandra Fuente

The hall was full of these 'toots'

Most pujas used to start at mid–day or in the afternoon then. That Saturday of the Shri Krishna Puja 1989, we were asked to gather and were told that Shri Mataji wanted the puja to start late on Sunday evening and She was worried if many people would have problems with this new arrangement. Very few hands were raised, so it was agreed to have the puja on Sunday evening. From the afternoon of Sunday, we were called into the main hall and told that Shri Mataji could come any time and we should get ready and meditate.

Night had already fallen when She came in to the sound of flute. She was with Sir CP, which at that time was an indication that the puja time had not yet come. They took their places on the stage and Shri Mataji announced that Sir CP had brought some presents for the children and they were going to be distributed. The atmosphere of the hall, after all the time we had been sitting in meditation, was a bit stern, but after a few seconds it totally changed, with the movements and voices of all the children getting on the stage to have their present, then returning to their parents to show it to them and to other kids, laughing and shouting. Moreover, some presents were T–shirts with little plastic designs of Mickey Mouse that made a noise when you pressed your finger on. The hall was full of these 'Toooots' and we became really in the mood for a Shri Krishna Puja. Shri Mataji said in the puja talk later how Shri Krishna had come to break all the conditionings that had been falsely imposed under the name of Shri Rama.

It was then a big fashion among Westerners to get an Indian name from Shri Mataji, but I had decided that I didn't care about getting one and avoided the big lines after each puja. That day two French boys from the same family had got the same Indian name, and they wanted to ask Shri Mataji if one of them could be given a different one. As they didn't speak English, I was asked to accompany them on the stage to translate their request. I don't remember anything about the conversation, but they got a name, and I found myself asking for one too. Shri Mataji looked at me attentively, and then, leaning Her head backward, She closed Her eyes. I just bent my head so that I could get lost into the vision of Her Lotus Feet, still decorated after the puja. I can't tell how long it lasted. When I raised my head again She said something that I couldn't understand. I think Baba Mama and his group were just playing a Qawwali loudly.

I couldn't get the name, so Shri Mataji called one lady attending to Her and asked for a little notebook. She wrote something, pulled off the page and handed it to me. I thanked Her and bowed down with the little paper in my hand.

> Devarshi
> Saint in The Gods

'Devarshi – Saint in the Gods,' was written on it. No need to say I preciously keep this little paper to this day.

Devarshi Abalain

Tell your mother to take her rebirth

We had a Shri Krishna Puja in England by the seaside in 1989, and I went to see Shri Mataji. It was shortly after my mother had died.

'Tell your mother that she must go and take her rebirth,' Shri Mataji said.

Patricia Deene

Breton music

For the Shri Krishna Puja 1989, in England, we had prepared a cassette of Breton music (Brittany is a part of France, in the north west of the country). We were going to give it to our dear Baba Mama. This magnificent puja lasted from midnight until six in the morning, and in the early morning, with Devarshi, another French Sahaja Yogi, we went to give a present to Shri Mataji.

It was very awe inspiring and we stayed in front of Shri Mataji for a long time. We told Her that Breton music sometimes had similarities to Indian music and She replied that it was because some Indians from Maharashtra had come to Brittany, a very long time ago. It was a very special feeling, to be there with Our Mother, simply, and talking about our common ancestors.

Marie-Joelle Coeuru

Chapter 19

1989: August to October Europe East and West

Helsinki

After Shri Krishna Puja in England in 1989, our Divine Mother travelled to Finland and the Soviet Union for programmes there. Shri Mataji's first port of call was Helsinki, where She arrived on Wednesday evening the 16th of August. The following morning a small puja took place, and in the evening four or five hundred people attended Mother's first programme in a Nordic country. Many enthusiastic and respectful seekers were in the audience, although many had been damaged by contact with false gurus. We stayed in the hall until after midnight helping to give advice and vibrations to newcomers.

Phil Ward

Love always knows

I was wonderfully blessed to attend Shri Mataji during Her visit to Helsinki in August 1989. By Her Grace I was also allowed to help do the puja to Her. We were just a few yogis in a hotel meeting room. Afterwards, She gave presents to the children, and I noticed that a little boy hadn't yet received one. I looked at the little brass Shri Ganesha statue on the table beside Shri Mataji, thinking that this would be a good present for him. She suddenly looked over at it, picked it up, and handed it to the little boy with a beautiful smile. Love knows everything!

Brigitte Saugstad

Russia

In 1989, we travelled from Helsinki to Leningrad (St Petersburg), pleasantly surprised by our reception in Russia. All through our stay in Russia we felt no problem in talking to people whom we met, nor did we feel any inhibition on their part in talking to us; a great change even from two years before, when Shri Mataji was in Moscow and some of the Sahaja Yogis were unable to meet Her as unofficial contact with foreigners was not allowed.

The hall in Leningrad, (St Petersburg) in the Palace of Youth, a large and rather drab building in the centre of the city, held 1,400 seats. Practically no postering had been done, but Shri Mataji had appeared very briefly on television earlier that evening at a peak–time what's–on–in–Leningrad programme. When the visiting Sahaja Yogis arrived about fifteen minutes before the scheduled start of the programme, the hall was completely full and we were obliged to stand at the back. We unfortunately had to turn away quite a few newcomers. Oleg gave an introduction and then translated Shri Mataji's address, at the end of which, after giving realisation in the usual way, Mother invited Her audience to ask the question whether Russia was going to lead the world in spirituality. Everyone felt the cool breeze!

That night all the Sahaja Yogis were instructed to go first to Shri Mataji's hotel for the distribution of presents. Mother had bought many warm and stylish clothes for our Russian brothers and sisters, and other gifts such as leather wallets and sunglasses, all very difficult to obtain in Russia, and these were distributed in Her hotel room which was crammed full of local and visiting yogis. The visiting ladies also received presents. At one point our Divine Mother corrected some of them for not observing Her protocol, chatting and giggling in Her presence. The local Sahaja Yogis would follow our example, She reminded us, and for ourselves we can make no progress if we do not bear in mind constantly in whose Divine presence we have the privilege to be. Shri Mataji mentioned with approval the example of Bruno's wife Misao, originally from Japan; every time she entered or left Mother's room she would bow to Her. That is the best way to make progress, by bowing, She told us.

Spontaneously, two more programmes were arranged for the following day, at 11 am on the steps outside the hall, and at 4 pm in the hall again. Shri Mataji was travelling by train to Moscow at ten that evening, with the Sahaja Yogis, so the programme could not be later. The morning programme attracted a few hundred people, and was preceded by a television interview outside the Palace of Youth. Shri Mataji spent a long time

P R O T O C O L
of intent between the Ministry of Health USSR
and the Life Eternal Trust International to
cooperate in the field of Research of Sahaja
Yoga method in the USSR

Moscow   August 9, 1989.

Meeting between Mr. V.I.Ilyin, representative of Main Administration for science and medical technologies of the USSR Ministry
of Health and Mrs. Sri Mataji Nirmala Devi, Mr. Yogeshvar Mohajan,
Mr. Brian Wells, Mr. Bogdon Shilovysh, representatives of the Life
Eternal Trust International has been held in the USSR Ministry of
Health on August 4, 1989. Both sides have drawn up mutual opinion on the
problem.
　　1. Sahaja Yoga techniques proposed by the representatives of the
Life Eternal Trust International are based on ancient traditions
of oriental (Indian) medicine. Those methods may be of great
interest for different specialists in the field of medicine.
　　Broad application of Sahaja Yoga methods in the USSR
requires profound scientific investigations and clinical trials.

2. The participants believe it's possible to define specific forms
for cooperation during 1989.

V.I.Ilyin
Main Administration
for science and medical
technologies
Ministry of Health
USSR

Yogeshwar Mahajan
Life Eternal Trust
International

Official recognition for Sahaja Yoga in the USSR, 1989

answering questions from Her audience, assuring them that communism
had done them no harm at all by comparison with the capitalism of the
Americans, which had made them completely stupid, a theme She repeated
several times over the different programmes.

Someone asked about Stalin; 'Forget the past,' was Mother's answer. Mr
Gorbachev is a realised soul, Mother said, and everyone should support
him and not oppose him for petty or nationalistic reasons. Meanwhile the
Sahaja Yogis were busy giving realisation to newcomers, behind where Shri
Mataji was sitting. We were all impressed with the quality of the people
who came; all seemed very intelligent and cultured.

The visiting Sahaja Yogis did not attend the 4 o'clock programme, as Shri Mataji had advised us all to visit the Hermitage Art Museum, one of the world's largest art galleries, full of great paintings by Rembrandt, Rubens, and many other realised artists, and the building itself is gorgeously and beautifully decorated. Behind the Hermitage stands a great square with an obelisk, to the far side of which is the Winter Palace. Shri Mataji said that Leningrad was the world's most beautiful city. It has many canals, like Amsterdam or Venice, and one splendid building after another laid out along wide avenues. Shri Mataji remarked, in Her hotel the evening after the first programme, that in those days people were able to build for posterity, and doubted that in modern times we could still do so, and perhaps the water flowing in the Neva and all the canals had something to do with this. Shri Mataji asked Lev and Dr Bohdan to return there after the Moscow programmes to take care of the follow-up.

Phil Ward

Shri Mataji in St Petersburg

Lining up to get realisation

In 1989 we were a group of people starting Sahaja Yoga in Finland, and after that we went to St Petersburg to attend the first programmes with Shri Mataji there. At that programme there were approximately two thousand people waiting outside the hall, because they did not have a ticket to come inside. Shri Mataji suggested they should come back the next morning. She received two thousand people in the hall of the place where we had been the day before. She spoke about America, smashing the ideas they had about it, and saying it was not the beautiful place they thought it was.

The people were lining up in long lines to get their realisation. We were a few yogis standing at the end of the lines, giving realisation. When the Kundalini was cool above their heads, then we went on to the next one. For hours we went on giving realisation to people. Shri Mataji was sitting on the stairs in the middle of that big crowd. People just kept on coming.

Gunter Thurner

Saint Petersburg

The year of Sahaja Yoga Centre establishment: Sahaja Yoga is officially considered to start spreading in Saint Petersburg since the summer of 1989 when Shri Mataji came to the city and did a public programme for the first time. She came to Saint Petersburg five times – first in 1989, and then in 1990, 1991, 1994 and 1996.

The first meeting of Shri Mataji with the people of Saint Petersburg took place in the Palace of the Youth in 1989. The hall was overcrowded. Mother told the audience about the subtle system and its connection with the physical body. Anyone who wanted could ask questions. Approximately one thousand people got their self realisation. In the following years, the programmes were held in the Saint Petersburg Sport and Concert Complex, the Palace of Sport 'Yubileiny', the House of Culture 'Vyiborgsky', and the House of Culture named after Lensoviet.

Anonymous Russian Sahaja Yogi

You have a tremendous job ahead of you

In Moscow we were again lodged with local Sahaja Yogis. Two programmes had been arranged in a hall in the centre of town, very comfortable but not very large – only 450 seats and room for a few more in the aisles. 5000 people applied for tickets at the box office! The halls were full to overflowing on both evenings, with very cultured and sensible people. In Her discourse Shri Mataji approached Sahaja Yoga in a very matter–of–fact way, not enlarging much on the 'religious' side. At one point, during the questions, She was asked who She was.

'It's rather embarrassing to say,' She replied, 'I'm a housewife.' We stayed in the hall until it closed, giving vibrations and talking to the new people, many of whom spoke good English, to our surprise.

During Shri Mataji's stay in Moscow, an article appeared in Trud, the Soviet trade union newspaper, with the largest circulation of any Soviet daily, about Sahaja Yoga, praising its curative properties and being very positive. A movie film was made of our Mother that would be shown throughout the Soviet Union on television later that year.

After going shopping in the GUM store and elsewhere, our Divine Mother left Russia for England on Tuesday evening. She hailed the Austrian contingent by saying that at last the Germans have conquered Russia, but in the true way, with love.

'You have a tremendous job ahead of you. But you asked for it!' She said, and promised to return in June 1990.

Phil Ward

A little TV

After St Petersburg we travelled on, to Moscow. We brought a lot of spaghetti and tomato sauce and olive oil from Italy. This was for food for our long trip. In Moscow, at the hotel we decided to cook for all the yogis who came and also for Shri Mataji. She invited a lot of us into Her room and at a certain point She switched on the TV. We saw some people killing each other and shooting and blood was going everywhere. It was a kind of a Wild West show, and we didn't know how to react.

'Oh, it is so relaxing to have a little TV!' Shri Mataji said after some time. This was while we were eating the pasta in that hotel in Moscow.

Gunter Thurner

Shri Mataji asked me about every person

In September 1989 I was able to phone Shri Mataji from Brazil. It was a long call, about half an hour, during which She asked me about every person She had met in Brazil, and about the collectives of Brasilia and Salvador. She particularly gave me instructions for people who had had experience with spiritualism. They were to put the right hand on the ground and say the mantra to Shri Mahakali. She said it would good if some of the seekers of Brazil could go on the India tour, and explained that it was not comfortable physically, but was for the spirit. She asked me to bring presents made of leather for the Indian Sahaja Yogis.

Duilio Cartocci

I will always love you

During the Navaratri Puja in Margate England in 1989, I was attending Shri Mataji with another yogini. At one stage I was alone in a room with

Shri Mataji and She was asking me some questions about myself. After a while I became aware of the expanse of the sky outside the window and a great silence.

'You know that I love you, and will always love you,' Shri Mataji said after a while.

Danielle Lee

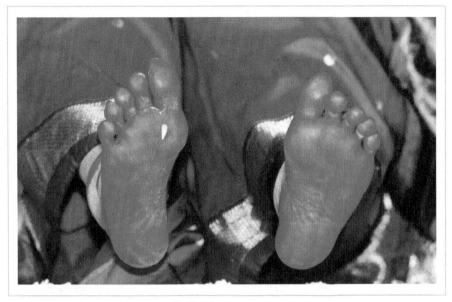

Navaratri Puja at Margate, England

Diwali Puja 1989, Montecatini (email report)

This year the Diwali Puja took place, by the Grace of our Divine Mother, in Montecatini, a resort town in the hills between Florence and Pisa, Italy. Several hundred Sahaja Yogis converged from many corners of the world on Pisa Airport to greet Shri Mataji and Her husband, Mr CP Srivastava, on their arrival from London. The small size of the airport meant that most of the people there were Sahaja Yogis. Shri Mataji arrived around lunchtime, to be greeted with flowers from all of us. She travelled to Montecatini in Her car, while the Sahaja Yogis followed Her and spent the afternoon settling into their respective hotels.

On Friday evening a sitar concert was held in a theatre in Montecatini, with Debu Chauderi and his son. They had flown from India especially for the occasion at Shri Mataji's request. At the end of the concert, after praising the musicians, Shri Mataji spoke on the role of music and art in Sahaja Yoga and how they are intended to entertain the Spirit.

On Saturday the Italians had laid on a special train for us to travel from Montecatini to Florence, to enjoy the city with its art galleries, palaces and ice–cream shops. The highlight for many Sahaja Yogis was the Uffizi Museum, which Shri Mataji always visits when in Florence, full of art done by realised souls such as Botticelli and Giotto, often depicting the Divine Mother with the Christ child in Her arms, and with beautiful vibrations.

During the afternoon our Divine Mother and Her husband also came to Florence, and spontaneously met up with the musicians near the Duomo cathedral, where a number of street artists were plying their trade. Shri Mataji and Mr Srivastava sat down to be painted by two of them, surrounded by a growing number of Sahaja Yogis. The likeness of Mr Srivastava was not good, and that of our Mother was even less accurate, and She spent a few minutes advising the artists as to how they could improve their pictures.

Shri Mataji in Florence

In the meantime another artist, with quite a big ego, was trying to sketch one of the musicians. It was hopeless. So Shri Mataji sat down before an easel and started to do the job Herself, spending twenty minutes or so sketching in Debu Chauderi's features as an astonished crowd of yogis and passers-by looked on. When She had finished, a Sahaja Yogi commented to Her that there were many other people who would like to be sketched by Her. Shri Mataji answered that She very much enjoyed painting, only Her time is so much taken up with travel, programmes, and other functions.

Phil Ward

Keeping up with Shri Mataji

In 1989, when Shri Mataji went to Florence, She went shopping, and my husband Henno and I were also there. We saw Shri Mataji on the other side of a market place but decided not to follow Her, so as not to disturb Her, but suddenly She came towards us and greeted us.

'With your French wife,' She said, while patting me on the shoulder, 'your children will not be too tall. You will have no problem to find clothes for them.'

On the same day we were a group of yogis following Shri Mataji on the street and Henno and I were at the back. Shri Mataji was walking normally but at times we had to run to be able to follow Her. Afterwards many yogis also said that they had difficulties to keep up with Shri Mataji, while She appeared to be walking normally.

Trupta de Graaf

Diwali Puja

In the evening, back at Montecatini, we made our way to a gymnasium that the Italian Sahaja Yogis were busy transforming into a puja hall, with saris, candles, lights, shrubs and flowers. When Shri Mataji and Mr Srivastava arrived we all stood outside the entrance to greet our Mother with a dazzle of sparklers, and a loud and brilliant firework display laid on by the Italians. Once inside the hall, Mother talked to us about how at the time of Diwali we are all meant to be joyful.

Shri Mataji announced that She wanted to give us all presents. First came the little girls, and then the little boys, who received tee–shirts decorated with a Mickey Mouse that squeaked when you pressed him. Then it was the turn of the teenagers, and then little by little the older yogis. Nearly everyone received a present in person from Shri Mataji; it was really fantastic. Bangles for the ladies, little decorated boxes for kumkum, leather purses, and many other sorts of gifts. After a while music started up in the audience, and with the bhajans we kept going on the vibrations of our Mother's Love until late in the night.

Sunday was the puja day. After the puja, which went on for several hours, Shri Mataji again distributed presents. Lev was very loudly applauded as he received his, for organising Sahaja Yoga in the USSR.

At the same time, Shri Mataji received many presents from the different countries and Sahaja Yogis. Shri Mataji spoke of the importance of oiling the hair, and stressed in categorical terms that all Sahaja Yogis should put a little coconut oil on the Sahasrara, every day. Otherwise we will go bald – and even those who are bald should put a little on. The Sahasrara is Her chakra, She said, and though we need not put on as much oil as She, we must still put a little. Mother suggested that we start a Sahaja fashion, with the hair oiled like this. Shri Mataji left Italy the following day by plane to Rome and Istanbul, for the programmes in Turkey.

Phil Ward

No wish left unfulfilled

In 1989 I was living in a Sahaja Yoga ashram in a European city. Shri Mataji's birthday was approaching and I had the idea to organise a card–decorating room. Many yogis and yoginis came to draw and paint beautiful, heart–felt artwork there for Her in the big room full of tables and art supplies. The vibrations became so strong that I felt I had been drawn up

Diwali Puja 1989

into a powerful wave of joy and clarity. In this state of connection to the Divine, I felt completely confident to ask Shri Mataji for a wish. As my wife and I had nothing lacking except for money, I knelt at the altar and asked Shri Lakshmi, sakshat Shri Mataji, for financial assistance. I definitely didn't expect my wish to be answered by God in person; but it was, and within just a few months.

At the following Diwali Puja, Shri Mataji saw my wife, Brigitte, and asked her to phone Her at Her London residence. We were invited by Shri Mataji to visit Her at Shudy Camps near Cambridge – the place we had called home the year before – as She wished to help us start a business. So, a few days after the Shri Lakshmi Puja, we found ourselves in the royal setting of Shri Mataji's suite, sorting through new oil paintings to sell. Shri Mataji gave us a total of fifty paintings. Over the following years, we tried to pay the money back to Her, but She refused each time, telling us to invest it in more paintings. About nine years later, we eventually deposited a sum onto Her account, and sent Her a poetic letter, declaring our undying gratitude. We were told that She read the letter and said that it had such beautiful vibrations, that She would accept our repayment.

A small incident at Shudy Camps showed me the powerful, motherly healing influence that Shri Mataji has over Her children. She was distributing presents to everyone who had helped with packing and sorting furniture and ornaments. As I hadn't helped, I waited downstairs, until someone suddenly called me up. I sat shyly at the back. Then a penetrating, confidence–inspiring voice commanded, 'Edward'. I felt my left Vishuddhi and my whole chest become light and clear at Shri Mataji's call, as I stood up and went forward to receive a token of my Mother's love.

Despite Shri Mataji's many universal spiritual concerns, She drenched us in much of Her priceless attention during our stay in the heart. Brigitte was very moved when Shri Mataji Herself phoned her to suggest that she could try hand–painting porcelain door knobs to earn a living. Since then, Brigitte has become a very successful artist, manifesting strong vibrations in her works.

Edward Saugstad

Shri Mataji was doing all this for me

My parents went to Shudy Camps to tell Shri Mataji that they were going to go and live in Scotland, and She spoke to them all about marriage. It was a time when I was having a lot of worries and confusion about getting married. I didn't see them for some time, but a bit later some of us went to the airport, and welcomed Shri Mataji, and when I gave my flower to Her She smiled at me so much, which I couldn't believe, because I was in such a state.

'Did you get My present?' She said.

'No, Shri Mataji,' I replied. When I got back home my mother said Shri Mataji had said to her, 'This is for your daughter, she looked after Me so well,' and I did not know what this meant, because I did not know when I had ever looked after Shri Mataji. It was when we came back from Finland, but I felt I hadn't done anything. Then my mum said how surprised she was that Shri Mataji had talked to them, an old married couple, all about marriage. I told her that I was going through the most tremendous dramas about getting married, and it turned out Shri Mataji was doing all this for me.

Katie Headlam

Does She really know everything?

Once Shri Mataji showed the doubting Thomas in me who She is. I was invited into Her room at Shudy Camps. I was sitting there and Shri Mataji had Her back towards the door and was going to have dinner with the people in the room. Somehow the mind started thinking, 'How special it is,' and so on, and Shri Mataji was talking very sweetly, telling stories. My mind started thinking, 'Does She really know everything that goes on around Her?' At one moment the door behind Her opened.

'And the door opened and at that moment the waitress came in with all the food,' She said, even though Her story was about something completely different. She could not see the door opening because it was behind Her. So I told myself, 'She knows everything!'

Henno de Graaf

Shri Mataji wanted me to stay for a week

One day I met Shri Mataji along with the other Sahaja Yogis of the UK, at the airport. I was feeling very ill. She came up to me and said She was feeling bad to see me in this situation, and I was to go to Her house near Cambridge (Shudy Camps). When I went there I thought it would be just for a few minutes or hours, but She wanted me to stay there for a week.

Twice Shri Mataji worked on me, and had me sit and cleared my left and right side. After those seven days She said I was alright and could go. The next day I saw Her at the airport, and She was happy to see me and said I was alright.

Joga Singh

Shri Mataji was thanking me

One morning at Shudy Camps in England, I was in such a hurry to serve Shri Mataji that I threw my sari on wrongly and couldn't even see that I had done so. Upon entering Her bedroom, I found Shri Mataji seated upon an armchair close to one of the windows, overlooking the garden.

'Ah, Marilyn,' She said, 'what a lovely sari you're wearing. It suits you so well. You're wearing it the wrong way round.' Somehow She was so gracious that I didn't feel silly. She then stood up and proceeded to remove my sari and then put it on again properly, circling me, tucking it in all around, pleating it and all the time saying to me, 'I don't know how to thank you. You've done so much for Me.'

Imagine, Shri Mataji was thanking me! How gently Shri Adi Shakti works out our Nabhi and Vishuddhi.

Marilyn Leate

Shri Shiva in Scotland

Shri Mataji told me that She wanted the main centre, which was then at Shudy Camps, to be in Scotland but some Sahaja Yogis were saying it was too far from London. She said that Lord Shiva was there and he would spread the vibrations down south if the ashram was there.

Derek Ferguson

The little pearls that Shri Mataji gives us

We were living at Chelsham Road in 1989, and Mother wanted to see me, so I had to get ready. At this time we were not wearing saris to go and see Her, but I wanted to look nice and elegant so I was frantically looking in my cupboard to match my clothes. When I left the house I realised I had not had the time to do a foot soak, because I had been so preoccupied about my external appearance.

I arrived at Shri Mataji's flat, near Victoria Station, and sat at Her Feet – my favourite place. Tea was brought in. I was so thirsty because of the trip in the tube train, but I wanted to wait until Shri Mataji started to drink Hers, and She looked at me smiling.

'Have it,' She said, and continued jokingly, 'you don't need to match your stockings with your skirt.'

'Oh Shri Mataji,' I said, and I was so enamoured and a bit confused.

These are the little pearls that Shri Mataji gives us to show us that we are constantly in Her benevolent attention, and it is so endearing.

Antoinette Wells

Chapter 20

1989: December India

Divine diplomacy

We had a public programme in December 1989 at the King George High School at Dadar, Mumbai. At that time there were many demonstrations in Maharashtra against what was termed as 'blind faith' cults, and some people decided that Sahaja Yoga was also one of these blind faith cults, so they came to the entrance of the place where Shri Mataji was having the public programme, and started demonstrating against Sahaja Yoga. Each new seeker who wanted to come to the programme was given a pamphlet against Sahaja Yoga. Throughout Shri Mataji's lecture these people were shouting outside.

After the talk was over, Shri Mataji told everyone, before doing the exercise for getting self realisation, that there would be a break for five to ten minutes, and those who wanted to could go out to have some tea or whatever, and then we would have realisation. We the yogis were surprised, as we had never seen Her giving a break during the public programme. Some people went out to the nearby shops to purchase some snacks. In the meantime people who were causing a disturbance thought that if people were going out it meant that the programme was over, and thus they left. Ten minutes after, when Shri Mataji gave realisation, there was no one shouting outside.

Without any words, She just showed us what divine diplomacy is.

Maneesha Shanbhag-Cruz

The exact point where Mother worked on me

In London, in the late 1980's, I had an attack of negativity on my left foot and hurt it, but did not take it seriously, so did not go to the doctor. The next night I dreamed of Shri Mataji, and She worked on my foot where it was injured. Then in the morning I thought that if Mother worked on me then must be something wrong there. I went to the hospital and they took an X–ray. I asked where the bone was broken and they showed me the exact point where Mother had worked on me in the dream. I was so thankful to Her for looking after me.

Later, in India, at Pratishthan, I saw Shri Mataji. A Sahaja Yogi told Her about my leg injury. She called me and put Her left Foot on the table, and told me to take vibrations. I took vibrations of Her Foot for about five minutes.

'You have cleared,' She said to me.

After this Shri Mataji arranged a lift for me, due to my leg injury, from Pratishthan back to Mumbai, as there was a Mercedes car belonging to a Sahaja Yogi going back to Mumbai empty. Millions of thanks to Her!

Then once, Shri Mataji was watching a Hindi movie of Shri Krishna, with some yogis at Pratishthan. I was sitting a long way from Her in the room. She spoke to me about the actor who played the role of Shri Krishna.

Shakuntala Tandale

Without the Spirit, there is no joy

This story is from when I had perceived myself to be 'away' from Mother and then had the wonderful realisation that She had been protecting me all the while under the generous palu of Her sari. I promised Her in my heart that from then on, whatever She asked, I would always do it – without question or hesitation.

In December 1989 we were near Pratishthan, sitting under a cotton canopy that did little to keep out the cold night air, yet gave a tantalising peek now and then of the magical Indian starlit sky as the cotton flapped open in the wind. My name had just been called out. Sahaj marriages were in the air. Without even hearing properly, the word 'No!' came from inside of me, thankfully no one around had heard it. You can't say 'No!' I told myself, what about your promise to Mother?

I had been matched with an Italian who wasn't on the tour, and I soon turned to the Milanese yogis to try and gain an inkling of my future. Their comments seemed a little incongruous with the auspicious surroundings of the ancient Maharashtran landscape.

'I've seen him at a few meetings – looks like the sort of chap who'd know how to mix a good cocktail.'

'He works out, looks like a model.'

'Very fashionable, wears Versace.'

All very interesting, yet I kept hoping for someone to say how deep he was and how much he loved Mother – but nobody did. According to the Sahaja Yogis we were 'engaged' and we met in London a few times. He was not quite settled into his yoga and had not recognised Shri Mataji. I thought he might grow in his understanding given time and held fast to my pledge of not saying 'No', believing this was Mother's choice and I was determined it could work.

After some months of feeling in a bit of a limbo, there was the exciting news that the UK was hosting Shri Krishna Puja, in 1990. I threw myself into stick dance rehearsals and stage decorations with gusto. Perhaps unconsciously I had chosen roles that avoided being involved in the preparations of Mother's rooms because then She couldn't ask me about my fiancé. On the Saturday of the puja, I was walking past Shri Mataji's cottage when I saw the leader standing outside looking a bit worried.

'Danya! Can you stand here a moment, all the ladies have disappeared and we need someone here in case anything is needed.' What could I do? I stood outside Shri Mataji's door and could hear many voices inside all sounding very serious. Suddenly the door swung open and one of the leaders handed out a tea–tray. My intention to discretely take the tray, refill and disappear was foiled when a very dear and familiar voice called from within.

'Danya! How is your fiancé?' Shri Mataji came straight to the point. Her laser beam eyes had spotted me in the corridor. 'Come and sit down.' I prostrated at Her Feet, red with embarrassment at interrupting the august gathering.

'He is well Shri Mataji, thank you,' I answered sheepishly.

Shri Mataji looked at me as only She could – with such intensity that it created a stirring in my heart to recall it even now. The room, and all the people in it, faded away and only She filled the space.

'Danya, what do you really want? Who do you want to marry?' She looked deeper inside me.

'Mother, I just want to marry a yogi.' By then I didn't mind who I married – as long as they loved Shri Mataji.

'You see!' She said triumphantly, 'Without the Spirit, there is no joy.' She gave a huge smile, making my heart dance.

I bowed again before Her Holy Lotus Feet feeling a million times lighter, and thanked Her.

'Now, you take it easy.' She said as I took my leave.

It was a wonderful feeling to know in that moment that my whole life was in Her Divine hands – whether I married that boy, someone else – or didn't marry at all, it really didn't matter! 'Without the Spirit there is no joy!' Her words, those sacred mantras, still echo in my ears.

Much later on I got the 'inside story' from someone who had been in Shri Mataji's room in Pune when names had come up relating to marriages. She had said, 'Danya loves Italy! She would enjoy living there. There is an Italian boy living in Milan who works in Olivetti.' I was matched to the only person who fitted the criteria, yet when his name was put forward, Mother said She wasn't sure and wanted to know what I thought. Shri Mataji later told me (whispering in my ear at Heathrow Airport as if it were all a great joke), 'They were all praising him, and I said I wanted to see what you thought!'

With humbling trust, She wanted to leave the choice up to me. I didn't get to hear that at the time of the 'announcements'. Through Her grace, I did marry an Italian (not the boy from Rimini). My husband Enzo and I have been happily married for over twenty years now – and in a twist of fate, he was also working in Olivetti and living in Milan – only at the time he had not yet come to Sahaja Yoga.

Danya Martoglio

A white dove

It was on one of the Indian tours, in December 1989, at a private high school in Kolhapur with our Holy Mother, while we were staying in a town with a university. The whole day we were walking through the streets, looking at the shops, informing people of the evening programme and then we went to the university.

The programme was in the open air. The stone stairs, which were going up at three sides of the venue, were full of Indian people. The sky turned black and as Shri Mataji said the affirmations for the different chakras, putting Her hand on all the places of Her body, it was totally silent. I was tired and instead of keeping my eyes closed and doing what everybody else did, I was looking at our Holy Mother and all of a sudden, while everybody put their hands on their Sahasraras, a white dove flew over the black sky directly above us for one circle and two circles above Shri Mataji, then it flew away.

As all the others had their eyes closed I couldn't exchange this with them. But I still see it before me, as if it happened yesterday.

Ramaa Reusch

The sari maya

Great excitement – 1989, my first trip out of Australia and my first time to see Shri Mataji. We had to supply our body measurements as She would organize saris, petticoats and blouses for us to be worn on the tour. The ladies were ecstatic, eagerly anticipating the beautiful silks, bright hues and patterns and gold and glittery embellishments.

We were all bubbling with excitement and anticipation on the day we were to receive our saris. They were wrapped in paper tied with string in knee–high piles, each with a name on them. We eagerly walked through the bundles till we came to our names, impatiently struggled with the string and ripped open the coverings. We could not believe what we were seeing; each of us had a pile of thin pastel coloured cotton saris! In a somewhat subdued manner we wrapped ourselves into our saris and in a short time they became crumpled and limp like used dish cloths. Later that evening Shri Mataji asked us if we liked them.

'Yes Mother,' we all replied in a flat monotone. Mother asked us again.

'Yes Mother,' we replied, trying for a bit more enthusiasm.

As the days and weeks ticked over, saris became the last of our concerns. However I started to notice that amongst the broad spectrum of pastels of the five or six saris in each package, everyone had a selection of colours that suited their complexion perfectly. Shri Mataji, half way through, again asked us if we liked our saris.

'Yes Mother,' we replied in a matter of fact way.

One day I was on a small hill overlooking the camp and river where a lot of ladies were doing their washing. The mass of pastel saris blended together, the scene looked like a moving Monet painting and I began to see why Mother had bought us washed–out cotton saris. Firstly, maybe, to calm down our Western egos that were very particular about fashion, maybe to identify us as a group or maybe they were just more practical as we moved every other day, but what I especially noticed was that no one stood out – we were visually truly collective and equal. Towards the end of the tour Shri Mataji again asked us if we liked our saris.

'Yes Mother!' we replied joyfully.

Leela Holland

How Moses parted the Red Sea

It was the India Tour, and I'd come from a city that was more like a large country town. It was my first trip to India, but also out of Australia, and hence I was struggling with the crowds and the personal space factor. One day we were walking and singing beside Mother in a bullock cart procession, part of a mass of Indians and Westerners jammed in together enjoying. Shri Mataji was in the cart, and myself and another yogini were to the left of Her. We received a message that She had requested all the Westerners to move to the front of the procession. My friend and I looked at each other aghast. All we could see was a sea of mostly Indian Yogis and no way through.

'There's no way I'm pushing and shoving through all those people!' I said.

I could feel Shri Mataji in my head and my brain. There's no other way to explain it. Her consciousness permeated mine, something I experienced on many occasions in conversation or in close proximity to Her. Then the people in front of us started to part – until we were looking at a path leading into the crowd.

We started walking and the path just kept opening up before us. Yogis were still walking, talking, laughing and singing and had no idea this was happening, really quickly. As we started walking in wonderment, I looked behind, and where we'd just walked through, those we had passed fell immediately into the space they'd just created, still talking and laughing like before, completely unaware how they had just created a passageway.

My friend and I kept looking at each other a bit nonplussed about what was happening, but enjoying it anyway, all the way to the front of the procession. It was then I understood how Moses parted the Red Sea.

Leela Holland

Shri Ganesha's mouse

Shri Mataji sent us to an Indian craft market to 'circulate and shop'. I was with a yogini from America, who bought a wooden carved statue of Shri Ganesha. It was about one foot tall, with lots of intricate detail. She had a desire for Shri Mataji to hold the statue and vibrate it. At one point, we looked up and there was Shri Mataji shopping, mingling amongst the shoppers. The American yogini got her statue held.

That night in the tent, we put the statue on our little altar, right at our heads. Later we were woken by scratching sounds coming from it. We looked, and in the pale light could see a little mouse sitting in the carving work at the feet of the statue.

Leela Holland

Keeping out of the sun

In India in the late 1980's, my friend and I were sitting by a lake in the midday sun chatting, when we both instantaneously had a sudden strong feeling to get out of the sun, to protect our Sahasraras. So we pulled up the ends of our saris over our heads. We stayed where we were and continued chatting, including about how Shri Mataji had talked about the heat being too strong and to stay out of it in the middle of the day. We thought that advice was for the Europeans who weren't used to the sun. Coming from the sub–tropics, we didn't think the advice was for us because we were used to it.

Twenty minutes later a yogi came up to us and said that Shri Mataji asked us to get out of the sun. She was staying at a bungalow at the side of the lake, and it would have taken the yogi approximately twenty minutes to reach us from Her bungalow. Shri Mataji had either been on the veranda watching us, or inside the house and She knew anyway.

Not long after we returned home, government media campaigns commenced to encourage people not to sunbake and to avoid sun exposure during certain hours, as our state had the dubious title of the skin cancer capital of the world.

Leela Holland

Vibrated liquorice

One time when most people on India Tour were coughing and spluttering for days and weeks together, we were cleaning our teeth beside a lake in the brisk early morning air, doing Allah Ho Akbah and gargling with salted water. A yogi arrived from Shri Mataji's residence, bringing small pieces of pure liquorice vibrated by Shri Mataji Herself for all of us with coughs. I put one in my mouth and sucked. Instantly the cough stopped. The passageways cleared, but also the chakra opened out and felt light, sweet and expansive. Also, at least temporarily, my voice changed. It was light, clear and sweet and I felt very detached, softly sweet, balanced and in the centre.

Leela Holland

The stone-throwing incident

Angapur is a village near Brahmapuri/Satara, on the banks of the Krishna River in Maharashtra.

'This Angapur has a very special feature about it,' Shri Mataji explained, 'you see, Shri Ramdas swami, the master of, the guru of Shivaji, found the statue of Shri Rama, Sita and Lakshmana in this river, at this point in the Krishna River. And this was such a remarkable thing, they didn't know how the statue has come there.'

The entire tour of this year was overshadowed by disturbances against us, brought forth by a group of people who called themselves Against Blind Faith. They appeared at public programmes and, while Shri Mataji was speaking, started shouting slogans from the back, causing disruption and confusion. This happened during the programme in Satara, Maharashtra, and when we heard that we would go to Brahmapuri next we felt that this place, being so remote, would give us a welcome break from being constantly followed by this group.

On December 29th, 1989, while in Brahmapuri, we were told that on that evening we would walk over to Angapur, about a mile and a half from our camp, to be with Shri Mataji at a public programme. It was already dark when we arrived and the local people helped us reach the village square where the programme was to be held. The stage was facing the dimly lit square, which was already filling with local seekers.

As I was part of the bhajans group we were sitting on the stage and bhajans were going on when Shri Mataji arrived. We finished our song, and She took Her seat on the stage. We musicians were waiting for Her instructions, whether we should leave the stage or stay – it was different in different places – this time Shri Mataji asked us to stay, and our fairly small group remained seated to the right of Her throne.

Shri Mataji started Her lecture in Marathi when after a short while I noticed a strange noise, like howling, or strange shouting, coming from almost every street leading into the central village square. First I did not pay much attention, but then saw a crowd of people emerging from several streets running towards us across the square. I noticed large stones being thrown towards the people sitting in front of the stage.

This created quite a commotion, but Shri Mataji, interrupting Her lecture, kept repeating through the microphone to stay calm, don't react, don't respond, everything will be all right – speaking both in English and Marathi. Meanwhile the Sahaja Yogis in front of the stage formed a circle, our sisters inside and their brothers around them to protect them.

I was looking against the light on a pole in the centre of the square and could see the stones raining down on this circle like a hailstorm. It was a frightening sight. Shri Mataji interrupted Her lecture, most of the local Indians left and stones were coming down on the Western Yogis, Shri Mataji kept repeating to stay calm and nobody would get hurt – when I noticed that the rain of stones was coming closer and closer towards the stage and Shri Mataji. It seemed they were actually aiming at Her – too much for me to bear!

I found the cover of our harmonium. It looked like a pretty useful shield, so I got up and placed myself in front of Shri Mataji, holding it up as a shield. I had no idea what would happen next, but I was ready to protect my Mother! Suddenly I heard Her speaking in a low voice behind me.

'Do you really believe someone could throw a stone at Me without My permission?'

I turned around and looked at Her smiling face. My bravery suddenly felt very awkward, I pulled my ears, put the harmonium cover back and quietly sat down. My head was spinning. How could I forget who I was sitting next to?

By now the rain of stones had subsided, the programme was obviously finished and there was considerable commotion in front of the stage where Shri Mataji was treating two yogis who got hurt while trying to push against the intruders, despite Her repeated requests to stay calm and not to react. One of them seemed to have suffered a broken rib and was in great pain. Shri Mataji asked him to lie down in front of Her and She placed Her Foot on his chest. After a few minutes She asked Dr Bogdan to see if he was all right, and to our amazement the yogi confirmed that he was fine, no broken rib to detect!

Herbert Reininger

Shri Mataji's explanation

The next day we all were still shaken and learned that despite more than 400 stones having being thrown at a very tightly packed circle of yogis only about seven got hurt, none of them life threatening and they were treated in a local hospital. Shri Mataji explained during Her puja talk later that day that those who got hurt were catching on that part of their body and their catch got worked out through this incident.

I remembered the incredible rain of stones falling down on such a small area and it was nothing short of a miracle that not more yogis got hurt. Shri Mataji simply said that the deities were there to protect us and only those got hurt who needed to.

Our camp was buzzing with activity that day as Shri Mataji had unleashed a huge campaign against the organizers of this incident, who were backed by a leading Maharashtran politician, and instigated by the Pune false guru. Many high–ranking officials and police commanders were ordered to come to this remote place of Brahmapuri and take note of Shri Mataji's request, for them to end this problem.

We yogis were staying as quiet as we could and at a certain point that afternoon I got called to where Shri Mataji was, a humble place, just two small rooms with a tin roof, now serving as the abode of Shri Adi Shakti. When I entered I noticed several people, some in uniform, and Shri Mataji was clearly in command. As soon as I closed the door behind me, and without warning, She began speaking.

'Why did you tell the Western yogis to run to the back and fight the intruders while I was asking everyone not to react?' Shri Mataji said to me in a very stern voice. She repeated it several times.

At first I did not understand why She was saying that. I wanted to respond that it wasn't me, but quickly realised She did not expect an answer. Shri Mataji had told me off before and I was always amazed and overwhelmed by the sheer power that could emanate from Her words. This time it was stronger than ever and I felt all the atoms of my being slowly started to dis-integrate. My eyes were firmly fixed on the ground, I did not dare to look up at Her and it felt I was in the midst of a giant hurricane and needed to hold on to something, anything, for dear life!

'I'm very disappointed with you! Get out now!' She said.

In a daze I folded my hands and left the room. Nothing really made sense. I don't know how long I remained in this state, but it felt like eternity.

I had tears in my eyes and desperately tried to understand what I had done wrong. I knew for sure I had not told any yogis to go and fight the attackers but realised that if Shri Mataji said so in front of so many official people, She must have had a good reason.

Then a yogi who was in Shri Mataji's room before came to talk to me. By that time all the official people had left. He said Shri Mataji wanted to let me know that Her anger was just a drama. She needed to have someone from our group to be the culprit to make sure the police officers understood that She was serious about Her request for us not to react to the violence. At first I was confused. But looking into the smiling, loving eyes of my brother helped clear the heavy clouds around my head.

'Shri Mataji probably picked you for this role because you seem to be able to bear it,' he added.

The following year Shri Mataji explained the broader background of this drama in a talk after the evening entertainment of the Easter Puja in Rome, Italy. By adding a much larger dimension to it, I understood that She was absolutely in control of every minute aspect of this drama, and of anything and everything throughout the universe.

The false guru died soon after that incident.

Herbert Reininger

This was the colour of Shri Mahalakshmi

It was 1989 when I was on the India tour, when we were at Brahamapuri, which was on the Krishna River, and I had the opportunity to walk close to Shri Mataji. She did some footage for a video, and I put my shawl on a rock where She was going to sit down. She vibrated it, and when I put it on afterwards it felt like being wrapped up in the whole universe – there were so many vibrations.

We followed Her back, and She was barefoot. She stopped and looked at the sky. She told us to look at the sky, and the sky changed through about eight different colours in about thirty seconds. At the end it turned this very dark pink colour.

'That is Me. When you see that colour, know that I am there,' She said, 'and this is the colour of Shri Mahalakshmi.'

Mohan Gulati

Mother had saved me!

On the India tour of 1989 – '90 all the ladies body soaked in the Krishna River. Even though I was only thirty I was amazingly stiff. Suddenly the message came that we had to put on dry saris, because Mother was coming to the river, and I was the very last. When everybody was already on the river bank I was still struggling with the sari. Some local ladies who lived there graciously helped me to dress. Shri Mataji and some yogis were grouping together because there was going to be a video–shooting of Shri Mataji.

'Out of the river! Get out of the river!' some men said, pointing to the right. I had to walk over the rocks but decided to do it as fast as I could because it was important was not to be in the way. At that very moment Shri Mataji called at me. (The distance between me and the others was quite far). She pointed at the opposite direction. There was no way to reach the bank of the river, on that side, but I would not be seen by any camera. The way Shri Mataji suggested had only flat stones placed like a path in the river. Immediately I followed Her suggestion, which was at the same time as simple as a genius. Instead of feeling embarrassed of my awkward position, I felt utterly happy.

Mother had saved me! It was the same moment when we all could see the image of Shri Garuda in the sky formed by the clouds. It was a very, very special moment.

Henriette Hagrasman

By the banks of the Krishna River 1989

Shri Shiva in the clouds

I was at Pratishthan and by Shri Mataji's grace I could show Her some photos I had taken on the India tour of 1989/90. In the photo we were on the banks of the Krishna River, and all the yogis were standing in a tremendous light, while the sky was dramatic with both light and dark colours. This was the reason I took it.

'Look, this is Shri Shiva with His hair in a knot,' Shri Mataji said, and showed me the image in the clouds. I was absolutely speechless and thankful.

Brijbala Samii

This is an enlargement of part of the photo above. Shri Shiva can be seen in the cloud on the left hand side, above the men in white kurtas.

Shri Shiva in the clouds above the Krishna River

Why do you think I brought you to India?

Just before returning to Australia, after the 1989/90 India Tour, it was New Year's Eve. Earlier that day I had walked up a hill, and observed Indians politely lined up to board a bus. A cow was standing across the doorway, and the people were respectfully waiting for her to move. The symbolism moved me, the respect for the feminine, the Mother. Later that day, in the evening, we waited for our Holy Mother to come. I felt sad about leaving Mother India, and did not want to go back to Australia, where the Mother is not respected. Shri Mataji arrived and started to talk.

'Why do you think I brought you to India? To fill you up with vibrations, so you could go back to the West and tell them about the Mother,' She said.

Heather Jeffrey

Contributors

Akbar Samii
Akshay Saxena
Ajit Kulkarni
Alan Morrissey
Albert Lewis
Alessandra Pallini
Alexandra Fuente
Amy Ahluwalia
Andrea Wicke
Angela Reininger
Anita Gadkary
Anna Mancini
Annegret Kaluzny
Annie Calvas
Antoinette Wells
Auriol Purdie
Barbara Martens
Barbara Napper
Barry Humphries
Bernard Cuvellier
Bernard Rackham
Betty Cooper
Bill Hansel
Brent Fidler
Brian Bell
Brigitte Saugstad
Brijbala Samii
Bruno Descaves
Bryce Clendon
Carol Garrido
Carolyn Vance
Catherine Hallé
Chris Greaves
Chris Marlow
Christina Rosi
Christina Sweet
Claude Ishram
Colette Desigaud
Danielle Lee
Danya Martoglio
Dattatreya Haynes
David Sharp

Deepa Mahajan
Derek Ferguson
Devarshi Abalain
Duilio Cartocci
Edgar Patarroyo
Edward Saugstad
Edwin Tobias
Elizabeth Matera Matthews
Frances Firth
Gautam Sarkar
Genevieve Brisou
Gillian Patankar
GK Datta
Graham Brown
Grazyna Anslow
Guillemette Metouri
Gunter Thurner
Guy Beavan
Gwennael Verez
Hardev Bhamra
Heather Jeffrey
Heidi Zogorski
Henno de Graaf
Henriette Hagrasman
Herbert Reininger
Ian Maitland Hume
Ingrid B
Janie Frith
Javier Valderamma
Jayant Patankar
Jean–Michel Huet
Jenny Brown
Joaquin Orús
Joga Singh
John Henshaw
Juan Vega
Judy Dobbie
Kamala Singh
Katie Headlam
Kristie Corden
Leanne Huet
Leela Holland

Lena Koli
Lene Jeffrey
Linda Williams
Lori Wills
Luis Garrido
Lyn Osterholzer
Maggie Burns
Maggie Keet
Mahima Saxena
Mahua Sarkar
Maneesha Shanbhag–Cruz
Mara–Madhuri Corazzari
Marie–Joelle Coeuru
Marie–Laure Cernay
Marilyn Leate
Mary Heaton
Matthew Fogarty
Michael Petrunia
Mohan Gulati
Mona Dale
Nanda Tagliabue
Nirmal Gupta
Pamela Mathews
Pascal Shrestaputra
Patricia Deene
Patricia Leydon
Patrick Lantoin
Paulette Oddo
Peter Corden
Phil Trumbo
Phil Ward
Prakash Khote
Pramod Shete
Pranava Fiorini
Prerna Richards
Ramaa Reusch

Raman Kulkarni
Mr Raskar
Ravindranath Saundankar
Reza Ghaffarian
Richard Payment
Rosalyn Tildesley
Rosemary Maitland Hume
Ruth Eleanore
Sahaj Singh
Sanjay Talwar
Sarah Frankcombe
Sarvesh Su
Simmi de Techtermann
Shakuntala Tandale
Sharon Vincent
Shoma Arcilio
Shruti Jalan Gupta
Shubhra Nicolai
Siddheshvara Barbier
Sigrid Jones
Sita Wadhwa
Spanish Sahaja Yogis
Stephen Day
Steve Jones
Suresh Nigam
T. Roy
Tereza Cartocci
Theodore Estathiou
Tim Bruce
Trisha Sharp
Trupta de Graaf
Videh Saundankar
Virendra Verma
Waltraud West
Wolfgang Hackl
Yogi Mahajan

CPSIA information can be obtained at www.ICGtesting.com
Printed in the USA
LVOW01s0306120514

385372LV00006B/22/P